COLOSSAL
GRAB A PENCIL®
LARGE PRINT

CROSS WORDS

RICHARD MANCHESTER

BP
BRISTOL
PARK
BOOKS

Please visit www.pennydellpuzzles.com for more great puzzles

This Bristol Park Books edition published in 2021

Bristol Park Books
3300 Park Avenue
233
Wantagh, NY 11793
www.bristolparkbooks.com

Bristol Park Books is a registered trademark of
Bristol Park Books, Inc.

Published by arrangement with Penny Press, Inc.

ISBN: 978-0-88486-751-7

Printed in the United States of America

PUZZLES

ACROSS

1. Glide on snow
4. Gore and Roker
7. Soft cushion
10. — in the neck
11. Sermon subject
12. Isn't honest
14. Knife injury
15. Bride's vow: 2 wds.
16. Grown-up
18. Rounded line
19. Notable time
21. Hamburger roll
23. Offstage hint
24. Hi-fi receiver
26. Patriot Paul
28. Matinee star
30. Contrary to
31. Marble chunk
34. Plugs up (holes)
36. Hugging limbs
40. Slippery critter
41. Zodiac cat
42. Acorn's tree
43. Month section
45. — Patrick's Day
47. Extremely
48. Rocker Clapton
50. Yawn widely
52. Moved to and fro
55. Flower parts
59. Thankful sigh
60. Fish catcher
62. Added fuel to
63. Small speck
64. Halloween giveaway
66. Hunting bird
68. Great distress
70. Economize
71. Deep sorrow
72. Folk tradition
73. Mom's man
74. Affirmative gesture
75. Junior, to 73-Across

DOWN

1. Pasta "gravy"
2. Related people
3. "Absolutely!"
4. Tibet's region
5. Jar cover
6. Aloof person
7. Neptune or Venus
8. Financial help
9. Low playing card
10. Harbor
13. Garble (words)
14. Existed
17. Golf-ball mound
20. Top of a house
22. Footed vases
25. Chest bone
27. By means of
29. Spring bloom
30. — for the ride
31. Close a seam
32. Kung-fu master Bruce
33. Beer cousin
35. Honolulu garland
37. Caviar base
38. Harm the surface of
39. Cloud's spot
44. Lock insert
45. Lateral edge
46. Adhesive strip
47. Dog doc
49. Leased
51. Bicycle propellers
52. Occupied a bench
53. Hostile conflicts
54. In front
56. Drape with decorations
57. Sole
58. Farm pen
61. Urban center
62. Escaped from
65. Glamorous Gardner
67. Court (a lass)
69. Sticky stuff

Crossword grid (filled answers, row by row):

1	¹S ²K ³I ■ ⁴A ⁵L ⁶S ■ ⁷P ⁸A ⁹D
2	¹⁰D A I N ■ ¹¹S I N ■ ¹²L I E ¹³S
3	¹⁴W O U N D ¹⁵I D O ¹⁶A D U L ¹⁷T
4	¹⁸A R C ■ ¹⁹E ²⁰R A ■ ²¹B ²²U N ■ ²³C U E
5	²⁴S T E ²⁵R E O ■ ²⁶R E ²⁷V E R E
6	■ ²⁸I D O ²⁹L ³⁰A N T I
7	³¹S ³²L ³³A B ■ ³⁴T I ³⁵L L S ■ ³⁶A ³⁷R ³⁸M ³⁹S
8	⁴⁰E E L ■ ⁴¹L E O ■ ⁴²O A K
9	⁴³W E E ⁴⁴K ⁴⁵S A I N ⁴⁶T ⁴⁷V E R Y
10	■ ⁴⁸E ⁴⁹R I C ⁵⁰G A P ⁵¹E
11	⁵²S ⁵³W ⁵⁴A Y E D ⁵⁵P E T ⁵⁶A ⁵⁷L ⁵⁸S
12	⁵⁹A A H ⁶⁰N E T ⁶¹? ⁶²F E D ⁶³D O T
13	⁶⁴T R E ⁶⁵A T ⁶⁶O ⁶⁷W L ⁶⁸A ⁶⁹G O N Y
14	⁷⁰S A V E ⁷¹N O E ⁷²L O R E
15	⁷³D A D ⁷⁴N O D ⁷⁵S O N

2

ACROSS

1. Big bustle
4. "Tiny" Dickens boy
7. Quick punch
10. Stroll in the surf
12. Rock of comedy
14. Mentally healthy
15. Equally distributed
16. Fail to be
17. Color lightly
18. Mansion grounds
20. Enchilada kin
22. College paper
24. Chafe
25. Broadcasts
27. Boot front
29. Giddy mirth
32. Commotions
34. Water barrier
36. Edge of a roof
38. "— my life!"
39. Narrowed gradually
42. Newsman Koppel
43. Boxing match
45. Hair goo
46. Compares (to)
48. Place to perch
50. Faceted stone
52. Express (emotion)
53. Cashew or pecan
55. Burger joint
57. Plane's "garage"
60. Ordinary
63. Rate of speed
64. Provokes
66. Modern-day Persia
68. Quite eager
69. Skyscraper floor
70. Funny Fey
71. Vibrant hue
72. Braying mammal
73. Bit of wet paint

DOWN

1. Humbling fear
2. Mr. Letterman, familiarly
3. Lofty poems
4. Menacing statement
5. Exasperation
6. Cooling candy
7. County prison
8. Green Gables gal
9. Wager in Vegas
11. Walks inside
12. Meowing beasts
13. Night twinkler
14. Horse's home
19. Prized quality
21. Coffee vessel
23. Yoo-hooed from an Alp
25. Motor vehicles
26. Debate topic
28. Pitcher part
30. Consumed, as brunch
31. Special occasion
32. Falsehood
33. Be droopy
35. Vocalist Tormé
37. McMahon and Bradley
40. Violin knob
41. Scuba enthusiast
44. Sun-toasted
47. Muppet frog
49. Harbor escort
51. Coal-digging pros
54. Paving substances
56. Overly curious
57. "— a heart!"
58. Caustic chemical
59. Moreno of film
61. Bone-dry
62. Lovely Turner
63. Golfing score
65. — Alamos, New Mexico
67. Catch suddenly

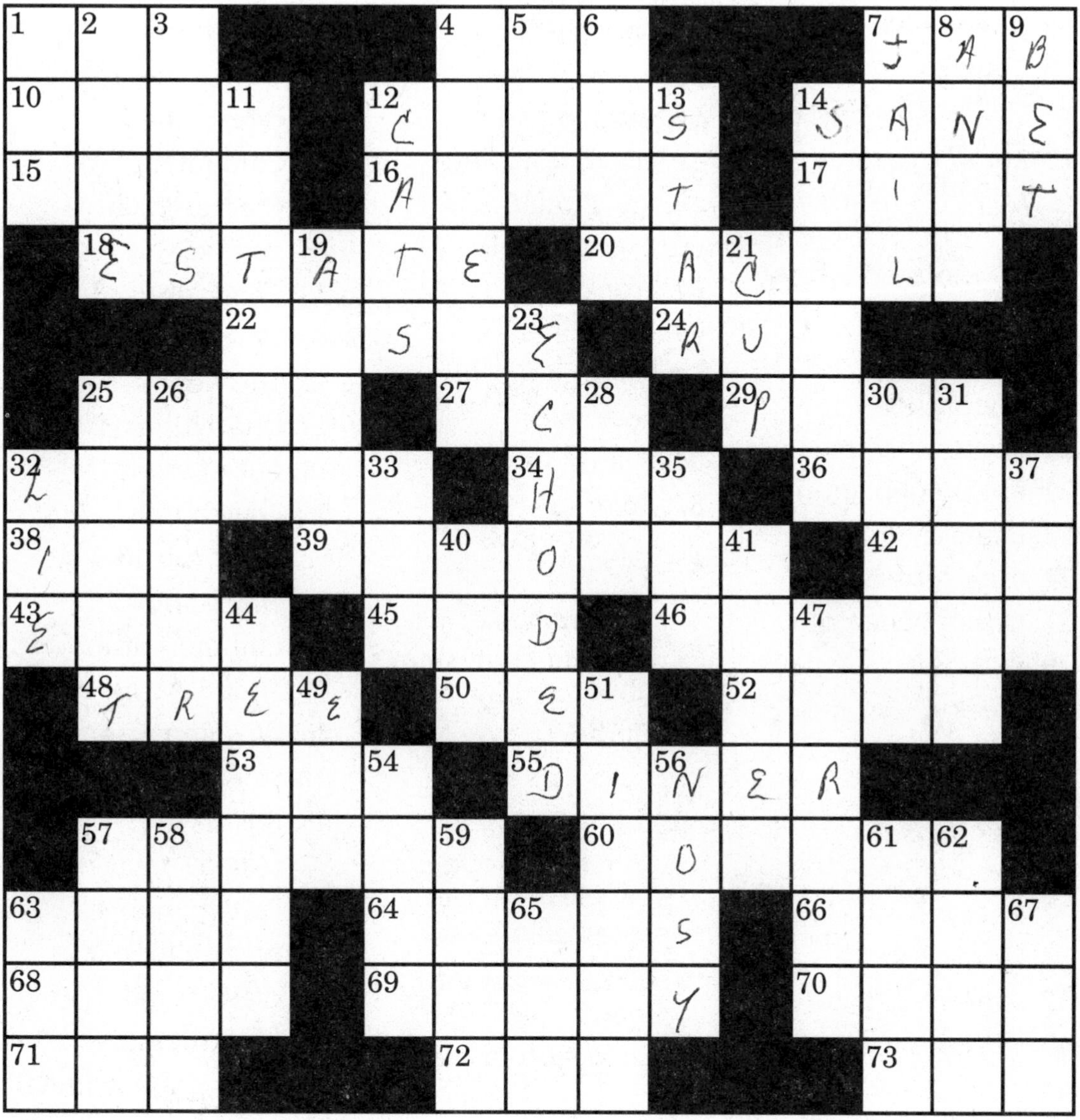

ACROSS

1. Wound reminder
5. Young lass
8. "The Sun — Rises," book
12. Felt sick
14. Friendly nation
15. Plow the field
16. Playhouse platform
17. Bagel center
18. Quite noisy
19. Coop clucker
20. Constant complainer
22. Put up (a painting)
23. Beam of light
24. Cute sprites
27. Ocean behemoth
29. Purpose
30. Meek
33. Pull along the ground
34. Asian grain
36. In addition
37. Decays
38. Fir growths
39. Group bus trip
40. Devoured lunch
41. Clock pointer
42. Labor
43. Snooze spot
44. "Of course!"
45. Slides on ice

47. Value
49. Oinking animal
50. Lima's site
52. Bread spread
54. Clothing label
57. Glowing review
58. Poncho kin
60. Explorer Polo
62. Frank
63. Mellowed
64. Hair tangle
65. Low voice
66. Flat denials
67. Colored (Easter eggs)

DOWN

1. Pageant contestant's ribbon
2. Quote
3. Actor Ladd
4. Ask for alms
5. Spherical model of the earth
6. 100%
7. Caustic substance in soap
8. Collection of maps
9. Maned hunter
10. Slimy garden crawler
11. Ancient
13. Window sticker

14. "That's it!"
21. Cereal grass
22. Skirt border
23. — to riches
25. Intertwined
26. Competes (for)
27. Created poetry
28. Loathed
30. Bend forward
31. Units of time
32. The New — Jets
33. Unexciting
34. Cut of beef
35. Cozy hotel
38. "Moonstruck" star
39. Tiny branch
44. Common pronoun
45. That 5-Across
46. Weaving frames
47. Small birds
48. Wishes
50. Mama's fella
51. Festive nights
53. Was a pioneer
54. Waiter's aid
55. Land measure
56. Costly yellow metal
57. Steal from
58. Food holder
59. In a past era
61. See 36-Across

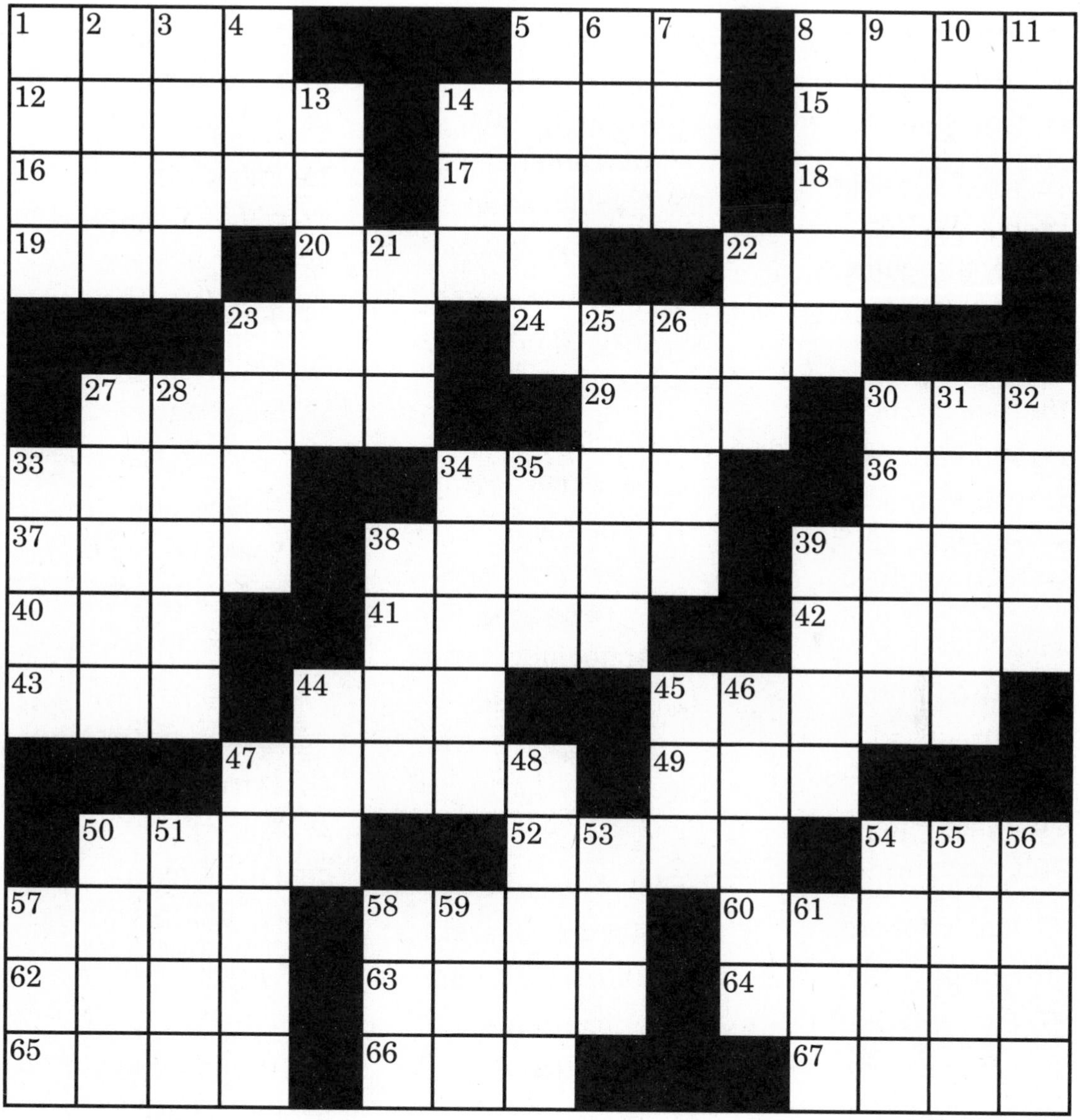

ACROSS

1. Hit with a palm
5. Urban taxi
8. Doctor's charge
11. Office notes
13. Lacking color
14. Toy figurine
15. Band together
16. Ready for harvest
17. Hazard
18. Thor or Zeus
19. Soon afterward
21. Place for a 45-Across
22. Order to remain
23. "Scram!"
25. Religious song
27. Passed over
30. Outline (a drawing)
31. Cheese with holes
32. Commit blunders
34. Hog's comment
35. Edible tubers
36. Pair plus one
37. Encountered
38. Loose change
39. Every 24 hours
40. Cruising the seas
42. Thin board
43. Movie part
44. Camera glass
45. Country's banner
47. Flat bell
48. Fast airliner
51. Fishhook attachment
52. Divulge (a secret)
54. Avoid artfully
56. Slope's summit
57. Sticky mud
58. "Home on the —"
59. Favorable vote
60. Have bills to pay
61. Glimpsed

DOWN

1. Annoyingly proud
2. Jay of comedy
3. Encircled by
4. Boiling vessel
5. A son of Adam
6. European peak
7. Summer buzzer
8. Aluminum wrap
9. Ultimatum word
10. Majestic deer
12. Establish roots
13. Fly, to a frog
14. Slump
20. Smoked meat
21. Explosive noises
22. Burlap bag
23. Slides on ice
24. Cat's warning
25. Snoops (into)
26. Jolly Claus
27. Flailed (a bat)
28. Spooky
29. Boring device
30. Male turkey
31. Backbone
33. Western star Rogers
35. Make grimy
36. Soaks up the rays
38. Sink problem
39. Jeopardy
41. Fuming
42. Fenced enclosure
44. Earring's site
45. Clock front
46. City in Peru
47. Look intently
48. Bride's month?
49. Limit
50. Young adult
51. Port's locale
52. Scornful shout
53. Melancholy
55. Scale steps

5

ACROSS

1. Enormous
4. Ladder rung
8. "M*A*S*H" star Alan
12. Unreturnable serve
13. Nautical call
14. About to depart
16. Commandments count
17. Pocket fluff
18. FM receivers
20. "Blood is thicker — water"
22. Tended the garden
24. Floor scrubber
25. Heaped (on)
27. Current style
28. Beer crate
29. Affirm positively
30. Wee lake
31. Provoked
32. Auto fuel
33. Weeps loudly
34. Word of denial
35. Main courses
37. Manhattan's locale: 2 wds.
41. Shade provider
42. Regret the absence of
43. Moving truck
44. Smell (a rose)
47. Pursue game
48. Used to exist
49. Coal weights
50. Quite smart
51. Number of Magi
52. Grill residue
53. Pretty Winslet
54. Item of winter footwear
55. Egg-whipping device
57. Army squad
59. Devilish kid
62. Had a snooze
63. Life companion
64. Cow's lament
65. Devours food
66. Daisy support
67. Female bleater

DOWN

1. Baseball club
2. Sprain soother
3. Least harsh
4. Meal of greens
5. Slim
6. Very long span
7. Large snakes
8. Be of like mind
9. Heavy burden
10. Completed
11. Zoo dweller
15. Gaggle member
19. Drove rapidly
21. Of that gal
23. Kooky
25. Leaf of a book
26. "Terrible" Russian tsar
27. Unruly crowds
28. Urban center
30. Metered verse
31. Plies the oars
33. Personal identity
34. Wren's abode
36. NBA officials
37. Four plus five
38. Pay for working after hours
39. Pink, as steak
40. Leg-bending joint
42. Places to view art
44. Dagger thrust
45. Snouts
46. Draw a breath
47. Broadway smash
48. "— is she?"
50. Skin blemishes
51. — pole, carved post
53. Held on to
54. Light snack
56. Morning brew
58. Melodic King Cole
60. Cut the grass
61. Author of "The Raven"

6

ACROSS

1. Wee tykes
5. Barely open
9. Supporting
12. Dubuque native
14. Models (for)
16. Federal rule
17. Place a call
18. Upper leg
19. "— you awake?"
20. Drops of grass moisture
22. Related a story
24. Digging tools
27. More nicely arranged
28. Frying pans
30. Blasting compound: abbr.
31. Suffer sickness
32. Corrects (text)
34. Poker pool
38. Radiance
40. Spice cookies
42. Tender affection
43. Church stand
45. Shred (cheese)
47. Anti
48. American symbol, Uncle —
50. Immense
52. Knocked sharply
55. Least free of pain
56. Think about
58. Parcel of land
59. Operate (a machine)
60. Bette of old films
62. Sprinted
66. Freudian self
67. Cut, as bread
68. Work very hard
69. Question from a reporter
70. Mailbox entry
71. Graceful bird

DOWN

1. Gratuity for a waiter
2. Exclamation of wonder
3. Half of four
4. Beach shoe
5. Quick to learn
6. Musician Lennon
7. From Seoul or Singapore
8. Rue
9. Flat dish
10. Not as common
11. Had a debt
13. Sewing device
15. Got smaller
21. Unwelcome plants
23. Upstairs room
24. Expertise
25. Airline captain
26. What 39-Down may do
28. Heroic account
29. Fixed gaze
33. Extends across
35. Mexican snacks
36. Stream fish
37. Deep urges
39. Cousins of bees
41. Seat at a bar
44. Rushing waters
46. Mistakes
49. Olympics awards
51. Lead and iron
52. Far from smooth
53. Be a pest
54. Evil personified
56. Boat's staff
57. Puerto —
61. Gel, as a mold
63. Crow's noise
64. *Señora* Perón
65. Wolf's abode

7

ACROSS

1. Defective
4. Restful resort
7. With it: slang
10. Catalog offering
12. Routine task
14. Ply a peeler
15. Absence of any
16. Talks madly
17. Fluttered down to a perch
18. Whodunit novel
20. Fracture wraps
22. Ooze (out)
23. Yearn for
24. Nasty odor
26. Ship's boss
29. Riding horse
30. Exposes to view
31. Achieved
33. Docking spot
34. College residences
35. Smudged streak
36. As of now
37. Austin's state
38. Showy bloom
39. Frozen dessert
41. Unaccompanied songs
42. Inch up to
43. A bit nippy
44. Sugary
46. Mexican entree
49. Sewing line
50. Fill with glee
52. Compass heading
54. Crave what another has
55. Mall events
56. Rural tower
57. Juice beverage
58. For each
59. Prune (a branch)

DOWN

1. Flour container
2. Molecule fragment
3. Contradict (a charge)
4. Keen, as a blade
5. Small 29-Across
6. Museum display
7. "Cease!"
8. Pigmented eye area
9. Family animal
11. More cluttered
12. Little brook
13. Flees, as from jail
14. Spaghetti, for example
19. Administer care to
21. Tiny insects
23. Raises the temperature of
24. Pig abodes
25. Pearly whites
26. Diamond weight
27. Arctic shelter
28. Sentence subjects
29. KGB employee
30. Ring athlete
32. Make an effort
34. Argues
35. Stomachs, informally
37. Apple-bearing plant
38. Far from rich
40. Opposing army
41. Skin wounds
43. Less unappealing
44. Post (mail)
45. Gesture hello
46. Cotton bundle
47. Dog's wagging appendage
48. Port of Norway
49. Vast expanse
51. — of luxury
53. Highest part

ACROSS

1. "Mayday!," at sea
4. Tavern barrel
7. Close chum
10. Metered cab
11. Lyricist Gershwin
12. "Open —!," dentist's request
13. Not as sullen
14. Most joyous
16. Fa follower
17. Cruel Roman emperor
19. Brief bark
20. Tattooing fluids
22. Vessel of 1492
24. Squints (at)
28. Nagging people
30. Canine companions
32. Rain globule
33. Under the weather
35. Peddle
37. Lupino of Hollywood
38. Battling pro
42. In the least amount of time
44. Noted Vigoda
45. Forms a knot
47. Large serpent
48. Give out cards
50. Unchanged
52. Longed (for)
56. Purse band
58. Bologna shop
60. She fibs
61. Fido's "foot"
63. Opera set in Egypt
65. Sob aloud
66. United
70. Heavenly being
72. Like some exams
73. Single bill
74. Will beneficiary
75. Spider's trap
76. Chime in with
77. — up to, admit

DOWN

1. Verbalize
2. Strong animals
3. Police warning
4. Japanese robes
5. Before: poetic
6. Indiana city
7. Apple pastry
8. Job listings
9. Permit to happen
10. Has a conversation
12. Cleared a windshield
13. Departed
15. Clothing flaw
16. Drink daintily
18. Free (of)
21. Move a spoon in
23. Becomes mature
25. Buffalo's Great Lake
26. Curtain poles
27. Lover's tiff
29. Narrow cut
31. Untidy fellow
34. Superman's gal
36. Circle of yarn
38. Lumps of gum
39. Help in crime
40. Back region
41. Scan (a bar code)
43. Metal spike
46. Made a streak
49. Suit flap
51. Yale coed
53. More agreeable
54. British noble
55. Far from wet
57. Butter square
59. The Gem State
62. "Halt, horse!"
64. Freshly
66. Drag (a car)
67. Mine extract
68. Shoot the breeze
69. Stop
71. Juniper-flavored liquor

ACROSS

1. Humorous Arthur
4. Scatter (seed)
7. &
10. Places (down)
11. Dinghy blade
12. Tress ringlet
14. Bunny cousins
15. Had a snack
16. Salad veggie
18. Quaint hotel
19. "Safe!" caller
21. Negative word
23. Night before a holiday
24. Ruin completely
26. President Jackson
28. Garment edge
29. Calf-roping loop
31. Experienced pain
34. Bandleader Arnaz
35. Havana's site
39. Dove murmur
40. Kitchen basins
41. — Diego, California
42. Write with a keyboard
44. Joins in matrimony
45. Immaculate
47. Serene joy
49. "I was right!"
50. Haircut pro
53. Ad phrases
57. Firewood tool
58. Wily
60. Draft spigot
61. Feel bad about
62. Wine vessel
64. Zoo denizen
66. Self-esteem
68. Canyon reverberation
69. Pint-size
70. Simplicity
71. Clucking fowl
72. Baby's rest
73. Tinting fluid

DOWN

1. Farm shelters
2. "Peeper"
3. Guaranteed
4. Full of suds
5. Stable tidbit
6. Small songbird
7. Oak nuts
8. Convent sister
9. Less damp
10. Bowling aisle
13. Deep passion
14. Stowed away
17. Freshly created
20. Dad's spouse
22. Desert garden
25. "In — beginning…"
27. Pal of Sneezy
29. Lets borrow
30. Inquires (of)
31. Play section
32. Modestly shy
33. Little jump
34. Expires, as a battery
36. "— it or lose it!"
37. Goat's cry
38. "Raggedy" doll
40. Whirl; eddy
43. Recede, as a tide
45. Minced (meat)
46. Dawdle
48. Unit of study
49. In imitation of: 2 wds.
50. Grocery sack
51. Wheel's rod
52. Extend a hand
53. High, as a price
54. Get out of bed
55. Totally naked
56. Watch
59. Sign of tedium
63. That 71-Across
65. Pod dweller
67. Brief glimmer, as of hope

10

ACROSS

1. Collect a harvest
5. Professional prizefight
9. Furious
12. New Haven university
13. Family dwelling
14. 33-Down dropping
15. Anon's mate
16. Keyboard key
17. Sharpen, as a razor
18. Release a breath
20. Emptied (a bathtub)
22. Deadly serpent
23. Direct (a camera)
24. Passed, as hours
28. Frightened shriek
31. Oinking beasts
32. Long-barreled gun
34. Box (with)
36. President Eisenhower, informally
37. Contend (for)
38. — de Janeiro
39. Dollar part
41. Insertion mark
43. Tuneful Turner
44. Little rocks
46. Rode a bike
48. Gain a victory
49. Capture (a criminal)
50. Believes in
54. Steel ropes
57. Lion's warning
58. Nero or Cicero
60. Midterm test
62. Canal locales
63. Alter to fit
64. Fork's prong
65. Completely
66. Behind time
67. Hearty soup

DOWN

1. Dark bread
2. Roof perimeter
3. "Jeopardy!" icon Trebek
4. "That's a possibility!"
5. Treat for Fido
6. "Scram!"
7. Put into play
8. Large patio
9. Earth orbiter
10. Bancroft of film
11. Title of land ownership
13. Aide
14. Clock bells
19. Wild donkey
21. Balloon filler
24. Sweeping account
25. Is fond of
26. Actor's representative
27. Opera soloists
28. Have a snooze
29. May preceder
30. Bangor's state
33. Fragrant pine
35. Car's path
40. Looms (over)
41. — America, Panama's region
42. Lease signer
43. Medicine pills
45. Small bit
47. Pat with a napkin
50. Sector
51. Fossil fuel
52. Funny Reiner
53. Fizzy beverage
54. Magician's cloak
55. Leave the stage
56. Rational
59. Gym pad
61. Feline comment

ACROSS

1. Burger bread
4. Till the soil
8. Hockey disk
12. Chorus singer
13. Brain flash
14. Cupid's weapon
16. Bearded animal
17. Inhale sharply
18. Trap for game
19. Different
21. Flour factories
23. Tormé of jazz
24. Undersea craft
26. Exclamation of excitement
27. Fiery gem
28. Impish child
31. Large village
33. Guy's date
35. Meadow tweeter
37. Powerful hit
39. Takes a breather
43. Roaring female
45. Cocktail base
47. Knight's protective suit
48. Peel (apples)
50. Confident
51. Scrooge's comment
53. Swerve abruptly
55. Tycoon Turner
56. Pouncing pets
59. "— been bad!"
61. Witnessed
63. Bitter brew
64. Clever
66. Bird's flappers
70. Evans of "Dynasty"
72. Small bucket
74. Car's rubber roller
75. Stone worker
76. Boldly gaze at
77. Jaguar's "toenail"
78. Attempt to find
79. Marsh stalk
80. "Psst!"

DOWN

1. Ink smudge
2. Provo's state
3. Brief letters
4. Seeded fruit
5. Funny Sandler
6. Quits a job
7. Syrup flavor
8. Football throw
9. Vase relative
10. Muscle pain
11. South —, Seoul's country
12. Before today
15. Oil derrick
20. Road furrow
22. Stool support
25. Short hairstyles for women
27. Fake butters
28. Famous Fitzgerald
29. Dragon's cave
30. Beginning at
32. Bee cousin
34. Circle section
36. Drawer pulls
38. Jack rabbit
40. Closed tight
41. Ripped (down)
42. Musher's post
44. Length of time
46. Spike and Bruce
49. Ordinary
52. That rooster
54. Like some sushi
56. Peaceful
57. Bogus name
58. Strained
60. Thin mist
62. Spell caster
64. Plummeted
65. Ceramic piece
67. River in Egypt
68. Ash-colored
69. Stitch up
71. Forest mama
73. Headed a tour

ACROSS

1. Especially talented
5. Divide by category
9. Force out
14. Borrowed money
15. Where Akron is
16. Theater feature
17. Gasp loudly
18. Lunch hour, for many
19. Borscht veggies
20. Escalator step
22. Eye drop?
24. Butterfly trap
25. Goldfish kin
28. Big piece
30. Speedy felines
34. Runs away: slang
38. "— Town," play
39. TV programs
41. Prop for a painting
42. Persia, nowadays
44. Walking pole
46. Eat in splendor
47. Misplaces
49. Nebraska city
51. Expected to arrive
52. Prowls (about)
54. Most meager
56. Seize hold of
58. Strike (flies)
59. Beaver construction
62. Cash box
64. Commence
68. Bring together
70. Human form
73. In addition
74. River mammal
75. Reedy woodwind
76. Govern (over)
77. Locales
78. Dabs liquid on
79. Cherry stone

DOWN

1. Swiss peaks
2. Rowed vessel
3. Glamorous Turner
4. Attract irresistibly
5. Male child
6. "Well, well!"
7. Uproar; tumult
8. Color shades
9. Warm hug
10. Baseballer DiMaggio
11. Equally matched
12. Name (an example)
13. Laboratory evaluation
21. Sewer rodents
23. Roker and Gore
26. Cheering yells
27. Camera's image
29. Thin nail
30. Spiral shapes
31. A Great Lake
32. Wipe off
33. Uses the pool
35. To the perimeter
36. Cafe lists
37. Ice pellets
40. Hits with the palm
43. Shipshape
45. Start to melt
48. Rink athletes
50. Baghdad native
53. Glide down a snowy slope
55. Is at the helm
57. Arm bender
59. Singing pairs
60. Debate stance
61. Oven glove
63. Ear region
65. Sticky stuff
66. Bit of land in the ocean
67. Requirement
69. Golf gizmo
71. Tiny speck
72. "Indeed I do!"

13

ACROSS

1. Arrives on shore
6. Facial arch
10. Deck 45-Down
14. Be ready for
15. Peru's capital
16. Composer Porter
17. Florida city
18. Mellowed, as cheese
19. Range chamber
20. Deep fury
21. Orange potato
23. Ignore
25. Hornets' home
27. Grid official
29. Mom's fella
30. Colored parts of eyes
33. Flower leaf
37. Serious plays
40. Excavated
42. Accomplished
43. Snack on
44. Shiny stone
46. Trim the lawn
48. "— my turn!"
49. State firmly
51. "— a chance!"
53. Dining surfaces
55. Push away
57. Kitchen closet
59. Nervous spasm
61. Hive insect
62. Per unit
66. "— of the Opera"
70. One of several
72. "Alas!"
73. Sushi grain
74. Wild pig
76. Higher than
78. Tributes in verse
79. Stairway banister
80. Collected (leaves)
81. Dirty disorder
82. Griffith of TV
83. Gown or frock

DOWN

1. Old language
2. Conscious (of)
3. Identifies
4. Dunk (chips)
5. Linger
6. Holds responsible (for)
7. Fix (an election)
8. Seer's portent
9. Moved in water
10. Criticized angrily
11. Interlaced
12. Talented Baldwin
13. Stooped
22. Up and about
24. Blank space
26. Comic Allen
28. Gave a meal to
31. Torn cloth
32. Addition total
34. Hard work
35. Poker stake
36. Fewer
37. Beloved
38. Talk madly
39. Over
41. Obtained
45. Floor wiper
47. Military fight
50. Damp quality
52. Cafe bill
54. "Adios!"
56. Set fire to
58. Almost
60. Hooded snake
63. Emerged from sleep
64. Small inlets
65. Pays mind to
66. School dance
67. Animal skin
68. Perfect serves
69. Pained cry
71. Grass plot
75. Assistance
77. Chocolate shape

14

ACROSS

1. Oversized
4. Performed (a task)
7. Gloomy
10. "Bells — Ringing"
11. Good-natured
12. Left ajar
14. Freight weight
15. Prayer closer
16. Clark's exploring partner
18. Brazenness
20. Blender top
21. Firm refusals
23. Cowboy Rogers
24. Police attack
26. Place to rest
27. Expand, as a business
29. Flexible pipe
30. Hazardous
31. "Thank —"
32. Press, as a button
33. Trouble
34. Voice-mail recording
36. Grad's reward
40. Tint
41. Major vein of ore
42. Standard level
43. Backless 26-Across
46. Diamond source
47. Sly look
48. Boxcar vagrant
49. Head coverings
50. Paving mixture
51. Positive reply
52. Because of
53. Aircraft detection device
55. Use one's nose
57. Weaving frame
59. Also
61. Amazed
62. Hooting birds
63. Outdated
64. Ames and Asner
65. — Aviv, Israel
66. Apple-colored

DOWN

1. Flying mammal
2. Laundry appliance
3. Opposite of selfish
4. Wee coin
5. Drink cubes
6. Lion's home
7. Densely packed
8. Copied
9. Grass droplets
11. Sea force
13. 9 9 9 9 9
17. Relax in a tub
19. Stadium tier
20. Be deceitful
22. Pig's abode
24. Fragrant bloom
25. Campfire dust
26. Window edge
27. Sports room
28. Halibut eggs
29. Extremely 1-Across
30. Ready to pick
32. Famous Revere
33. Nurse's helper
35. "Go away!"
36. Puts on (clothes)
37. Switchboard employee
38. Entertainer West
39. Noah's boat
41. Teacup rim
43. Far from bold
44. Boot tips
45. President Barack
46. Make imperfect
47. Paper tablet
49. Winter maladies
50. Highlands hats
52. Turned tail
53. Bread bun
54. Function
56. Woolly mom
57. Fortune
58. Have creditors
60. Uncommon

ACROSS

1. Maiden
5. Noggin warmers
9. Casual talk
13. Briny deep
15. Operatic song
16. Deli sandwich
17. Humiliate
18. Opposite of short
19. Highway exit
20. Coveted gymnastics score
21. "For — the Bell Tolls"
23. Greased
24. Hawaiian necklace of flowers
25. Sour chemicals
28. Clutches
31. Wedding vow: 2 wds.
32. Cherry stone
35. Wakeful
36. Theatrical pro
38. Weed chopper
39. Puzzle entry
40. Shelled slug
41. Wolf's wail
42. Gardner of Hollywood
43. Book's backbone
44. Artificial watercourse
45. Money of Japan
46. Bolt fastener
47. Director Spielberg
49. Pickford and Martin
51. Fruity cooler
52. Hold securely
54. Food fish
56. Disobedient
59. Horse's leash
60. Daddy deer
62. Salary boost
64. Riveted by
65. Yank on
66. Shiny material
67. Pub brew
68. With facility
69. Radiators provide it

DOWN

1. Was defeated
2. Feel pain
3. Oscar recipient Penn
4. American Uncle
5. Heavenly glow
6. Smell
7. 37-Down metal
8. Hang down
9. Evert of the courts
10. Be on the mend
11. Military squad
12. Upper part
14. Most modern
22. Waist joint
23. See 6-Down
24. Rendered fat
26. Big towns
27. Revered figure
28. Baseball mitt
29. Showed on TV again
30. Soundness of mind
32. Call up
33. Dubuque dweller
34. Make known
35. Absent
37. Soup container
40. Cowboy-boot accessory
41. Own
43. Crackle
44. Fragrant woods
48. Beige hue
49. One under 18
50. Procrastinate
52. Heredity unit
53. Altar ceremony
55. Repulsive
56. Nibble
57. China's region
58. Fender bend
59. Barbecued morsel
60. Luxury resort
61. Bathing vat
63. Relieved sigh

16

ACROSS

1. In poor health
4. Macabre American author
7. Metered car
10. Leg bender
11. Purge (of)
12. Begin —, start over
14. Factions
15. Cotton-gin inventor Whitney
16. Sipping aid
18. Muhammad of boxing
19. Declare
21. Walking baby
23. Entertainer Gabor
24. Locations
26. Military gestures
28. Single condos
31. Pub barrel
32. Part of speech
35. Martial —
37. Form, as clay
41. Wordy Gershwin
42. Dorothy, to Em
44. Comedian Aykroyd
45. Gave guns to
48. Ground grain
49. Gelatin pan
50. Valuable rock
52. Took the wheel
54. Proper behavior
58. Baked tuber
62. Name hidden in "sabers"
63. Caspian or Red
64. Door locker
65. Grown boy
66. Bell sounds
68. Delivery truck
70. Exclusively
72. Forest plant
73. Self-love
74. Heavy cymbal
75. "HELP ME!"
76. Adjust (a clock)
77. Breakfast staple

DOWN

1. Gandhi's land
2. Civil War general
3. Diminish
4. Hunter's quest
5. Frying fat
6. Corrects copy
7. Princely homes
8. Picnic pest
9. French cap
10. Shut off (an engine)
13. Ocean crest
14. Pine's liquid
17. "I — just joking!"
20. Like Thai food
22. Durable 72-Across
25. Little bear
27. "Oh, no!"
29. Clip (a beard)
30. Spirited mount
32. By a route through
33. Goof up
34. Ewe's mate
36. Injury mark
38. Big ruckus
39. Close friend
40. Final chapter
43. Marry secretly
46. Eternity
47. Frocks and gowns
49. NYC baseballer
51. Before, to Burns
53. Trip on a ship
54. Road chart
55. Assist in a crime
56. Approaches
57. Rescues
59. Surrounded by
60. Sharp flavor
61. Half a pair
64. Rope creation
67. Horoscope cat
69. A vital statistic
71. Bit of lumber

ACROSS

1. Celebrities
6. Of the mouth
10. Region
14. Christmas tune
15. Was a jockey
16. Depraved
17. Excuse for a suspect
18. Intense wind
19. Coat holder
20. Spot for sleep
21. Scrape along
23. People
24. Roaring females
27. Upward climb
30. Crabby Stooge
31. Ewe's bleat
34. Threw a punch
35. Clutch at
37. Battle weapons
38. Cattle group
39. Human spirits
40. Chatters
41. Sea wrigglers
42. Yuletide 14-Across
43. Book's name
44. Be a mole?
45. Towel monogram
46. Dusk event
47. Duplicating
50. Happen
53. Patch (socks)
54. Pitcher's edge
57. Astronaut Shepard
58. Lunch meats
60. Escape from
62. Car corrosion
63. Came safely to earth
64. Soup dipper
65. Witnesses
66. Fruit from a palm
67. "Home, — home!"

DOWN

1. Wound remnant
2. Fanciful yarn
3. Extremely dry
4. Stick up (a bank)
5. Diving into base
6. Piano cousin
7. Cheek coloring
8. Paid notices
9. Give an OK to
10. Worst possible test scores
11. Football-shaped
12. Shaving injury
13. Benevolent order members
22. Decay
23. Charge for a service
24. Grants temporarily
25. Wee
26. Weeps out loud
27. Fireplace powder
28. Ply a broom
29. Cohort of 30-Across
31. Obnoxious tots
32. Walkunhurriedly
33. Desirable quality
35. Honking bird
36. Deeply regret
37. Growing older
39. Cut, as hair
43. Underground passages
45. Yonder lass
46. Gent's address
47. Tiniest pups
48. Confess (to)
49. Sample (food)
50. Rowing poles
51. Helpful hint
52. Flute box
54. Quite impolite
55. Lazy
56. Encounter
58. Owned
59. Patterned after: 2 wds.
61. Courtroom field

ACROSS

1. Frog leap
4. Yonder lass
7. Riotous crowd
10. Firewood splitter
11. Perceive by feeling
13. Great wonder
14. Still
15. Made calm
17. Demolition substance: abbr.
18. Entertainer Wayne
20. Martini fruits
22. Bush's anchor
23. Pod legumes
24. Carried a debt
26. First Lady Truman
27. Knocks softly
30. Informal restaurant
32. Lobe sites
36. "— is it?"
37. Brewery tub
38. Equal score
39. Granola grains
41. Burger unit
43. Feline remark
44. Steeped drinks
46. Harvard's longtime rival
48. Alpine evergreens
49. Hair neatener
51. Is worthy of
53. Where a choker is worn
55. Instantly
56. Vie (for)
58. Bar of iron
60. Impersonate
61. Remainders of ancient buildings
62. Tropical snake
63. — capita
64. Procure
65. Crafty

DOWN

1. Horse feed
2. Yoked cattle
3. Pan of fiction
4. In a bit
5. Small cabin
6. Reflection of sound
7. Spouses
8. Possesses
9. Casino wager
11. Blew a whistle
12. Assistant
15. Pack (away)
16. Fizzles out
19. Courts (a sweetheart)
21. Flower holder
25. Opera stars
26. White or Ford
27. Number of sides on a coin
28. "Eureka!"
29. Kettle cousin
31. Jazzy King Cole
33. Patronized a 30-Across
34. Brazil port, for short
35. Close a seam
40. Blend with a spoon
41. Church head
42. Luxury boats
43. Brief letter
45. Bluesy Clapton
47. Tribal wisdom
48. Less (than)
50. Nasty comments
51. Sulk about
52. Too confident
53. Camp dwelling
54. Fix-it utensil
55. Catch 40 winks
57. Filled dessert
59. 24-hour span

ACROSS

1. Block of bread
5. Exact image
9. Pool distance
12. Tuneful Fitzgerald
13. Theater cheer
14. Square of hay
15. Cowardice
16. Made public
17. Completed
18. Hanks of "Big"
19. Insect pest
20. Speak proudly
21. Liking company
23. Prejudice
25. Dancing Miller
26. Convey (mail)
27. Itty-bitty
30. Plucked instrument
33. Canvas window protection
35. Lovely Lupino
36. Climbing plants
38. Greedy person
39. Soothes, as pain
41. Young child
42. Indian clans
45. Landlord's fee
46. Bible lady
47. Hosiery flaws
48. Billiards rod
50. Slugger Ruth
51. Bagel seed
54. Back street
57. Grape's stem
58. Little demon
60. Lane in "Superman"
61. Spry
63. As soon as
64. "Quit it!"
65. Quacking birds
66. Shoe fillers
67. Fitting
68. Tinting agents
69. Release from jail

DOWN

1. Abandoned
2. Butter substitutes
3. Texas mission
4. Remote
5. Courtroom hearing
6. Toad bump
7. "— missed you!"
8. Gesture "yes"
9. Volcanic rock
10. Foamy brews
11. Lively
13. — cream pie
14. Ghosts' shouts
19. Rummy variation
20. Police emblem
22. Dracula's cloak
23. Sandy color
24. Lodging place
26. Uppity folks
27. Learned
28. Home for 46-Across
29. Rising sun's direction
30. Mountain walk
31. Tel —, Israeli port
32. Go by pony
34. Peevish cry
37. Lost animal
40. Tract
43. Be a masseur
44. Play parts
49. Application
50. Finest
51. Costly fabrics
52. Gold-rush figure
53. Game-show host
54. Talented Alan
55. Circle of tape
56. Clothing fuzz
57. Wicked conduct
59. Noted Sampras
61. Compute a sum
62. Fellow
63. Light-switch setting

ACROSS

1. Guy's date
4. Bear's "hand"
7. Yet
10. Nevada neighbor
12. Hebrew prophet
14. Unshakably confident
15. Musical symbol
16. Distraught
17. Home for ducks
18. Award of honor
20. Hunters' lures
22. Metallic shine
25. In support of
26. Formal fight
28. Shred, as paper
30. Shade trees
33. Strictly forbids
34. Dallas natives
36. High peak
38. Arrow's path
39. Big —, London clock
40. Dull routine
41. "Wow!"
42. Become solid
43. President, Ronald —
45. Observe
46. Talented Arnaz
48. Clump of turf
49. Nape's place
50. Now — then
52. Devil
54. Cruise ships
57. From Dublin
60. Deck member
61. Catalog entries
64. Trim (11-Down)
66. "Fine!"
67. Wee skin openings
68. Gutter-mounting spot
69. Calligraphy tool
70. Kitchen skillet
71. Request charity

DOWN

1. Holstered weapon
2. Powerful particle
3. Tardy
4. Cork noise
5. Burro
6. Unwanted plant
7. Ocean marker
8. Coffee dispensers
9. "Chopped" host Allen
11. Shrub borders
12. Army mascot
13. Dance move
14. Film reel
19. The whole crew
21. Summit
23. Boxing venues
24. Blend together
26. Took a chance
27. Mom's brother
29. Festive march
31. Houdini's forte
32. Smooth; glossy
33. Sack or tote
34. Driving-range prop
35. Convent lady
37. Seat in church
39. Salt water
44. Sermon topic
45. Italian canal city
47. Covered with grit
49. Neither trailer
51. Faucet leak
53. Be off target
54. Fishing locale
55. Tehran's site
56. Halt
58. Concrete chunk
59. Bees' shelter
60. Peace officer
62. Span of time
63. Checkers pieces
65. Wooden nail

21

ACROSS
1. Acute sorrow
6. Disney pooch
10. Play segments
14. Town native
15. Lake near Cleveland
16. Ark captain
17. Sung drama
18. Intentions
19. Slangy denial
20. Exchange rings
21. Floor cleaners
23. Wisecracked
24. Bridge ploy
25. Opinion piece
28. Military branch
32. Crow's squawk
33. Capone and Jolson
36. On the side of
37. French capital
39. Forest female
40. Tasks
41. Knotted (up)
42. Hold a stance
43. Cry of glee
44. Extend (a lease)
45. Healed (the sick)
46. Urban pest
47. Writing fluid
48. People who make points
50. Noisy explosion
52. Belonging to us
53. Markswoman Oakley
56. Draped on
58. Gridiron judge
61. Viewed
62. Public vehicle
64. Depart
66. Nudge
67. Ancient
68. Anxious
69. Boy children
70. Physical being
71. Strict

DOWN
1. Look radiant
2. Catch with a lasso
3. Chilled (champagne)
4. Corn spike
5. On fire
6. Frog's jump
7. Greet the morning
8. Fairly dark
9. "Agreed!"
10. Test the patience of
11. Prepare dinner
12. Adhesive
13. Molt (fur)
22. Serious poem
23. Shark film
24. Grain boxes
26. Threaded nails
27. "Enough —!"
28. Army rank
29. Oahu welcome
30. Automated worker
31. Punishes Junior, old-style
33. Love madly
34. Race also-ran
35. Plants-to-be
38. Fighter pilot
41. Singer Horne
42. Cat's murmur
44. Provoke
45. Pairs
49. Dove's sound
50. Ties
51. Put a surcharge on
53. Scary serpents
54. Notorious fiddler of Rome
55. City sign gas
57. Neaten (up)
58. Furious anger
59. Always
60. Bouquet extra
62. Bar bill
63. In days past
65. Enjoy pickles

44

ACROSS

1. Wood strip
5. Site for a castaway
9. Food fish
12. Single step
13. Remain
14. One who fibs
16. Asian bear
17. A few
18. Star Bancroft
19. Ancient
20. Chunky
22. Pedaled a cycle
23. School exam
25. Affirmative vote
26. Funny Allen
27. Color variant
29. Bed for a baby
31. Gym surface
34. Oregon city
37. At that time
38. Explorer Marco
39. Typical instance
41. Most unearthly
43. Otherwise
44. English noble
46. Choir voices
47. Caress
48. Taxi cost
49. Female sheep
50. Annoy
51. Went first
53. Board cutters
57. DeVito or Glover
60. Untrue
62. Cup edge
63. Enthusiastic
64. Refer to
65. In the know
67. Skeleton part
68. A Baldwin
69. Hollowed out (an apple)
70. Candle material
71. Relax
72. Skirt bottoms

DOWN

1. Hardly fresh
2. Countries
3. Help
4. Animal snare
5. Magazine edition
6. Organ of digestion
7. Desk light
8. Needle slit
9. Assert
10. Pig grunt
11. Great —, dog breed
12. Blot
15. Scarlet
21. Harsh cleaner
22. Neck napkin
24. Main topic
26. Fork prong
28. "Out!" caller
30. Film spool
31. Verse writer
32. Too
33. Round specks
34. Trickle (out)
35. Wheel shaft
36. Final
37. Rip
38. Stacks (up)
40. Pipe problem
42. Uncooked
45. Tells (a tale)
48. Sauté
49. Asner and Sheeran
50. — finger, pointing digit
52. Vote in
54. Clock buzzer
55. Electric cords
56. Drove fast
57. Tiny bit
58. Admit openly
59. 1492 ship
60. Manicure tool
61. Every
64. Auto
66. Deep sadness

ACROSS

1. Cut (a lawn)
4. Noah's boat
7. Jar top
10. Verdi opera
11. Comic Rickles
12. Mecca resident
14. Objects to
15. Carry debt
16. Heredity factors
18. Citrus punch
19. Thigh joint
21. Sway, as a dog's tail
23. Feline pet
24. Admire
26. Cure
28. "— you nuts?"
29. Playground attraction
31. Sets of shoes
34. Pest on Fido
35. Fond hope
39. Inquire
40. Bank offerings
41. Half of a quartet
42. Those folks
44. Car
45. Little rock
47. Plentiful
49. Hive insect
50. Points a finger at

53. Cradle tune
57. "That feels nice!"
58. Bed support
60. Senate affirmative
61. Fish eggs
62. Fun surprise
64. Weaken
66. Royal hat
68. Letterman, to pals
69. Dark bread
70. Scottish caps
71. Father
72. Singer Tormé
73. Health resort

DOWN

1. Coal caverns
2. Peculiar
3. Laundromat machines
4. Take in (a child)
5. Sound-alike of 61-Across
6. Was sure of
7. Fell behind
8. Anger
9. Waltz or polka
10. Helper
13. Rosary orb
14. Disfigure
17. Pigpen

20. Frozen water
22. Diva deliveries
25. Golf score
27. Kitten noise
29. List of candidates
30. Famous Jay
31. Butter square
32. Cigar residue
33. Eisenhower's nickname
34. Disgusting
36. Wedding words
37. Our star
38. Weeding tool
40. Slight goof
43. Sweet potato
45. Chooses
46. — Aviv, Israel
48. Thawed
49. Purchase
50. Flying mammal
51. Cooking fat
52. In the future
53. Clothes tag
54. Smell
55. Fancy knots
56. Strong urge
59. Disease cause
63. Ms. Gardner
65. "Adios!"
67. Sharp knock

24

ACROSS

1. Minor quarrel
5. Dull pain
9. Call for help from a ship
12. Arm joint
14. Cry of grief
15. Morning haze
16. Pearly whites
17. Casino stake
18. Leer at
19. Used a sofa
20. Tall bloom
22. Small fish
24. Make a sweater
25. Dollar fraction
26. Current style
28. Mexican cloaks
31. Tearful
32. Bazaar stall
33. Awful
35. Departure door
36. Soup vessels
37. Retail event
38. Price label
39. Removes the rind from
40. — says, game
41. Canvas shoe
43. Enclosed car
44. Grows older
45. Window square
46. More cottony
49. Boys
50. Space between two 16-Across
53. Quite skilled
54. Russian tsar
56. Clear (a slate)
58. Satellite of earth
59. Long periods
60. Bette or Sammy
61. Stitch
62. Swing in the wind
63. Tidy

DOWN

1. TV receivers
2. Emotional appeal
3. Assist(a criminal)
4. New walker
5. Be ready for
6. Pantry tins
7. Considerable success
8. Basic parts
9. Highway guide
10. Capital of Norway
11. Hearty dish
13. Horse noise
15. September, for one
21. Dispose (of)
23. Ruler measure
24. Retained
25. Loses heat
26. Dallas's state
27. Govern
28. Great force
29. President Barack
30. Beauty parlor
31. Dripping
32. Tiresome folks
34. Lions' lair
36. Bread shops
37. Agree (with)
39. Book leaf
40. Felt instinctively
42. Already consumed
43. Depressed
45. Garden flower
46. Houston and Snead
47. Clarinet kin
48. Gush
49. Noted Turner
50. Donated
51. Huge continent
52. Annoying sort
55. Take an oath
57. Moved swiftly

ACROSS

1. Unrefined, as petroleum
6. Air pollution
10. Perimeter
14. Show on TV again
15. Midwest state
16. Toad kin
17. Wrath
18. Easter bloom
19. Snake tooth
20. Crabby Stooge
21. Big fusses
23. Ear sections
24. Self-esteem
25. Thin candle
28. Shrill scream
32. Wobbles
36. Young person
37. Church table
39. Confederate general
40. Lubricates
41. Creep about
42. Long story
43. Half of two
44. "The Sound of —," film
45. Daisy feature
46. Baby 16-Across
48. Bits on a cob
50. Leg joint
52. Animal doctor
53. Electric flash
56. Harvest
58. Common virus
61. Possess
62. Cain's victim
64. "Goodbye!"
66. Unlock
67. Tie holder in a closet
68. Wash lightly
69. Segment
70. Bath rugs
71. Concluded

DOWN

1. Study hard
2. Nevada city
3. Strong yen
4. Payable now
5. Furious
6. Farm tower
7. Slightly wet
8. Wise bird?
9. Carefree
10. Determined attempt
11. Dull
12. Auction shout
13. Custard base
22. Disney dwarf
23. Crafty smile
24. Thin fish
26. Military raid
27. Top
28. "Leave!"
29. Beijing's nation
30. Stirred up
31. Gretel's brother
33. Fill with joy
34. Fit for a queen
35. Closes firmly
38. Hawaiian garland
41. Pout
42. Dispatched
44. Abbey resident
45. Get ready
47. Mom or dad
49. Ms. Gabor
51. Build (a barn)
53. Mall business
54. Father, to a tot
55. Say clearly
57. Lodge members
58. Discover
59. Fail to win
60. — car lot
62. Give guns to
63. Ram bleat
65. Unbearable racket

ACROSS

1. Commenced
6. Pecan, for one
9. Blast noise
12. Royal castles
14. Some
15. Gershwin of Broadway
16. From Mecca
17. Walked quietly
19. "— a gift!"
20. Pull along
22. Adolescent
23. Mesh snares
25. "Blue —," old song
27. Allows
30. "— or treat!"
32. Goof up
33. Slumber
34. Ice-cream serving
36. Grocery reminder
38. Bit of sunshine
39. Long journey
41. Winter garment
43. Existed
46. Grand film
48. Dog variety
51. Bonus
53. Arrest
55. Lion pro
57. Male suitor
58. Special talent
60. Office note
61. Raise
63. Requirement
65. Steal from
66. City roads
69. Provoke
71. Contains
72. Ocean
73. Mexican dish
74. Hill insect
75. Scheming
76. Extends credit

DOWN

1. Trades
2. Stretchy
3. Talk a lot
4. Lab chemical
5. Gets close to
6. Name hidden in "nominate"
7. Motel rooms
8. Sort; kind
9. Trailblazing colonist
10. Mine find
11. Roll of bills
12. Emulate Picasso
13. Serpent
18. Relate (a story)
21. Lass
24. Kilt wearer?
26. Viking explorer
28. Hot drink
29. Secret agent
31. Divided Asian peninsula
33. First square of a board game
35. Brisk energy
37. Cry softly
40. Knotty twist
42. Sports squad
43. Spider snare
44. Hatchet kin
45. Least fresh
47. Son of Adam
49. Green gem
50. Reduces in rank
52. Destroy
54. Sheep sound
56. Choir attire
58. Girder material
59. Okay by the rules
62. Be cranky
64. Ten-cent coin
66. "Eureka!"
67. Delivery truck
68. Utter
70. Light brown

27

ACROSS

1. Wound traces
6. Facial spasms
10. Mature, as fruit
14. Have a spat
15. Singer Fitzgerald
16. Adam's garden
17. Big
18. Alda of TV
19. Winter toy
20. Consumed
21. Tree fluid
23. Annoys constantly
25. Hart or stag
27. Fishing stick
29. — Grande
30. Joins together
33. Pony gaits
37. Spinets and grands
40. Be dishonest
42. Sinister
43. Ms. Landers
44. Tells the meaning of
47. Giants great Manning
48. Plant stalk
50. Henpeck
51. Bellowed
53. Planted (seeds)
55. Rush of excitement
57. Even score
59. Foot digit
60. Arthur of tennis
64. Accumulates
68. Arid
70. Bowling target
71. Toledo's state
72. Italian city
74. Separately
76. Manor master
77. Margarine
78. Less narrow
79. Recolors (a shoe)
80. Decomposes
81. Very poor

DOWN

1. Dish of greens
2. Packing box
3. Concur
4. Small carpet
5. Glances at
6. Hot-drink server
7. Sick
8. Applaud
9. Not as crazy
10. Give back
11. Inactive
12. Squint (at)
13. Finales
22. Cropped up
24. Take a chair
26. "— for your lives!"
28. Great joy
31. Head motion
32. Moral offense
34. Completed
35. Floor square
36. Coasted
37. Gridiron throw
38. Division term
39. Freshly
41. More surreal
45. Chunky
46. Scale tone
49. Set procedures
52. Like: 2 wds.
54. Wither away
56. Cowboy shows
58. Mistake
61. Garden digger
62. Engaged
63. Diary excerpt
64. Jewelry metal
65. Nautical yell
66. Grow weary
67. Fly alone
69. Appear drowsy
73. Convened
75. Key lime —

ACROSS

1. Easter meat
4. Commercials
7. Photographic device
13. Mythical Baba
14. By way of
15. Egg dish
16. Hollering
18. Healthy, green veggie
19. Go underwater
20. Cultivated a garden
21. Golf peg
22. Agenda entry
24. Custer's Last —
26. Helsinki native
27. Facial features
29. Large truck
30. Mail drops
31. "Believe it or —..."
32. Bucket
34. Compared to
35. Ring of light over an angel
36. Cowboy shoe
37. Stringed instrument
38. Look stunned
39. This girl
42. Slumber sound
44. Barbecue hunk
45. Scrub (a tub)
47. Be apt (to)
48. Exists
50. Overdue
51. Feeling of inspiration
52. Barn ornament
53. Partly open
55. Answer
57. Keyboard player
60. Impressive home
61. Hardy tree
62. Convent lady
63. Current fashions
64. Beast of burden
65. Receive

DOWN

1. Dried grass
2. Pub brew
3. Least harsh
4. Tel —
5. Has supper
6. Droop
7. Dealt (with)
8. Surrounded by
9. Adult guys
10. Sheer joy
11. Up-to-date
12. Greek capital
17. Citrus fruit
18. Tune
20. Icy shower
22. Rural hotel
23. Besides
25. Music combo
26. Blown-out tire
28. Extra
30. Foot protectors
33. Swiss peak
34. Acme
35. Challenging
36. Yankee Ruth
37. Truthfulness
38. Donate
39. Flying high
40. Crude cabin
41. Prior to, to poets
42. Gawks (at)
43. Most contemporary
44. Orange layer
46. Big family
48. Country roads
49. Ship's sheets
52. Ballot
54. Bread spreads
56. Crony
57. Podded edible
58. Take to court
59. Common explosive: abbr.

ACROSS

1. Steep, as tea
5. Massage
8. Upon
12. Roof edge
13. Exchange vows with
15. Volcano flow
16. Moth-eaten
17. Orphan of comics
18. "Grace" finale
19. Conclusion
21. Flower bed
23. Clinging vine
24. Tear up
25. Gleam
28. Quick humor
29. Plane driver
33. Opposite of short
34. Peke cry
35. Canal city of Italy
36. Plus
37. Lock unlocker
38. Lass
39. Five pairs
40. Loud sounds
42. Large rodent
43. Lamb or pork
44. Leftover mark
45. Grocery sack
46. Alerts
47. Ms. Winfrey
49. Strong liquor
50. Less distant
52. July follower
55. Castle ditch
56. Terrible pain
58. Landed (on)
60. Formerly
61. Is in front
62. Bean variety
63. Foamy drink
64. Blue expanse above us
65. "— lively!"

DOWN

1. Arthur on TV
2. Intense anger
3. Still
4. Vegas chapel event
5. Chimed
6. Fancy planter
7. Illuminated
8. Disney film with a genie
9. Domesticated
10. Baking machine
11. Bad review
13. Several
14. 365-day unit
20. "— done it!"
22. Drive off
24. Wee taste
25. Tilt
26. Great respect
27. New Delhi's nation
28. Milky —, galaxy
30. Soda amount
31. Briny deep
32. Camp shelters
34. "You're on!"
35. Dyeing tub
37. Hangs on to
38. Funny stunt
41. Vehicle for a kid
42. Sidelines shout
43. Instruction booklets
45. Flat-bottomed boats
46. Head covering
48. Authentic
49. Fellows
50. Pine dropping
51. Veil trimming
52. "Toy Story" boy
53. Narrow cut
54. Clock reading
55. Unruly crowd
57. Acorn source
59. Sink faucet

ACROSS

1. Tool set
4. Sty grunter
7. — Angeles
10. Common metal
12. Poetic works
14. Mom's sis
16. Show courage
17. Holiday song
18. Lead actors
20. Less messy
22. "How vile!"
24. Regret
25. Mr. Orbison
26. Epoch
27. Emcee Trebek
28. 49-Across area
31. Young ladies
33. Absent
34. A conjunction
35. Pen's partner
38. For each
39. Fido's "hand"
40. Lay wagers
41. Used a shovel
43. Movie premiere
45. Took a spouse
46. Animal skin
47. "— we stand…"
49. Lodging place
50. Bit of data
53. Contend
54. Ruby or topaz
55. Ms. Lupino
56. Golfer Hogan
57. French caps
60. Guitar kin
62. Receive pay
64. Be a nomad
66. Yell of pain
67. "Scram!"
68. Comfy couch
69. Potato bud
70. Asner and Sullivan
71. Journalist Koppel

DOWN

1. Young goat
2. Shah's realm
3. Ripped
4. Tea sweetener
5. Smell
6. Cry of awe
7. Eyelid hair
8. Diamond shout
9. Canine warning
11. Close at hand
13. Veiled insults
15. Accurate
19. Gender
21. Plaything
23. Inhaled suddenly
26. Hearing organ
27. African snake
28. Drink (up)
29. Carried loans
30. Unclothed
31. Despicable
32. Enjoy food
34. Locally born
36. Revise (text)
37. Impolite
39. Verbal joke
40. Catnap locale
42. Harden
44. However
45. Itty-bitty
46. Baseball feats
48. Fork prongs
49. That princess
50. White lie
51. Eden fellow
52. Narrow boat
54. Chaps
56. Femur, for example
57. Hunky Pitt
58. Whistle blast
59. Wall vault
61. Comic Leno
63. Air-show pilot
65. Angry

ACROSS

1. Was dressed in
5. Stadium level
9. Oil container
13. British noble
14. Land measure
15. Facilitate
16. Heaven resident
17. Blood vessel
18. Liberate
19. Senate affirmative
20. Imitate
22. "I just had the — feeling..."
24. They sleep noisily
27. Take the gold
28. Contract negotiators
30. Cat comments
34. See 9-Across
37. Line of seats
39. Let fall
40. "— we there?"
41. Chose (to)
44. Pretty Gardner
45. Made knots
47. Mom's guy
48. Bank clerk
50. Less dangerous
52. Crawling bug
54. Brief craze
56. Snow vehicles
59. Hone
63. Circle part
64. Cry of glee
66. Tijuana snack
67. Cushiony
69. Direction sign
71. — and crafts
72. Joint above the shin
73. Sample (a stew)
74. Superior
75. Finch food
76. Female sheep

DOWN

1. Weakens
2. Keyboard instrument
3. Fish eggs
4. Got bigger
5. Neighborhood bar
6. Arctic scenery
7. A Great Lake
8. Extend
9. Explained the meaning of
10. Hard to find
11. Employs
12. Encounter
13. Ocean inlet
21. Pared
23. Saucer edge
25. Rowing pole
26. Giant steps
29. Clump of dirt
31. Of a mouth
32. Interlaced
33. Fight (with)
34. Flying mammals
35. Opera solo
36. Coral ridge
38. More humid
42. Metered car
43. Fragile
46. Thaw
49. Chair support
51. Loud knock
53. Very pleased
55. Office tables
57. It neighs
58. Golf strokes
59. Piercing injury
60. Tortoise foe in a fable
61. Behaves
62. Opposite of all
65. Be in debt to
68. Bank charge
70. Entirely uncooked

32

ACROSS

1. Wound cover
5. Jaw part
9. Casual greeting
12. Sum
14. Jay of TV
15. Nat King —, 1950s singer
16. Hilo hello
17. Bothers
18. Show emcee
19. Sweet potato
20. Rounded roof
22. Location
23. Thick piece
24. Mournful cry
26. Sugary
28. European land
31. Dull pains
32. Blaze of light
33. "HELP!"
35. Rigid support
36. Egyptian city
37. — into, meet
38. — Aviv, Israel
39. Address for a lad
40. Serious play
41. Matrimony
43. Every 24 hours
44. Simple
45. Shape
46. Live in tents
48. Pisces or Scorpio
49. Mr. Rather
52. Boxcar rider
53. She fibs
55. Rub out
57. Fateful predictor
58. Skin problem
59. Actress Bette
60. Moist
61. Words of parting
62. Tidy

DOWN

1. Remain
2. Soda flavor
3. Tiny particle
4. "Ridiculous!"
5. Scale (a mountain)
6. In this place
7. Pen liquid
8. Verbal rejections
9. Owl sound
10. Otherwise
11. But
13. Soup scoopers
15. Spicy dish with beans
21. Cereal grain
22. Exhale sadly
23. Ooze
24. Tired
25. As well
26. Threaded nail
27. Complete
28. Eyelid movement
29. Customary
30. Daddy's wife
31. Likely (to)
32. Far from plain
34. Health resort
36. Racket from pigeons
37. Hat edge
39. Hit with an open palm
40. Mended (a sock)
42. Evil creature
43. Barking pet
45. Shoots (a gun)
46. See 52-Down
47. Aid (a crook)
48. Rational
49. Columnist Barry
50. Big continent
51. Bird home
52. With 46-Down, "Why?"
53. Science room
54. Very cold
56. Jogged fast

ACROSS

1. Drink counter
4. Leg bone
7. Give cash to
10. Biblical king
12. Cairo resident
14. Keep for later use
15. Wed secretly
16. Roman ruler
17. Mirror image
18. — Jersey, shore state
19. Tent stake
21. Assigned task
23. Dense mist
24. Cloth scrap
25. Snapshots
28. On the spur of the —
31. Urgent appeals
32. Defrosts
34. Italian-dressing ingredient
36. Attendance list
37. Bridal accessories
38. Greater in quantity
39. Wise bird?
40. Wild fowl
41. Stationed (at)
42. Flew high
44. Like some pretzels
46. Disfigure
47. Round speck
48. Jewish clerics
51. Comic Knotts
52. Lamb's lament
55. Find a buyer for
56. 1492 craft
58. Oddly amusing
60. Poker stake
61. Glisten
62. Closes firmly
63. Cow sound
64. Have
65. Cook in fat

DOWN

1. Cotton bundle
2. Announce
3. Tear
4. Suspend
5. Exasperation
6. Peel (away)
7. Lowly chess piece
8. Eager
9. Tokyo money
10. Hibernation site
11. Bus stations
13. Takes for a time
14. Phase
20. Conceit
22. Runs into
23. Barn baby
25. Farm tools
26. "Greetings!"
27. Frisky mount
28. Bachelor-party guests
29. Rope loop
30. Weary
31. Expert golfer
33. That guy's
35. Blazed a trail
37. Swerving
38. Actor Dillon
40. Get ahold of
41. Fair-haired folks
43. Meander
45. Commotion
48. Nevada city
49. Choir voice
50. Rural skyscraper?
51. Daybreak
52. Tusked pig
53. Comrade
54. Pacino and Unser
55. Historic Houston
57. Immediately
59. Hockey judge

ACROSS

1. Served a meal to
4. Dinner check
7. Warsaw natives
9. Chick peep
11. Loses light
13. Most earsplitting
15. Accumulate birthdays
16. Thinks about
18. Absence of peace
19. Screw (up)
21. Daniel of the frontier
22. Depend (on)
23. "Cut it out!"
25. Scarlet
26. Disease cause
27. Figures out
29. Tiny terrace crossers
30. Must have
31. Burn black
32. Thrash
33. Shreds (cheese)
35. Sculpted portrait
36. Macabre author
37. Cloth bag
39. Raise
40. Paved paths
42. Anagram of 29-Across
44. Assistant for Santa
45. Less clean
47. "— for Two," song
48. Helium or oxygen
50. Blew a whistle
52. Smelled bad
53. Bellybutton
54. CIA agent
55. Golf score

DOWN

1. Wooded areas
2. Big deer
3. Profound
4. So
5. Financial help
6. Wisconsin team
7. Book leaves
8. Uppity jerk
9. Apple center
10. Holy hymn
11. River blocker
12. Was a noisy sleeper
13. Give for a bit
14. Attempt
17. Performs
20. As early as possible
22. Fall back, as troops
24. Kilt fold
26. Pesky insects
28. Cat doctor
29. "Gotcha!"
31. — card, alternative to cash
32. All-you-can-eat spreads
33. Farm critter
34. Strew
35. Bird beaks
36. Harbor town
38. Bend to pray
39. Martial artist Bruce
40. Place to play hockey
41. Stitched
43. Far from happy
45. Contradict
46. Harvest (a crop)
49. Atlas diagram
51. Pretty Longoria

ACROSS

1. Inquire
4. Use the eyes
7. Big snake
10. Eat less food
12. Unaided
14. Acid
15. Be jealous of
16. Comes to rest (on)
17. Urban oasis
18. Kitchen pans
20. Makes a scarf
22. Snide smiles
23. Meter face
24. Decompose
25. Reno regulars
29. Mr. Vigoda
32. Pet name?
33. Go offstage
34. Mint or basil
36. Heavy strings
37. Cowgirl Evans
38. British title
39. Sacred
40. Litter sound
41. "West Side Story" and "Chicago"
43. Talk a lot
46. Phoenix team
47. Fond embrace
50. Many times
52. Remarks (on)
54. Competent enough
55. Avoid cleverly
57. Spot for a diving board
58. Docile beast
59. Lung sections
60. Song for one
61. Tinting agent
62. Mower fuel
63. Chapel bench

DOWN

1. Stand drinks
2. Descends
3. Bacon of film
4. Wood strips
5. Many millennia
6. Extreme tip
7. River vessel
8. A possessive
9. Noah's boat
11. Mary — Moore
12. Watchful
13. Native Alaskans
14. Overflowed
19. Zodiac cat
21. Seize; arrest
23. Father
25. Young women
26. School final
27. Stir to anger
28. Hearty dish
29. "Excuse me!"
30. Suitor of old
31. Does wrong
32. Silly folks
35. Foot woe
36. TV station
42. Stage prompt
43. Friendly competitions
44. Biceps site
45. Pager alerts
47. Sets of laws
48. Be a busybody
49. Pilfered
50. Comply with
51. Run away from
52. Havana's nation
53. Like a turtle
54. Determine a sum
56. Bit of timber

ACROSS
1. Dawn droplets
4. Butter square
7. Buddy
10. Russian tsar
12. — de Janeiro
13. Noble address
14. Hands (to)
16. Lode mineral
17. Bed linen
18. Jumped high
20. See 65-Across
22. Prescribed substance
23. Mouth parts
24. Uptight
26. Flowing cloak
27. Back section
30. Tales of adventure
32. Beach grit
36. Like antiques
37. Deprive (of)
38. Flower loop
39. Plate or record
41. Adored folks
43. Refer to
44. Landers and Sothern
46. Repetitive sound
48. Mr. Clapton
49. Points (a dart)
51. Athletic award
53. Attract
55. Throws
56. Adam's rib, supposedly
58. Glasgow natives
60. People
61. Feel bad
62. "He's — a hard worker!"
63. Chair cushion
64. Owns
65. With 20-Across, African desert

DOWN
1. Excavate
2. Villainous
3. Gestured goodbye
4. Push
5. Balloon filler
6. Foot digits
7. Long docks
8. Region
9. Allow
11. More intimate
13. Geometric forms
15. Potato, to some
17. Big boat
19. Hen products
21. Exclamation of dismay
25. There are 100 between end zones
26. Wire cord
27. Curtain pole
28. A Whitney
29. Billboards' contents
31. Sticky stuff
33. Famous boxer
34. After-tax take
35. Cease to live
40. Christmas ditties
41. Yardstick segment
42. Radar display
43. Sunday funnies
45. Little bites
47. Top 40 songs
48. Was at fault
50. Indian guide
51. Sushi fish
52. "You bet!"
53. Long fish
54. Impress deeply
55. Jump like a kangaroo
57. Through
59. "Ain't — Sweet"

ACROSS

1. Bath basin
4. Fireplace powder
7. Lyricist Gershwin
8. Buzzing insect
9. See 19-Down
11. Stands at a slant
13. Sick
15. Scale tone
16. Suburban tree
17. Funny person
20. Guided trip
22. Reminds constantly
24. NFL commentator Ditka
25. Water vapor
27. Green growth on a rock
29. Prayer end
30. Twirl a spoon in
32. Indian tents
34. Muscle twitch
36. Express agreement
37. Top's opposite
40. Care for
43. "Stop, horse!"
45. Pub brews
47. Doctor's assistant
50. —, line, and sinker
51. Neighbor of Nevada
53. Sign of crying
54. "I agree!"
55. Actor Hanks
57. Complete collection
59. Had lunch
60. Writer Mark
62. Employed
64. 100%
65. Chest bone
66. Crafty
67. Weep aloud

DOWN

1. Fasten with string
2. Greek vases
3. Conductor's stick
4. Son of Adam
5. Garment joint
6. She clucks
9. Assortment on this page
10. Close loudly
11. Decrease
12. Enjoys a pool
13. "— not my fault!"
14. Land parcel
18. Eisenhower's nickname
19. With 9-Across, dime's value
21. Urban rodent
23. Received
24. Funny West
26. Oven glove
28. Location
31. Lovely Hayworth
33. Bible garden
35. Pillar kin
37. Push up
38. See 16-Across
39. Encountered
41. Bolt go-with
42. Great fear
43. "— did the chicken cross the road?"
44. Weeding tool
46. Fabric belt
48. Made a lap
49. Before, in poems
52. Folks in a will
55. Statuesque
56. Slick with grease
58. Music group
61. Existed
63. Weaken

38

ACROSS

1. Serious vows
6. Jump lightly
10. Office note
14. Sound of pain
15. Ore deposit
16. Pizzeria appliance
17. Singer Ronstadt
18. Persia, today
19. Do a Vegas job
20. Harris and Asner
21. Italian city
23. Comedian Jack
24. Winter bug
25. Role player
28. Eggy brunch orders
32. Female in a pride
36. Dwelled (in)
37. Stinky smells
39. Tell fibs
40. Creative spark
41. Come up
42. Tip off
43. Service truck
44. Drama segment
45. Referred to
46. Elaborate properties
48. Unlocks again
50. Wipes down
    furniture
52. Positive vote
53. :
56. Huge sandwich
58. "— was that?"
61. Profess
62. Tel —, Israel
64. Sampled
66. DNA holder
67. Face wrinkle
68. Simplified
69. Special times
70. Squint (at)
71. Tool huts

DOWN

1. Leer at
2. Bone-dry
3. Scads (of)
4. — on, wore
5. Tangled, as hair
6. Slender
7. Divided Asian
   peninsula
8. Ms. Lupino
9. Autographing
   implement
10. New
11. Balanced
12. Hateful
13. Just
22. Not at home
23. Spooky cries
24. Fido biter
26. Less far
27. Become drowsy
28. Popeye's love
29. Mythical king
30. Happening
31. Most offended
33. Cheer up
34. Wailing alarm
35. Conveys
38. Noisy racket
41. Cockpit stars
42. Towel off
44. Fill with awe
45. Wolflike creatures
47. Is mad about
49. Hearing organ
51. Glow
53. Parrot housing
54. Superior to
55. Talented Horne
57. Always
58. Very smart
59. Listen to
60. Gambling stats
62. Swiss mountain
63. Contend (for)
65. Bowl cheer

ACROSS

1. Fail to hit
5. Mama's man
9. Punch hard
13. Above
14. Not as comfortable
15. Country byway
16. Wound trace
17. Say
18. Make changes in (text)
19. Seafood treat
21. Most sluggish
23. Short rests
25. Smack (flies)
26. "— speak louder than words!"
29. Pizza pieces
33. Evergreen tree
34. Classy curtain
36. Posed humbly
37. Father of Abel
39. General direction
41. Was generous
42. Fight back
44. Dined
46. Drink a bit of
47. School themes
49. Dwells (at)
51. Pair (up)
53. Asian grain
54. Winter Olympics racer
57. Leased car
61. Volcano output
62. Stood
64. Corn Belt state
65. For the mouth
66. Lacking
67. From the beginning
68. In the pink
69. Article in the paper
70. See 66-Across

DOWN

1. Catholic service
2. Need to scratch
3. Fly in the clouds
4. Run swiftly
5. Deep pan
6. Martial —
7. Orange skins
8. Cupid's darts
9. Raining icily
10. Young fellows
11. Army squadron
12. Obtain
14. Uphold
20. Hotel worker
22. Stroll
24. Trap
26. They help
27. Grouchy folks
28. Sharp lance
30. Discontinue
31. 1950s icon Presley
32. Recipe instruction
33. Travel cost
35. Come in
38. Sphere on spaghetti
40. Wants
43. Harsh liquids
45. Good-natured
48. Popular cold cut
50. Opposing statement
52. Worthiness
54. Uncovered
55. Egg-shaped
56. Completed
58. Color variation
59. Overwhelms
60. Crooks break them
61. Ankle-high
63. Total

40

ACROSS

1. Violin knob
4. Science room
7. Star Gardner
10. College test
12. Neon and hydrogen
14. Fibbed
15. Rub (out)
16. Grow mature
17. Lemony drinks
18. Bank clerk
20. More loving
22. Bran source
23. Kuwait export
24. Police emblems
27. Show up
30. Randall of sitcoms
31. Public area in a hotel
33. Conceited person
35. Irritate
36. — de Janeiro
37. Full of mirth
38. Slim swimmers
40. Have a debate
42. Lowly; humble
43. Assistant to a sheriff
45. Tall, thin candles
47. Blaze residue
48. Did nothing
49. Urban road
52. The movies
55. Adult filly
56. Majestic
58. Hostile takeover
60. Eager
61. Wipe grease on
62. "Whose — are you on?"
63. Jazz (up)
64. Ply a needle
65. Mr. Aykroyd

DOWN

1. Bench for praying
2. Opposite of entrance
3. Look stunned
4. Dragon's dwelling
5. Deadly snake
6. Hamburger meat
7. Staff member
8. Swerve wildly
9. Commercials
11. Tune
12. Sister of Hansel
13. "Peanuts" beagle
14. Soup scoopers
19. Drop behind
21. Wee pinch
24. Uninterested
25. Foot joint
26. Apologetic
27. "It's — time!"
28. Wrath
29. Laughs loudly
30. Lace (up)
32. Large
34. "See ya!"
39. Had mercy on
40. Greece's capital
41. Less difficult
42. Taxi devices
44. Avail oneself of
46. Frying vessel
49. Keep for a rainy day
50. Stumble (over)
51. Male cats
52. Eagle's talon
53. Domestic employee
54. Opera heroine
55. Road chart
57. Garden buzzer
59. Scout unit

ACROSS

1. Stealthy soldier?
6. Boot attachment
10. Brief trends
14. Happen
15. Pond relative
16. Loads: 2 wds.
17. Said a third time
19. Midwest state
20. Wild donkey
21. Great: 2 wds.
22. Bible book
24. Pharmacy item
25. Tar kin
26. Wholeheartedly: 2 wds.
29. Preference
30. Creature
31. Place in rows
33. Propping peg
36. Concern
37. Austrian composer of "The Seasons"
38. Sketch
39. Chic resort
40. Thick liquid
41. Baseballer Pee Wee
42. Showroom model
43. More timid
44. Craftsperson
47. Hunky Johnny
48. Brain cell
49. He fibs
50. After: 2 wds.
53. Heredity unit
54. Sympathizes (with)
57. Festive nights
58. Rock's Turner
59. Exodus peak
60. For fear that
61. "You bet!"
62. Surplus

DOWN

1. Ibsen heroine
2. Freezes (up)
3. Mark Harmon series
4. Protrude
5. Floor protector: 2 wds.
6. Informal language
7. Rich spread
8. Little guitar
9. Make a new blueprint for
10. Theology topics
11. Don Ho hello
12. Wooden pin
13. Inception
18. Conquer
23. Reach across
24. Accomplished
25. Remain (with)
26. Kindergarten lessons
27. Graceful jump
28. Old Pisa dough
31. Slugger Hank
32. Drain opener
33. Go on foot
34. Poise
35. Water vessel
37. Benevolence; goodwill
38. Extending far below
40. Mexican coin
41. Perform again
42. Most dreadful
43. Ham or veal
44. Halo wearer
45. Actor Christopher
46. Ditties
47. Ms. Shore
49. Olin of films
50. "If it — broke..."
51. Tragic Shakespearean king
52. Nepal's site
55. Lose force
56. Remedy

ACROSS

1. Basinger of cinema
4. Polishing cloth
7. Mineral nutrient
9. Actress Downey
10. Blue shade
11. Glimpse
12. Scared shriek
15. Enemy
17. Air-rifle ammo
20. Twisted awry
22. Shopping binge
23. Minute skin opening
24. Artery fluid
26. Holbrook of Hollywood
27. Bert's roomie
28. Pieces of bacon
30. Forte of a siren
32. Warbling Yoko
33. May honoree
34. Check out the scene, at a party
37. Modernize
40. Covered with fine grit
41. Jelly glass
43. Build (a house)
45. Norway's capital
46. Flavoring plants
48. Tall tale
49. Average grade
50. Tenor Pavarotti
52. Dull routine
53. Emporium
54. Carpet piles
56. Becomes sick
57. "CHiPs" star Estrada
58. Spoken pauses
59. Luau souvenir

DOWN

1. One's family
2. Islamic country
3. Changes location
4. Comedian O'Donnell
5. Current measures
6. Joyful
8. Nature goddesses
9. Offer again
12. Grow weak
13. Reef dwellers
14. Entanglement
16. Special time
17. German city
18. Ship's jail
19. Be witness to
21. Home of the NHL's Maple Leafs
23. Chief
25. Begrimed
27. Disintegrate
29. Official candidate: slang
31. Baseball VIP
34. Inspiring figure
35. Land surrounded by water
36. Ousts
37. Suave
38. Weeper's drop
39. Hose hue
40. Sleepy's pal
42. Nickname for Onassis
44. Demolition substance
46. Throws
47. Growl fiercely
50. Crooks' den
51. Ron Howard TV role
53. West of film
55. — chalet

43

ACROSS

1. Unlocking aid
4. School theme
9. Auto style
14. Spanish cheer
15. Kitchen item
16. Custom
17. Every drop
18. Saltwater snails
20. Bouncy tune
22. Firetruck hue
23. Most roguish
24. Takes on faith
26. Mine car
27. Ghostly word
28. Brilliant jewels
32. Bit of junk
35. Minty drink
36. Cry of wonder
37. Reporter Lane
38. Suppress
39. Slugger Sammy
40. Muffin grain
41. Business attire
42. Queued (up)
43. Man-made materials
45. The Chicago White —
46. Full of frills

47. Compromised
51. Waylay
54. Show on TV
55. Sharpen
56. Unaffected by emotion
59. Tapper Miller
60. Cheek coloring
61. Diva Ross
62. Egyptian king, for short
63. Was at fault
64. Took a chance
65. Towel monogram

DOWN

1. Aussie marsupial
2. — Island, N.Y. immigration center
3. Shouts
4. Clairvoyant skill
5. Audio system
6. Tender areas
7. Gung-ho
8. Wood for bows
9. Tanning device
10. Igloo dweller
11. Famous Evans
12. Generations
13. Snug retreat

19. Jewish nation
21. Brass basses
25. Floor swabber
26. Cash drawers
28. Ditties for a pair
29. Lunch hour, often
30. Serum portion
31. Food fish
32. Hogs' grub
33. Glowing ember
34. Glamorous Hayworth
35. Like a ripe melon
38. Eggy dish
39. — sense, eerie talent
41. Hidden away
42. Property site
44. Muddy deposit
45. Calm
47. Indian instrument
48. Unwilling (to)
49. Boredom
50. Fender dings
51. Deed measure
52. Boggy spot
53. Fuzzy image
54. Tenor's big solo
57. Supplement
58. Family VIP

ACROSS

1. States firmly
6. Soaks through
10. Troubles
14. Musical show
15. James of "Misery"
16. Ark figure
17. Muscle pain
18. "That's awful!": 2 wds.
19. Park path
20. Finale
21. Ballet skirt
23. Tanzania neighbor
25. Most secret
27. Bias
28. Plains Indian
29. Brewed drink
30. Crunch targets, for short
33. Salad veggie
36. Tour de France vehicle
37. Shade; tint
38. Young gents
39. Small salamanders
40. Gaelic speaker
41. 63-Across, to a biologist
42. Large, saltwater fishes
43. Fails onstage
44. Precious find
45. Pretentiously bohemian
46. Comic Caesar
47. Table scraps
48. Made a bet
52. Bahamas capital
55. Woody's boy
56. Much fuss
57. Madame Bovary
58. One-of-a-kind
60. Unspoken
62. Totally wild
63. Omelet base
64. Choose (a candidate)
65. Roman robe
66. Chimney ash
67. Mud-covered

DOWN

1. Curved
2. Author Jules
3. Dodge
4. Common liquor
5. Singing groups
6. Baio of TV
7. Hawaiian site
8. Shallow pot
9. Underwater breathing tubes
10. Sibling's spouse: hyph. wd.
11. Borrowed sum
12. Touch ground
13. Former Mets stadium
22. Operate
24. Existed
26. Face: slang
27. Religious factions
29. Side road
30. Throaty sound
31. Lamp need
32. Adjusts
33. Drain problem
34. Praise highly
35. Dutch cheese
36. Pennies
39. Fosters
40. System of symbols
42. O'Hara abode
43. Narrow-minded
46. "My Gal —"
47. Japanese port
48. Forcibly take
49. Track athlete
50. Public decree
51. Crazy
52. Orderly
53. Military supplies: slang
54. Choking haze
55. Jason's boat
59. Prior to today
61. Frazier's foe

45

ACROSS

1. Broadness
6. Vatican VIPs
11. Bikini half
14. Farewell
15. Unattended
16. Torso bone
17. Queen's domain
18. Pattern on Wall Street?
20. Lacking color
21. Slightly curled
22. Belief
23. Stage in life
25. Is the king
26. Revolutionary Hale
29. Adolescent
30. In progress
31. Zeus's wife
33. Roguish guys
37. Show glee
38. Plot again
39. Fluish feeling
40. Shoe bottom
41. Simple
42. Search about blindly
43. Sonny's former partner
45. Jeopardy
46. Attack vigorously
49. Singer Abdul
51. Celery unit
52. Sprint
53. Start to melt
57. Foolish state
59. Princess's headdress
60. Room addition
61. Actor Nick
62. — system
63. Quite cunning
64. "Excellent!"
65. Drawer pulls

DOWN

1. Twist out of shape
2. Vague sense
3. Clock face
4. Bell made the first: 2 wds.
5. Bee's buzz
6. Fathers
7. Martini fruit
8. Polo equine
9. Three letters in 19-Down
10. Parlor piece
11. Provide
12. Mature, as a banana
13. Aids in crime
19. Hindu 22-Across
21. 20-Across, in a sickly way
24. Sombrero or bowler
25. Gather grain
26. Annoys
27. Full hairdo
28. Work hard
29. Cafeteria platter
31. Get the news
32. Type measures
34. Keyed up
35. Hoodwink
36. Visionary one
38. Spool of film
42. Damsel
44. On a nature walk
45. "Obviously!": slang
46. Wild donkeys
47. Motionless
48. Astronaut Ride
49. Penne or ziti
50. Good quality
52. Erase, to a printer
54. Saint's aura
55. Fast horse
56. Big conflicts
58. Negative word
59. "For shame!"

46

ACROSS

1. Intentions
6. Greek sandwich
10. Frosted (a pastry)
14. Distraught
15. Maui event
16. Numerical info
17. Cafe drink
18. Urgent occurrence
20. "Alice" role
21. Sicily spewer
23. Solemn vows
24. Formed a web
25. Almond-shaped
27. Links bend
30. Inept person: 2 wds. (slang)
34. Baseball flub
35. Realities
37. Raced on foot
38. What winds do
39. Famed Gardner
40. Insignificant
41. Tier of seats
42. Certain office clerk
44. Ms. Zellweger
45. Replies
47. Postpones
48. Downwind

49. — pro quo
50. Barely: 2 wds.
53. Unopened flowers
54. Youngster
57. Simple game: 3 wds.
60. Burn lightly
62. Author Rice
63. Give off goo
64. Labor group
65. Salon employee
66. House portal
67. List item

DOWN

1. Deep chasm
2. Fiery stone
3. Regarding: 2 wds.
4. Rent
5. More sloped
6. Bandleader Miller
7. Arizona town
8. Charlotte of sitcoms
9. Created by us
10. Perfect examples
11. "I — stand it!"
12. Carve in acid
13. Week parts
19. Prods
22. Harbor hauler

24. Hardly swift
25. Writer Wilde
26. Brewing tank
27. Actress Messing
28. Acrylic fiber
29. Gets bigger
31. Hockey venue
32. Singer Mariah
33. Joints above the ankles
35. Artificial
36. Hymn word
40. Blend
42. Bloke: slang
43. Ill temper
44. Circulate again
46. Cronkite of journalism
47. Bum bomb
49. Odd
50. Some: 2 wds.
51. Miniature
52. Skin blemish
53. Classic TV clown
54. Make a sock
55. Composer Stravinsky
56. Reject (a claim)
58. Edible fish
59. Also
61. Country motel

ACROSS

1. Poet
5. Alabama city
10. Train sound
14. Burn remedy
15. Fun surprise
16. English noble
17. Piece of coal
18. "— you excited?"
19. Phone wire
20. Charlatan; fake
22. Reluctant
24. Author Bellow
25. Wound remnant
26. Alleges
29. India neighbor
33. Apartment fee
34. Singer Carpenter
35. The — that got away
36. Enjoys lunch
37. Church official
38. Outer border
39. Hellenic character
40. Final inning, usually
41. Nullify (a check)
42. Drawings with acid
44. Runs after
46. Pub requests
47. Flunk
48. Nog spice
51. Mumbled
55. Dreaded exam
56. Residence
58. Ventilated
59. Mean monster
60. Finger bands
61. Heavy book
62. Maintained
63. Oxen harnesses
64. Greek letters

DOWN

1. Island near Java
2. College grad
3. Frolic
4. Sets down
5. Social class
6. Flynn of film
7. Lustful look
8. Adult lad
9. Violent person
10. Stars, briefly
11. Head strands
12. Certain vases
13. Elation
21. Cooke of soul
23. Egotistical
25. Isaac's mom
26. Thin pancake
27. Minimal
28. Silly prank
29. Mutual agreements
30. Commotions: hyph. wd.
31. Actress Dickinson
32. Lacks
34. Louis XVI and Richard II
37. Ill-tempered
38. Assess
40. African river
43. Small village
44. Light stroke
45. That 51-Down
47. Gooey chocolate candy
48. Room's corner
49. Drive (on)
50. Rain cover
51. Abbey member
52. Mob melee
53. Ms. Bombeck
54. 11-Down tints
57. Individual's history

ACROSS

1. Chip dip
6. Trim with a razor
11. Polar pixie
14. Marine environment
15. Log cottage
16. Floral loop
17. Chump: slang
19. — Cruces
20. Mental range
21. Green hue
22. Of Dublin
24. Pub drink
26. Ruling family's reign
28. Heat measure
31. Facial cosmetic
32. Extemporaneous quip: hyph. wd.
33. Sudden fancies
34. Popular pooch
37. Quite cozy
38. Cello relative
39. Ticket cost
40. Lunch meat
41. Feeling dizzy
42. Stale
43. Glue kin
44. More piercing
45. Actress Kerr
48. Connected
49. Sidestep
50. Crow noise
51. Towel word
54. Journey stage
55. Far from real
60. Before, before
61. Cleverly 49-Across
62. Singer Lena
63. Piggish pad?
64. Was furious
65. Rising agent

DOWN

1. Foot covering
2. Yearn
3. Boxer Spinks
4. Cutting tool
5. Yet
6. Threaded bolt
7. Sound of amusement: hyph. wd.
8. Judge Fortas
9. Through
10. Finales
11. Perry of fashion
12. Fewest
13. Questionable
18. Dueling sword
23. Charlotte of TV sitcoms
24. Nautical jail
25. Jewish Mister
26. Lace mat
27. Arizona city
28. Brief sprint
29. — St. Vincent Millay, poet
30. Morose
31. — Island
33. Diameter
34. Stretched out
35. Johnson of "Laugh-In"
36. Sudsy 24-Across
38. Passport addition
39. Dino's owner
41. Ava of film
42. Ball holder
43. Luau food
44. "Hairy" fruit
45. Small valleys
46. Chris of tennis fame
47. Golf score
48. Strained
50. Yield formally
51. Deity in "The Iliad"
52. Lodging spots
53. Printing term
56. Germ cells
57. Harp at
58. Retiring
59. Boot segment

49

ACROSS

1. Sir Guinness
5. Gusto
9. Swedish group
13. Swanky car
14. Jane of fiction
15. Senses
17. 19-Across of a klutz
19. Quality
20. African country
21. Wee tykes
23. Bass horn
24. Objective
25. Blaze a trail
28. Bar liquor
29. Nil
30. Actress Witherspoon
32. Hatcher of Hollywood
35. Noshed
37. Hesitated
40. Put in rows
42. Cut (down)
44. Old-fashioned
45. Having goose pimples
47. Lovely Novak
49. Can defect
50. Author Anne
52. Fill up
54. Chi follower
56. Additional
58. Meadow call
61. Skinny
63. Haughty one
64. Works for
66. Remove a knot from
68. Fame's opposite
70. Placid
71. Funny Jay
72. Adams of song
73. House pests
74. Took (a card)
75. Tree home

DOWN

1. Identical
2. Fine cloth
3. Revise (text)
4. Transcribe
5. Buddhism branch
6. Certain canine
7. Burning crime
8. Holt of news
9. Toward the stern
10. Ernie's buddy, on "Sesame Street"
11. Foreign Legion screen classic: 2 wds.
12. Cover story?
16. Comic Laurel
18. Bandage (up)
22. Ooze slowly
26. A savings plan
27. Hind section
29. Spicy: slang
31. Soft leather
32. Create doilies
33. A football Manning
34. Movie dog: 3 wds.
36. Scared yell
38. Shore flier
39. Tiny spot
41. Fitzgerald of music
43. Thanksgiving prize
46. Craves
48. Siren West
51. Mr. Reagan
53. Deuce topper
54. Bonus
55. Yule visitor
57. Facial product
58. Wedding star
59. Those against
60. To date: 2 wds.
62. Plaid skirt
65. Church echo?
67. Raised tracks
69. Today

50

ACROSS

1. Blunders
5. Drinking tube
10. Pencil end
13. — canal
14. Fragrance
15. Loving lines
17. Lacking in emotion
19. Entertainer Falana
20. Least dull
21. Pot kin
23. Yes: French
24. Balkans native
25. Broadway sign
28. Bloom origin
31. Thingamajig
35. Flirt: 2 wds.
38. From Scandinavia
39. Presently
40. Kitchen gizmo
42. Fanfare blast
43. Welding device
45. Communication aid
47. Followed immediately
49. Mean remark
50. During each
51. Horn honk
53. Bolt fastener
55. "Our Gang" kid
58. Motorcycle attachment
62. Verse crafter
63. Wipe out
65. Canine in Oz
66. Fierce stare
67. Messy dresser
68. Equal footing
69. Planted (wheat)
70. Stately trees

DOWN

1. Estrada of TV
2. Italian locale
3. Braided cord
4. Dictation secretary
5. Most impudent
6. Pony's gait
7. Howard of film
8. Gather
9. Took a stroll
10. Turnpike stop
11. Adored celebrity
12. Soccer great
16. Pulled up a stool
18. Employ again
22. Curling tool
25. Roofingrock
26. Prattled: 2 wds.
27. Foul smells
29. Pour forth
30. Agatha Christie and Judi Dench
32. Slump
33. In harmony: 2 wds.
34. Forestall
36. Place for a preemie
37. Singer Carter
41. Got back together
44. Shoe part
46. Priggish individual
48. Clears (a windshield)
52. Painter Picasso
54. Concise
55. Well-chosen
56. Lasso feature
57. Salty cheese
58. King's title
59. Summon via 45-Across
60. Elemental bit
61. Yankee foes, for short
64. Civil rule

51

ACROSS

1. Snow runners
5. Parlor seat
9. Break to bits
14. Links vehicle
15. Secret plan
16. "Greetings!"
17. Realm
18. — of March
19. Yule helpers
20. Zealous fan
22. Peddle
24. Impress
25. Plastic pattern sheet
27. Is unwell
29. Bundle, as of papers
31. Flair
35. Create a hem
38. Exam format
40. Rebound, as a billiards ball
41. Onstage item
43. Dallas native
45. Rooftop gauge
46. Oahu welcome
48. Summarize
50. Family fellow
51. Savor
53. Minuscule mammal
55. Essence
57. One learning the ropes
61. Grill residue
64. Niger neighbor
66. Autumn blooms
67. Robot-novel genre: hyph. wd.
69. Maximum
71. Coop cluckers
72. Divided land
73. Cheese option
74. Ms. Falco
75. Refined iron
76. Give lip to
77. Bakery loaves

DOWN

1. Cons: slang
2. Gold measure
3. Singer Cara
4. Discolorations on a shirt
5. Least mild
6. Obsolete
7. Opponents
8. On the briny: 2 wds.
9. Shiny finish
10. Comic Brooks
11. Menlo Park middle name
12. Whole lot
13. Flexible pipe
21. Nagging discomfort
23. Illuminated
26. Powerful beam
28. Croat or Serb
30. Phone-line transmissions
32. Notable times
33. Taboo subject: hyph. wd. (slang)
34. Special agents: hyph. wd.
35. Box playfully
36. Writer Stanley Gardner
37. Warm material
39. Luxury boat
42. Greek letters
44. Tells (a story)
47. Hardly gregarious
49. Pod legumes
52. "What?"
54. Shrivel
56. Sheep babies
58. Impoverished
59. Bert's buddy
60. Three letters in 76-Across
61. Seeks answers
62. Dundee denizen
63. Take on board
65. Animated explorer
68. Set cost
70. A sibling, for short

ACROSS

1. Film lioness
5. Sudden deluge
10. Metric measure
14. Rifles, for example
15. Desert refuge
16. Choir gown
17. Overabundance
18. Digital storage units
19. Neglect
20. Residential district
22. Satisfactory
24. Golf gizmos
26. Religious sister
27. Take care of: 2 wds.
31. Apple drinks
35. Thomas of "That Girl"
36. Small bay
38. Victory sign
39. Comply with
40. Opposing forces
41. Bee cousin
42. Verbal denials
43. Indispensable
44. Arm bones
45. Church reading
47. Rose Bowl locale
49. Flock fellow
50. Violin holder
51. Boldly disrespectful
56. Desire for water
60. Appear
61. Clamorous
63. Ark builder
64. Luxury auto
65. Singing range
66. Forum garment
67. Yale grads
68. January toys
69. Indication of the future

DOWN

1. Quiche must
2. Doozy: slang
3. Social slight
4. With shrewdness
5. Wept aloud
6. Spend (money)
7. "The Thin Man" dog
8. Fastened (laces)
9. Gists
10. Soil
11. Italia's capital
12. Some: 2 wds.
13. — out, allot
21. Nevada gambling mecca
23. Discontinue
25. Give sparingly
27. Between
28. Forbidden
29. Lock of hair
30. From the keg: 2 wds.
32. Elude
33. Pine product
34. Rusty shade
37. Spring flower
40. Afflictions
41. Begin with vigor: 2 wds.
43. Tender meat
44. Reckless
46. Ad-campaign spots
48. Mythical woodland creatures
51. Cruise sight
52. Mr. Diamond
53. Big rig
54. Christmas
55. Antler point
57. Hotel booking
58. Old, wise one
59. Comparing word
62. Lawn strips

ACROSS

1. Dessert order
4. Gavel sound
7. Helpful device
8. Eye boldly
10. Stewed fruit
11. Rendezvous
13. Will figure
14. Sleuth's hint
16. Soak with liquid
18. Injure
19. Make amends (for)
20. "—interested!"
22. Onassis nickname
23. Irritating, as fumes
24. Fiery bean concoction
26. Fundraising broadcast
28. They may be wild
29. "Crazy" bird
30. Presage
31. Music deity
34. Narrow passage
38. Deadly
39. Hunger for money
40. Hasten
41. Dynamite kin
42. Window shade
43. Weakling: slang
44. Sawbuck
46. Alan of old film
47. Puts on (clothes)
48. UFO detector
50. Like bacon
52. Hunter's prey
53. Debt notes
54. Nap site
55. Holiday drink

DOWN

1. Dispense tea
2. Altered atom
3. Charged particle
4. Plump
5. Concur (with)
6. Thickness
7. Dress edging
9. Snaky letter
10. Great danger
12. Invigorating potion
13. Swift mammal
15. Pork cut
17. Flag spot
18. Boater or tam
19. Sneeze noise
21. "— the season…"
23. Coral island
24. Surrendered
25. Lewis of 1980s rock
27. Scat diva Fitzgerald
28. Dished (out)
30. Becomes one of the crown: 2 wds.
31. Ship's end
32. Breathe fast
33. Furry swimmer
34. Quite dry
35. Prone to complaining
36. Aspirations
37. Slangy assent
39. Stared fiercely
42. Find fault with
43. Chinese pans
45. Torment
47. Magician Henning
49. Quick smear
51. Cow's lament

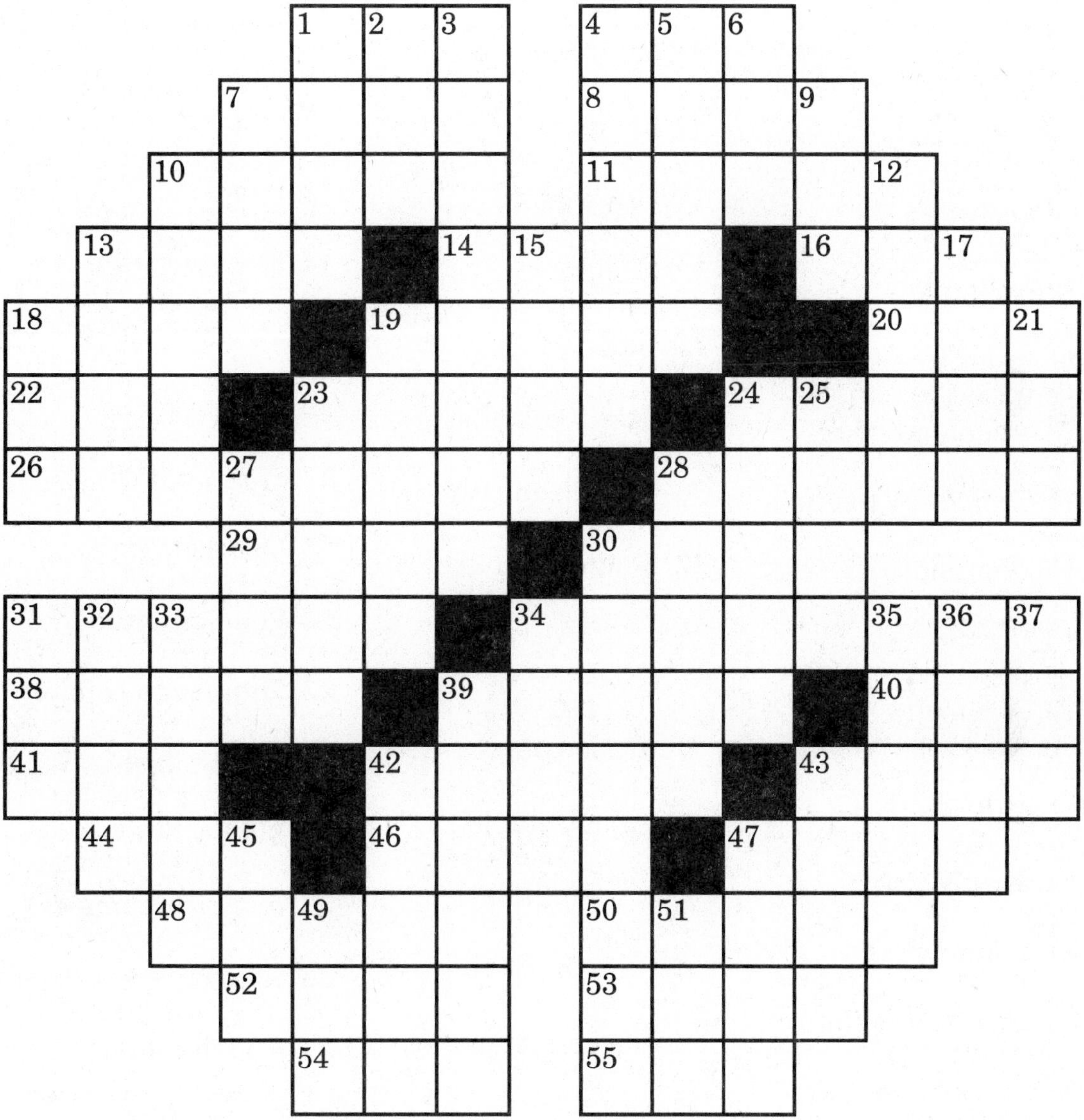

54

ACROSS

1. Writer of "The Raven"

4. Tightwad: slang

6. Comic Chaplin

8. Vocalist Ross

9. Young lass

11. Trunk of a body

12. Animated ogre

14. Temporary peace

15. Contour

17. Vacation isle

18. Like many newspapers

19. Cask wood

21. Powdery soil

22. Window sealer

23. Play beginning: 2 wds.

24. "Ready?"

25. Hiding place

26. Reserved

27. Changes the phrasing of

29. Loud alarm

30. Removes, in printing

31. Fish-fry fish

32. Prohibit

33. Gloss

34. Uses a colander

36. Canonized one

37. Bradley and Begley

DOWN

1. Organ cousin

2. Gumbo staple

3. Sushi option

4. Growth stage

5. In a correct manner

6. About

7. Ahead of time

8. Uncertainty

10. Floral gift

11. Had faith in

12. Luxurious hotel accommodation

13. Rapped

14. More accurate

15. Sworn pledges

16. Devoured

17. Public notices

18. Quacking birds

20. Reunion attendees

22. Those with children

23. Duelist Burr

25. Bubbly drinks

26. Auto foursome

28. Silken snare

29. Hound's trail

31. Lower legs

33. Spoken

35. — Dawn Chong

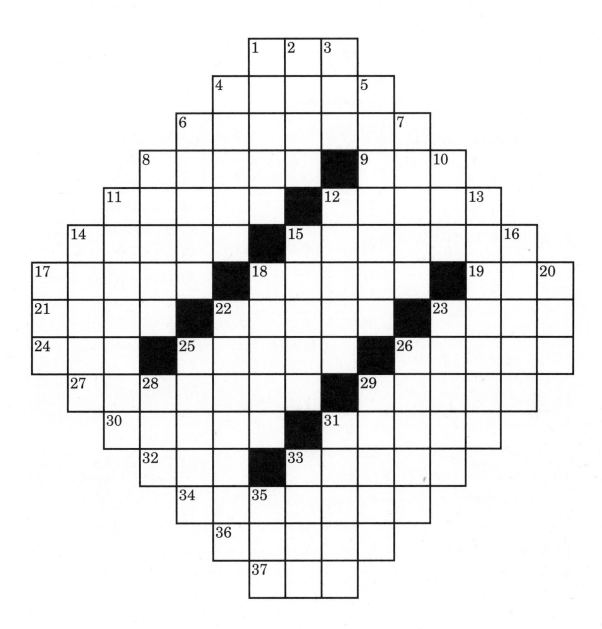

55

ACROSS

1. "— in Boots," children's story
5. Wild frolic
10. Nile biters
14. Honeymoon spot
15. Smug folks
16. Bat (a fly)
17. Scorch
18. Mechanical man
19. Make content
20. Large fleet
22. Altitude
24. Play on words
25. Fruit skins
27. Disreputable person: 2 wds. (slang)
30. Legacy
34. Rhyming boxer
35. Neither trailer
36. Safari sight
37. Is mad about
40. Kimono sash
41. Farewell
42. Pass (a law)
43. Be deceptive
44. Stag's mate
45. Miss: Spanish
47. Computer adjuncts
50. Some sculptures
51. At all
52. Wolf cousin
55. Teeter-totter
59. Germ cell
60. Pays (up)
64. Short length
65. Surrealist Salvador
66. Vacate
67. Alaskan port
68. A Baldwin brother
69. Genders
70. Pop star Stefani

DOWN

1. Italian city near Florence
2. Manipulative friend
3. Slam (a door)
4. Mexican shawl
5. Leaped
6. Positive vote
7. Umbrella spine
8. Self-conceit
9. Swimmer Williams
10. Helped out
11. Decorative drapery
12. Forest walkway
13. Editing term
21. Delved deep
23. Henry Higgins' pupil Doolittle
25. Exaggerated fears
26. Ghostly
27. Field bundles
28. "Home —," 1990 flick
29. Armless couch
31. Stand fast
32. Bride's spouse
33. Slackens
35. Nick of Hollywood
38. Of money management
39. Show off
46. Perfect models
47. Throngs
48. Inseparable
49. Salon service
52. Ending of a musical refrain
53. Track-shaped
54. Christmas
56. Wintry flakes
57. Apex
58. "What time?"
61. Born
62. IRS concern
63. Bible lady

ACROSS

1. Copycat
5. Greek consonant
10. Baseballer Musial
14. Actress Moore
15. Leafy vines
16. Old story
17. Pull heavily
18. Steam exits
19. Applications
20. Sky shiner
21. Ms. Garr
22. Rouses from sleep
23. Funny Rock
25. Textile pro
27. Akron citizen
29. Encourage
32. Answer
33. Meal platform
34. Jazz session: slang
36. Assassinate
37. Eagle's abode
38. Nuts: slang
39. Decide (to)
40. Nautical "Halt!"
41. Salsa chip
42. Concerned only with personal gain
44. Lurch from side to side
45. Roof perimeter
46. Composer nicknamed Papa
47. Painter Degas
50. Alpine evergreens
51. Refrain part
54. Pathetic
55. Backyard item
57. Joyce's isle
58. Lendl of tennis
59. "Unhand me!": 2 wds.
60. Paddy grain
61. Highlands native
62. Agrees with
63. Harbor craft

DOWN

1. Finds a sum
2. Where Lima is
3. Set free
4. Convoy member
5. Yield: 2 wds.
6. Declares
7. Tiny skirt
8. Ran across
9. Pack animal
10. — Little, famed mouse
11. Assigned job
12. Toward shelter, at sea
13. Crimefighter Eliot
21. Cafeteria aid
22. Took place
24. Blessed
25. Ledger entry
26. Connecticut university
27. Roughly: 2 wds.
28. Promotes
29. Overly severe
30. See 42-Across
31. Small recess
33. Rib playfully
35. Thug: slang
37. Tel —, Israel
38. Frying fat
40. Some ways off
41. Negative votes
43. Caught wind (of)
44. Ships' freight
46. Depend (on)
47. Grand film
48. Peace bird
49. Hockey coup
50. Conforms to
52. Puerto chaser
53. From the top
55. Calculating
56. Petite
57. Pause sounds

ACROSS

1. Frosts (a cake)
5. Speedy
10. Friendly talk
14. Kindly
15. Beyond plump
16. "It hurts!"
17. Stitched fold
18. Transfer picture
19. Grimm monster
20. Early years
22. Turner of film
24. Old Pisa cash
27. "Misery" star James
28. Burn soother: 2 wds.
32. Knife case
36. Knee-high
37. Mrs. Archie Bunker
39. Houston pro
40. Life phases
42. Duped: 2 wds.
44. Straight cut
45. Gambling game
47. Garfunkel's former partner
49. Enjoyed orzo
50. At the actual location: hyph. wd.
52. Carnival ride
54. Church leader
56. Sign brightener
57. Romantic letter: 2 wds.
61. Ship bottoms
65. Comic King
66. Laundry drop
69. Small bottle
70. Convey (mail)
71. Marsh bird
72. Funny Bombeck
73. Beanbag throw
74. Obeys a yellow light
75. Spiffy: slang

DOWN

1. Adventurer Jones, to pals
2. "Goodbye!"
3. Beige color
4. Colonize
5. Curtain shaft
6. Mr. Vigoda
7. Casual kiss
8. Hayes of soul
9. Nile deposits
10. Indifferent quality
11. Jumbo
12. Field unit
13. Afterward
21. Bee's pad
23. Laugh sound: hyph. wd.
25. Fiery hues
26. Zodiac ram
28. Texas fort
29. Enter a computer password: 2 wds.
30. Olympics sprinter Jesse
31. Dusty spot
33. Geography aid
34. Hackneyed
35. Lodging place
38. "To err is —..."
41. Fixed allowances
43. Skin opening
46. A prep school
48. Cozy niche
51. Time periods
53. Irregular
55. Lucy's cohort
57. Endure
58. Ersatz butter
59. Moving trucks
60. French bread?
62. The Emerald Isle, poetically
63. Buddhist monk
64. Lattice strip
67. Drag behind
68. Print measures

ACROSS

1. Farm harvest
5. Mental picture
10. Sturdy string
14. Arizona Indian
15. More polite
16. Garfield's dog pal
17. Baking spot
18. Blood vessels
19. "Run — Run," movie
20. Journeyed
21. Attempted
23. Delhi wrap
25. Father deer
26. Do great on
28. Nasty-looking
31. Pretty bloom
35. Mayday signal
36. Dismal
38. Wants
39. — exam
41. Merits (a salary)
43. Fluctuate
44. Titles
46. Entanglements
48. Yonder ewe
49. Chooses (to)
51. Exchange goods
52. Parking space
53. Bell sound
55. Speak crazily
57. Student of flora and fauna
62. Craving
65. Unlatched, perhaps
66. Conclusive
67. Corset strip
68. Neck area
69. Mom's brother
70. Care for
71. Wood choppers
72. Sports data
73. Funny Johnson

DOWN

1. Food: slang
2. Wander
3. Ali Baba's command: 2 wds.
4. Historic ship
5. Persuade by using trickery
6. Manner
7. Vinegary
8. Hereditary units
9. Synthetic
10. Perfume varieties
11. Foul scent
12. Irritate
13. Lacking life
22. Self-absorbed
24. Clean (off)
26. Together: 2 wds.
27. Atoll growth
29. Pipe problem
30. Knitting buys
32. Certain periodical
33. Nevada neighbor
34. Up to now: 2 wds.
37. Have the info
40. College speeches
42. Shocks
45. Mix (a drink)
47. Gym amenity
50. Mishaps: slang
54. Sparkle
56. Outlook
57. "Peter Pan" pooch
58. "The Iliad" hero
59. Adhesive item
60. Ancient Andean
61. Shaker filler
63. Are unable to
64. Jekyll's evil half

ACROSS

1. Salon service
5. Recite aloud
8. Czech or Pole
12. Precinct
13. Piano lever
15. Make off with
16. Hair dye
17. Pure white
18. Cast forth
19. Directive from a boss: 3 wds.
21. Arranges tidily
23. — and hers
24. School exams
25. Son of Eve
27. Goat baby
28. Wild hog
31. Rowing sport
32. Fade away
33. Plane garage
35. Ambience
36. Boy king of Egypt, briefly
37. Purchase
38. Creeping vine
39. Church district
41. Calf's site
42. Delight
43. Poet Teasdale
44. Fish "arm"
45. Mall denizen
46. Desi of TV
48. — pal
49. Small window over a door
52. Gala garb
56. Retro stereo: hyph. wd.
57. Metal bolt
59. Corsage bloom
60. Brain wave?
61. Assumed moniker
62. Without work
63. Stitched
64. Tuberous root
65. Chick's cage

DOWN

1. Taps fondly
2. A Great Lake
3. Painter Magritte
4. Broderick of film
5. Conveyed (mail)
6. Disturbance
7. Acted bored
8. Ranch hat
9. Shiny fabric
10. Related
11. Farm doctors
13. Greek letters
14. Harsh liquids
20. Saudi export
22. Unable to escape: 2 wds.
24. Connect
25. Opera melodies
26. Yankee Yogi
27. Set of tools
29. In shape
30. Black bird
31. Head cover
32. "Obviously!": slang
33. Embrace
34. Cereal crop
36. Russian despots of yore
37. Performer Vereen
40. Tehran native
41. Gossip Smith
42. Having no brand name
44. Clan
45. Crooner Ritter
47. Nick's sleuthing wife
48. Deposits
49. "— Old House"
50. Fair attraction
51. Some: 2 wds.
52. Baseball club
53. Extinct avian
54. Norwegian hub
55. Flow slowly
58. By a route through

60

ACROSS

1. Abominable Snowman
5. Writing task
10. Coif of the 1960s
14. Imitates
15. Explosive liquid, briefly
16. Beastly abode
17. Breed (animals)
18. Reject scornfully
19. Famed lioness
20. Go off the tracks
22. Main text
24. Dawson of football
25. Greek vowel
26. Garden chore
28. Elevation standard: 2 wds.
33. Crops waterer
34. Uncommon
35. Allots (out)
37. Friendly greeting
40. Cheap bar
42. Crisp cookies
44. Warty leaper
45. Calm
47. From Seoul or Singapore
49. Compete (for)
50. Slalom runners
52. Fills with cheer
54. Get stylish: 2 wds.
57. Fashioned after: 2 wds.
58. Cup feature
59. Junior Guthrie
61. Banks (on)
65. Weathered the years
67. Mold and mildew
69. Ames' locale
70. With 46-Down, da Vinci painting
71. Revue host
72. Hearty entree
73. Creatively pretentious
74. Lurches
75. Sound sensors

DOWN

1. Gridiron gain
2. Heavy foil
3. Muscle injury
4. Tel Aviv's nation
5. Subjugates
6. Little drink
7. Ticket part
8. Bow and —
9. Over there
10. Dublin draft
11. Become smitten: 3 wds.
12. Ascended
13. Long-armed primate
21. Single object
23. "Right!"
27. Eat less food
28. Grassy swatches
29. Change (copy)
30. Consideration
31. Sicilian peak
32. Rental paper
36. Revolve
38. Been supine
39. Keats works
41. Forest giants
43. Regular wages
46. See 70-Across
48. Aswan's river
51. Waves enthusiast
53. Luggage piece
54. Serious movie
55. Strictness
56. Showy feather
60. Story start
62. Tiny quantity
63. Large pitcher
64. Cuts planks
66. Calendar box
68. Salon supply

61

ACROSS

1. Expense tally
4. Pilfer
9. Map specks
14. Amazement
15. Puccini opera
16. String instrument
17. Pooch
18. In a rash manner
20. UFO occupants
22. Mineral rocks
23. Cheap metal
24. Yule drink
25. Grab quickly
26. Merely okay: hyph. wd.
27. Musical Loretta
29. Your: poetic
30. Fabric flaw
32. Yes, in France
33. "Pardon me!"
34. Smells
38. Loss of memory
40. Printed copy
41. Long knife
42. Son of Zeus
43. Hairy antelope
44. Pump fluid
45. — Angeles
46. Brady brother

47. Overtake
50. Fashions lace
52. Thick snake
53. Picnic cooler
54. At this point
55. Salon perch
58. Thoughtful
61. Bother incessantly
62. Scout collective
63. "I'll — tell!"
64. Spanish shout
65. Certain Slavs
66. Patriot Samuel
67. Composer Rorem

DOWN

1. Revealing comment: hyph. wd.
2. Army baddie
3. Start
4. Sharp pain
5. Male felines
6. Eerie ability
7. 2-Down, for example
8. Dern of drama
9. Burl of film
10. Moral lapse
11. Gambling game
12. Designer Perry
13. Reject: 2 wds.

19. Breaks down
21. Interminable stretch
25. Former Flushing stadium
26. Recognize
27. Laundry unit
28. City in Arizona
29. Had a strong craving
31. Elegant bloom
33. On a cruise
35. Birds' semiannual flight
36. Tops: 2 wds.
37. Warm and cozy
39. Omelet items
40. Love god
42. Remade
46. Achieved
47. Official agreements
48. Be devoted to
49. Sir, in Spain
51. Soccer site
52. Bar orders
54. Pelvic bones
55. Leaf support
56. A Gardner
57. Pieced (out)
59. Cry heartily
60. See 56-Down

124

62

ACROSS

1. Zeus's wife
5. Early anesthetic
10. Sagging flesh
14. Dubai native
15. Small and bright, as eyes
16. Nevada betting setting
17. Pitcher rims
18. River craft
19. Excited about
20. Sea creatures
22. Suave
24. Hanker (for)
26. Pharmacy offering
27. Gaming mecca: 2 wds.
31. Builds (a tower)
35. Four pairs
36. Mountain lions
38. Collide with
39. Wee bit: 2 wds.
40. Lukewarm
41. Lucid
42. Fat source
43. Units of medicine
44. Cuban dance
45. Gushed forth
47. Detoured
49. Remnants
51. Cut (grain)
52. Noted folk-rocker: 2 wds.
56. Trample: 2 wds.
60. Mocked
61. Eat away at
63. Grand lady
64. Ceramic piece
65. Disentangle
66. Plains tribe
67. Retained
68. Shoulder wrap
69. Confined

DOWN

1. Angelic light
2. Comic Idle
3. Enthralled
4. Pardoned, as sins
5. Tidal movement
6. Asian export
7. Quite firm
8. Sidled
9. Deli purchase: 2 wds.
10. Border of threads
11. Lovely Horne
12. Pro opponent
13. Oaf
21. Lyrical bard
23. Made by us
25. Gawks
27. Borrowed sums
28. Behave badly: 2 wds.
29. Assert
30. "Fantastic!"
32. Intone
33. Faint color
34. Place
37. Pinchpenny
40. Little kids
41. Like a hot rod: 2 wds. (slang)
43. Repudiate
44. Winter jacket
46. Married
48. Unload for cash
50. Ms. Jessica Parker
52. Relaxing soak
53. Mayberry lad
54. Door buzzer
55. Certain star
57. Meat spread
58. Warning sign
59. Finch's home
62. Dawn dampness

63

ACROSS

1. Dundee native
5. Luau greeting
10. Loud explosion
14. Numbers game
15. Admit: 2 wds.
16. Impulse
17. Points out
19. Pickling herb
20. — Plaines
21. Colony builders
22. Tightly crammed
24. Yonder folks
25. New —, India
26. Rare articles
29. Floral decorations
32. On reserve
33. Ebbs
34. Happy sigh
35. Speed contest
36. Circular
37. Director Preminger
38. Vanity
39. Far from cool: slang
40. Wool source
41. Unbeknownst to others
43. Disagreeing: 2 wds.
44. Squirrel away
45. Humdrum: slang
46. Weak
48. Go on a quest
49. Downcast
52. Play opener: 2 wds.
53. "So it would seem"
56. "How soon?"
57. Confidence
58. Dexterity
59. Signals approval
60. Categorizes
61. Stepped (on)

DOWN

1. Slide noisily
2. Formally surrender
3. Dollar bills
4. Shipping weight
5. Straightens, as type
6. Southpaw: slang
7. Elevator inventor
8. Make haste
9. Responded
10. Eastern religious figure
11. Began
12. Lustful look
13. Pinochle term
18. Nevada lake
23. House wings
24. Coastal flow
25. Mr. DeVito
26. Feels concern
27. Habit
28. Bounced, as a bullet
29. Ostentatious
30. Trite
31. Mall units
33. Whole universe
36. Withdraws from a battle
37. "My bad!": hyph. wd.
39. Patricia of film
40. Tent securer
42. Spring songbirds
43. Cautions
45. Large animal
46. Doe's baby
47. Audio effect
48. Cowboy's goad
49. Badge shape
50. Besides
51. Treated with henna
54. Favoring
55. Marine snare

64

ACROSS

1. Mean comment
5. Show stress
10. Passport adjunct
14. Sensible
15. Garden soil
16. Damaged-wares sign: 2 wds.
17. Pious reply
18. Say "Yes!"
19. Tide term
20. Scoundrel: 2 wds. (slang)
22. Tally
23. Rare stones
24. Pleasing
26. Andean nation
28. Gratis items: slang
32. Openings for elevators
36. Chaney of horror
37. Quite clumsy
39. Synthetic fiber
40. Energy field
42. Cluster
44. Spreadsheet info
45. Cache
47. — boom, explosive noise
49. Through
50. Noggin protector
52. North American tribal game
54. Flat chunk
56. Read hastily
57. Scrape mark
60. Rude chap
62. Athenian characters
66. Volcano fluid
67. Athlete Shaquille
69. Aged beverage
70. Grand work
71. Caribbean dance
72. Aid (a crime)
73. "— Got Tonight"
74. Bogus name
75. Evergreen shrubs

DOWN

1. Sailor's mop
2. Bean variety
3. Broken in
4. Back out
5. Like some vessels
6. Tail gesture
7. Deviates
8. Devoured: 2 wds.
9. Main topics
10. Front line
11. "Ah!": 2 wds.
12. Thailand, formerly
13. Nile cobras
21. Asian desert
25. Antlered beasts
27. Greek letter
28. Blink
29. Chosen path
30. Register
31. Cable holder
33. Envelope parts
34. Cloth bags
35. Animal trap
38. Yellowfin and albacore
41. Cold War contest: 2 wds.
43. Kin of flutes
46. Flexible fish
48. Study hard
51. Puget Sound city
53. Ticket option: hyph. wd.
55. Trite
57. Huge torrent
58. Riding cloak
59. Tel chaser
61. Moore of film
63. Scoff (at)
64. From scratch
65. Tennis rounds
68. Arab robe

65

ACROSS

1. Velvety forest growth
5. Knitted item?
9. Cat comments
14. In a frenzy
15. Princess played by Carrie Fisher
16. Beta preceder
17. Pablo's affirmative: 2 wds.
18. Big vases
19. Precipitous
20. Sci-fi hit: 2 wds.
22. Tea cakes
23. Movie mansion
24. Turkish title
25. Rhoda's mom
28. A Knight
29. Neither's pal
30. Attach
33. Seven-voyages sailor
35. Mall tenant
37. Pretty Turner
38. Scatter seeds
39. Greased
40. Vivacious
43. Muss
45. With 66-Across, screen legend
46. Territory for 33-Across

47. Get into (clothes)
48. Paving glop
49. Con: slang
50. Numbered work
52. Shrill scream
55. Detectives: slang
59. Lament
60. Vagabond
61. Veggie pod
62. Young hooter
63. Food scraps
64. Wading bird
65. Small valleys
66. See 45-Across
67. Little cutie

DOWN

1. Catholic rite
2. Skip
3. Homerun champ Sammy
4. Garment for a girl
5. Fuzzy
6. Peruse again
7. Sty squeal
8. Occurred
9. Eyelash enhancer
10. John of music
11. Accessible
12. "What fun!"
13. Plant fluids

21. "Cheerio!": hyph. wd.
22. Flu injection
24. Recognized
25. A religion
26. Famous Ross
27. Redheaded orphan
30. Sought-after party guests: hyph. wd.
31. Actress Reese
32. Laundry machine
34. "Kapow!"
35. Curtain bar
36. Debt paper
38. Fabric joint
41. Upward climbs
42. Elegant wood
43. Highest
44. Full burden
47. Reservations
49. Warning noise
51. Brief
52. Urban blight
53. Wolf's cry
54. Basic law
55. Strip in a 4-Down
56. Just fine
57. Mr. Estrada
58. Auction goal
60. "— now, brown cow?"

ACROSS

1. TV program
5. Query word
9. Wild crowds
13. Final passage
14. Puerto —
15. Celestial streaker
16. Artist Warhol
17. Look forward to
19. Darling of baseball
20. Cookie fruit
21. Dillydally
22. Loud knock
23. Learned
25. Reformist Turner
27. Ancient tale
28. Laboratory organisms
33. General feelings: slang
35. Bit of old Italian bread?
36. Funny Garr
37. Hail, to Nero
38. Paul of pop
39. Quite chubby
40. Hindu garment
42. Food heater
43. Lasso loop
45. Fettered
47. Fall heavily
48. Floral wreath
49. Sheens
52. Chichi resort
55. Gun (a V-8)
57. Enjoyed chili
58. Color shading
59. Building designers
62. Mental anguish
63. Ike's love
64. Western pact
65. Rural hotels
66. Viewed
67. Government agents: hyph. wd.
68. Boundary line

DOWN

1. Intimidate
2. Dignity
3. 1, 3, 5, and 7: 2 wds.
4. Milky —
5. Apparition
6. Door pivot
7. Assume a role
8. Hard work
9. Unruly hairdo
10. Literary Khayyám
11. Greek letter
12. Pace length
15. Cuban export
18. Parisian dance
20. Tantrums
24. Salon product
26. Young kid
28. Played charades
29. Crease maker
30. In advance
31. Key periods
32. Venue
33. Urn kin
34. Court star Lendl
35. In person
38. — Union
41. Causing harm
43. Plane point
44. Diamond call
46. Alpine home
47. Dons: 2 wds.
49. Espresso drink
50. Filled with regret
51. Taste or touch
52. Identical
53. Address God
54. Pinnacle
56. Air shaft
60. Kept secret
61. Engine rod
62. Crusted treat

67

ACROSS

1. Attempt to charm
4. Furthermore
7. "Bye!"
8. Pine's anchor
10. Year division
11. Stair noise
13. Tip the scales at
14. "Cheers" role
15. — soup, dense fog
17. Appearances
18. Fish features
19. Bank offering
21. Appropriate
22. Portion (out)
23. Consumed, as a snack
25. Capone's foe
27. Type; sort
28. Parentless child
29. Sleeping
31. About: 2 wds.
32. Proverbs
35. Petty lie
36. Lecture leader, briefly
40. Fracas
41. Washington insiders: slang
42. Tycoon Onassis
43. Rug protector
44. Wild-animal collections
45. Kick back
47. Brimless hat
49. SOS request
50. "— be sorry!"
51. Hindu rulers
53. All choked up
54. Actor Richard
55. "Sesame Street" cutie
56. Get hitched to
57. Raised tracks

DOWN

1. Glider parts
2. Vow in court
3. Cry of joy
4. Esoteric
5. Social standards
6. Fawn mama
7. Mint minting
9. Light strike
10. Bumps into
12. Urban of music
13. Clean (a windshield)
14. Smooth fabric
16. Geometry term
17. Adult bloke
18. Perform a laundry task
20. Dancer Miller
22. Stops living
23. Hesitation sounds
24. Per piece: 2 wds. (slang)
26. Stuffing herb
28. Spherical objects
30. Garden buzzer
31. Squeak cures
32. Rock accessory
33. Hard of hearing
34. Birch tree
35. Grocery buys
37. Pregame event
38. Mouth-related
39. Predicament
41. Calm
44. Congo, once
45. Is a nomad
46. Currency in Paris
48. Sharp turn
50. Shout loudly
52. Never used
53. — off, anger

68

ACROSS

1. Block
5. Slugger Willie
9. Party giver
13. Ames' state
14. Jai —
15. Input (data)
17. Make ready
18. Atlas pages
19. Confused: slang
20. Piano pieces
22. Aviv header
24. Fair grade
25. "Indeed!"
26. Chess markers
27. Oahu strings
28. Austin native
31. Sack fabric
33. Dinghy pair
34. Disallow
35. Published
39. Refrain word
40. Isaac Bashevis Singer's language
42. Go schussing
43. Carved gems
45. Renoir's work
46. Look to be
47. Chant
49. Old hat
50. Consequently
53. Canapé topper
54. Fellow: slang
55. Bunny feature
56. Veggie hull
57. Street hazard
61. Calculus letter
63. — Lane
65. Cut copy
66. Control a car
67. Patronizes a 34-Down
68. Funny Fey
69. Wasting time
70. Collar insert
71. Visualizes

DOWN

1. Little gulps
2. Bull, in Spain
3. A Wilson brother
4. Tropical fruits
5. Nursery figures
6. Unfortunately
7. Sharp bark
8. Family member
9. Afterlife place of torment
10. Yoko of music
11. Soup base
12. Sioux tent
16. Deli breads
21. ATM emission
23. Join, as the army
26. Ordinary
27. Increases
28. Animal in Oz
29. Gain by merit
30. Medical photo: hyph. wd.
31. Dog reprimand
32. Timber tree
34. Small restaurant
36. Applies
37. Pushes (out)
38. Silvery coin
40. Craving
41. Hot temper
44. Characters from Homer?
46. Perfumed bags
48. Lots
49. Loving touch
50. Hardy heroine
51. Caribbean country
52. Encouraged
54. Lichen-covered
56. Ply a peeler
57. Falafel wrap
58. "Garfield" pooch
59. Bus route
60. Athenian vowels
62. Crooner Tormé
64. Horse morsel

69

ACROSS

1. Vim
4. Pound sound
7. Blemishes
11. Eastern canal
13. Fauna go-with
15. Ladd of film
16. Tiny cut
17. Defiant person
18. "Behold!": hyph. wd.
19. Court typist
21. Narcissist's focus
23. Slacks mishap
24. Lofty poems
25. Deli buy
27. Chivalrous title
29. Thames school
32. Warm embrace
33. Taro dish
34. Conceited one
36. Fizzy drinks
40. Idaho neighbor
42. Exciting game result
43. Make a contribution
44. Narrow valleys
46. Cold capital
48. Scale tone
49. Deep furrow
51. 36 inches
53. Nocturnal predator
54. Unlock again
57. Paint clumsily
59. "2001" computer
60. Verbalizes
62. Bordered
64. Feverish state
66. Santa —, California
68. Harsh cleaning liquids
70. Completely overhaul
71. Suite spot?
72. Casual assent
73. Paradise
74. Flanders of "The Simpsons"
75. Like sawdust

DOWN

1. Buddhist sect
2. Gladiolus kin
3. Magazine feature
4. Saloon order
5. Is a thief
6. Unchains
7. Doorway find
8. Fire warning
9. Spokes
10. Sharp break
12. Squeezed (out)
13. Ices (a cake)
14. Muslim God
20. By birth
22. Viral ailments
26. In awe
27. Starchy tuber
28. Small bit
30. Aware of: 2 wds.
31. Quite loud
35. Composer Bartók
37. Was a 17-Across
38. Promise
39. Auction off
41. Brave warrior
45. Dines
47. Severe trial
50. Instruct
52. A parent
54. Stormed
55. Duck
56. Strong fabric
58. Hideous
59. Speedy hopper
61. Cloy
63. Loving word
65. Billion years
67. Brick color
69. Demure

70

ACROSS

1. Leather punch
4. Detail
8. A Fitzgerald
12. Garden tool
13. Nick Charles's wife
14. Florida city
16. Gender
17. Extensive
18. Aromatic trees
20. Ache soother
22. Fencing gear
24. Stun: slang
25. Fancy tie
27. "— been bad!"
28. "— Lisa"
29. Formless mass
30. Old pronoun
32. Confrontational encounter: hyph. wd.
33. Fire: slang
34. Oratory spot
35. Call for aid
36. Methods
38. Lab supply
42. "No —, ands, or buts!"
43. Egg on
44. Early August birth
45. Chosen few
48. Mild oath
49. Lithe
50. Yucky stuff: slang
51. Half a quartet
52. Peevish cry
53. Champ of note
54. Section
56. Slangy affirmation
57. Baseball shelter
59. Austen novel
61. Undersea boat
64. Stylish
65. Huge melee
66. Aussie bird
67. 1970s do
68. Proofreading directive
69. Covert agent

DOWN

1. Sigh sounds
2. Melancholy
3. Vocabularies
4. Water passage
5. Superfluously
6. Coastal flier
7. Crow cousins
8. Show host
9. False stories
10. Lass's pal
11. South American river
15. Tehran native
19. Cross over
21. Corn castoff
23. Holiday prelude
25. Kindergarten topic
26. Amuse: slang
28. Strong scent
30. Highlands hats
31. Bathrobe ID
32. Atlas listing
34. Skillful
35. Auditorium fixture
37. Check mark
38. Fluffy scarf
39. Geometric ovals
40. Horse leash
41. Approximately
43. Produce vendors
45. "Good gravy!"
46. Doozies: slang
47. Perplexing matter
48. Expected now
49. That ewe
51. Likewise
52. Marshal Earp
54. Cat's murmur
55. Send forth
58. Big klutz
60. Bossy Stooge
62. Sports judge
63. Pay money for

71

ACROSS

1. Sets in semis
4. Bruin Bobby
7. Greens dish
9. Entreat
11. Military processions
13. Made
15. Football blitz
16. Like some eyebrows
18. Nickname for Hemingway
19. Undivided
20. "Norma —," film
21. Male 26-Across
22. Joyous sound
24. Star, for short
26. Furry friend
27. Quartet voice
29. Ruined: slang
31. Fragrant tree
32. Saturate
33. Book of maps
35. Upstairs room
37. Fellow
38. Rent contract
40. Medic: slang
42. Crude abode
43. Unwelcoming
44. Hamm of soccer
46. Soot-covered
48. Midleg joints
50. Goes (for)
51. Police spy
53. Experiences a prickly feeling
55. Pipe instrument
56. Erases, to a printer
57. Certain sibling, briefly
58. Cowboy's handle

DOWN

1. Child safety device: 2 wds.
2. Dull: slang
3. Blue
4. José's "Rah!"
5. Gain via hard work
6. Machine-gun noise: 3 wds.
7. Spa feature
8. High-society girl
9. Employ a crowbar
10. Drop-off spot
11. Compensated athlete
12. Less doubtful
13. Facial area
14. Sire's mate
17. Bando on the diamond
23. Large and powerful
24. Reef growth
25. Moisten (meat)
26. Roman god
28. Zilch
30. Betting pool
33. They write
34. French river
35. Until now: 2 wds.
36. Intricate
37. Great vigor
39. Playing card
41. Quotes
42. Grasps
45. Wild burro
47. Catcher Berra
48. Family
49. Caesar of TV
50. Look at hungrily
52. Musical tones
54. Clear profit

72

ACROSS

1. Copied
5. Forest father
9. Military truant
13. Chile neighbor
14. — over, read carefully
16. Impelling force
17. Software engineer
19. Bruce or Laura
20. Hat: slang
21. Merino mamas
22. Spring blooms
24. High dice rolls
26. Underway
27. Asner and Koch
28. Multitalented Moreno
29. Escorted
32. Potent tastes
35. Who you are
37. Brain flash
38. Solitary figure
40. British queen
41. Court confrontations
43. Tea additive
44. Print measures
45. Brief correspondence
46. Jog swiftly
47. African charger
49. Close companion
53. Fashion
55. Be suspended
56. Smelted stuff
57. Broke ground?
58. Superficial amount
61. Offshore land
62. Hotel division
63. Bangkok's continent
64. Cheeky talk
65. Graph-paper design
66. Command to a pooch

DOWN

1. Crunchy fruit
2. Danger
3. Chip away at
4. Plied a spade
5. Deposits (eggs)
6. Heavy books
7. Arsenal cache
8. Cry of awe
9. Of sound
10. Sport with pins
11. Giant monster
12. Contact —
15. Nomad
18. Grass stems
23. Flecked horse
25. Las —, Nevada
26. School helper
28. Wash casually
30. Sicilian spouter
31. Tinting expert
32. Mosaic piece
33. Comic Sandler
34. Movie preceders of yore
36. Ridicule
38. Pride female
39. German king
42. Troop group
43. Sharp increase
46. Spoke wildly
48. Demon's domain
49. Ms. LaBelle
50. Hullabaloo
51. Bert's cohort
52. Of a monarch
53. Frat letters
54. Heroic Parks
55. Minute margin
59. Large cup
60. Hearty cheer

73

ACROSS

1. Quickly
5. — Francisco
8. Easter finds
12. Grads of 39-Across
13. Brownish-yellow
15. Crooner Nat King
16. Noted Jedi
17. Blood sucker
18. Store away
19. Mother —
21. Display deference
23. Creamy white
25. Heavy swell
26. Ms. Keaton
29. Fool: slang
31. English paper
35. Assigned task
37. Thus far
39. Harvard rival
40. Liquor choice
41. Make a doily
43. Pinch off
45. Vigor
46. That: 2 wds.
48. Brynner of the stage
50. Ness 53-Down
52. Book holder
54. Shopping sack
56. Alarm noise
57. Charged atom
59. Annoying ones
61. Echo
64. Wobble unsteadily
67. Historical Wyatt
68. Field rodent
70. Nose stimulus
72. Liver secretion
73. Sup at home: 2 wds.
74. City of Peru
75. Oozed
76. Thieves' lair
77. Thespian Connery

DOWN

1. Funny Tina
2. Plenty: 2 wds.
3. Box section
4. Empress of Russia
5. Grease marks
6. Vigoda of "Fish"
7. Throat site
8. Rapture
9. Attend: 2 wds.
10. Radiate light
11. Form a seam
13. Ditto
14. Greek characters
20. Big occasion
22. Itsy-bitsy
24. Crowd cheer
26. Painter of ballerinas
27. From Dublin
28. Golfer Palmer, familiarly
30. Inkwell item
32. Enjoy deeply
33. Straighten
34. Oman neighbor
36. Calendar unit
38. Muscle twitch
42. Washing vat
44. Thick glue
47. Paged (through)
49. Track circuit
51. Small guns
53. Adversary
55. Enters (a car): 2 wds.
58. Identify
60. Observed
61. Fence support
62. — Stanley Gardner, mystery writer
63. Pond dweller
65. Actress Falco
66. Capital of *Italia*
67. Fall back
69. A Shoshonean
71. Rushed

74

ACROSS

1. Chest muscles, briefly
5. Versatile Murphy
10. Stomped
14. Dull pain
15. Steadfast
16. Traveling worker
17. Bygone Mets venue
18. Like laws that fail to be imposed
20. Twisters
22. Japanese city
23. Meter man?
24. Elton of music
26. Protect
29. North American body of water: 2 wds.
33. Ms. Dunne
34. Enemy spotter
35. Heavy planter
36. James of "The Godfather"
37. Comfortable and familiar
38. Alum
39. Curvy turn
40. Filled fully
41. Packing case
42. Smoke —, safety device
44. In the pokey
45. Deviate
46. Had existence
47. French — soup
50. It dines on ants
54. Reverses a position
57. Legendary tsar
58. "Oh!": 2 wds.
59. Harmonize
60. Cruel emperor
61. Old sailors
62. Wee
63. Flourished

DOWN

1. Yesteryear
2. Cavern sound
3. Single-named songstress
4. "Mystic River" star: 2 wds.
5. Evaded
6. Prohibition words
7. Tints
8. Dramatic McKellen
9. Impish child
10. Ruler's post
11. Sway gently
12. Listen to
13. Extinct bird
19. Different
21. Super: 2 wds.
24. World-weary
25. Adequate
26. Cubed (veggies)
27. Dump (data)
28. Lavish meal
29. Less believable, as an excuse
30. Bucolic
31. Plenty sore
32. Finalized
34. Dynamo part
37. Ugly emotion
38. Activity for a mourner
40. Fragrance
41. Funny person
43. Calls forth
44. Stretchy fabric
46. Get up
47. News notice
48. Houston institution
49. Bakery pro
50. Zoning unit
51. State as true
52. Scarce
53. Recognize
55. Furry pest
56. Time of life

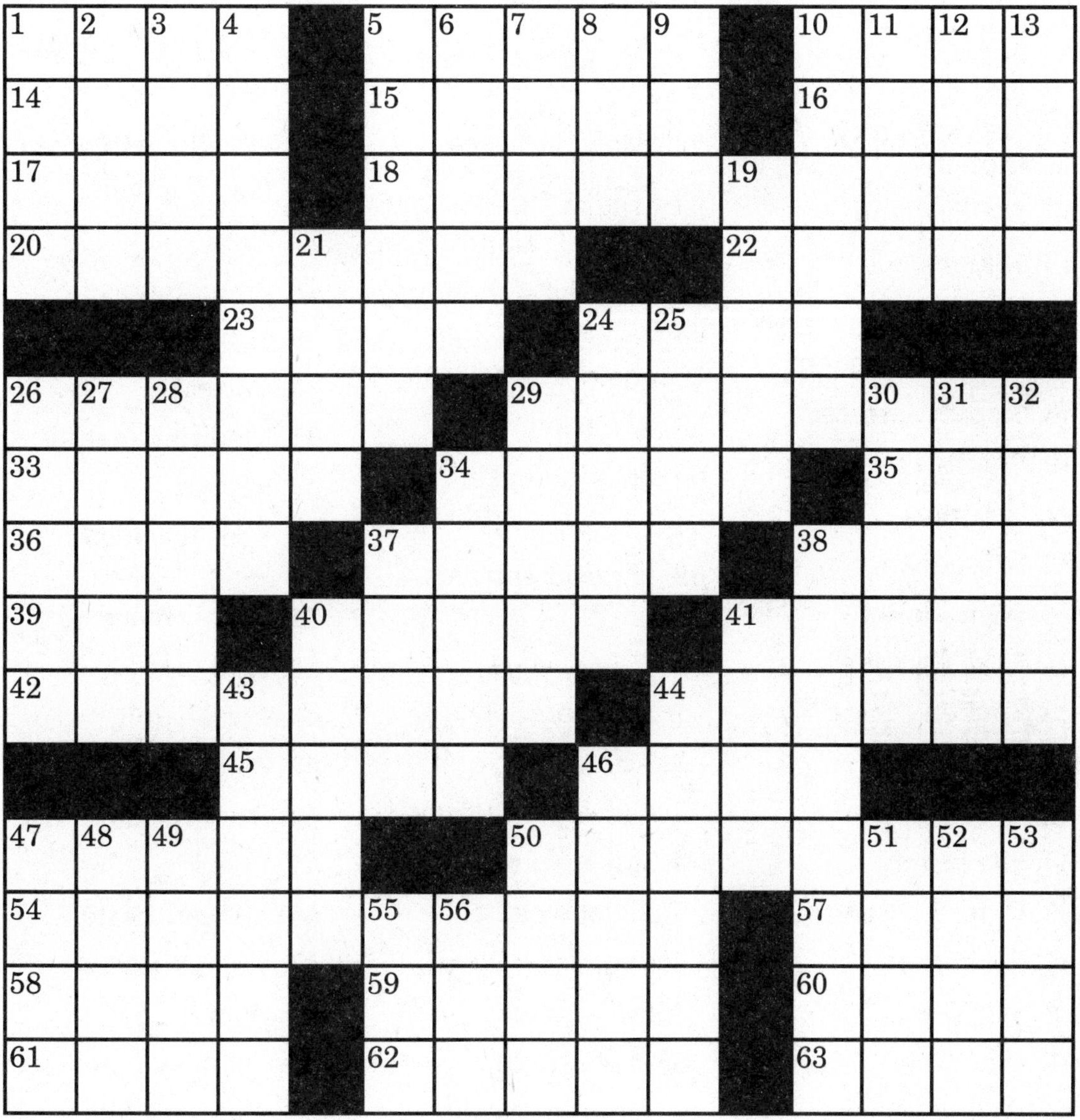

75

ACROSS

1. Grain husk
5. Leg region
9. Breton or Scot
13. Cork's country, formerly
14. Atelier stand
15. Solo melody
16. Cruising
17. Authorized agent
18. Sloping surface
19. Comfort food choice
21. Hesitates
23. Subsequent
24. Swift blows
25. False doctrine
28. Kitchen cabinet
32. Squirrel away
33. Urban lane
34. Life history
35. Oxford fellows
36. Flight part
37. Silly stunts
38. Giant Mel
39. Calling device
40. Utilize a tub
41. Baby bird
43. French caps

44. Be optimistic
45. Soccer aim
46. Personify
49. Heat sources
53. Weaving frame
54. Patriot Ethan
56. Biblical skipper
57. Baseball star Sammy
58. Put into service again
59. Water plunge
60. Curved lines
61. Eat sparingly
62. Iditarod entrant

DOWN

1. Smile broadly
2. Advance in rank
3. Carpeting calculation
4. Tidy quality
5. Jewel weight
6. Ever since: 2 wds.
7. Evil Luthor
8. Sticky snare
9. Tenor Enrico
10. Generations
11. Drink twist
12. Bugle strain

14. Strong adhesive
20. Diminishing word?
22. "Dear" columnist
24. Actress Andrews
25. Wore: 2 wds.
26. Play the ham
27. Talks wildly
28. Ringing noise
29. Ebb
30. Correct
31. Medicine measures
33. Repent
36. Spot for building ocean vessels
37. Floral chains
39. Walk heavily
40. Coffee unit
42. Poet Dylan
43. Transported
45. Visitor
46. Ms. Lanchester
47. Tie (a boat)
48. Winter pear
49. Chimney pipe
50. Curl (around)
51. Gutter site
52. Tool house
55. Hula necklace

76

ACROSS

1. Road charts
5. Healing ointment
9. Fill the tank: 2 wds.
10. Another name
12. Cower
13. Certain relatives
15. "Common Sense" scribe Thomas
16. Expand
18. Congeal
20. Eye pencil
21. Shiny metal
22. Package sealer
23. &
24. Bit of data
26. Funny Foxx
27. Capone pursuer Eliot
29. "Oh, no!"
30. Seoul native
31. Note in Nice
33. Gore, once
34. Sounds of rusted hinges
37. Clamor
38. Trucking rig
42. Illinois hub
43. Religious order
44. Cleanse (of)
45. Connect the —
46. Total
47. Petite
49. Paid promos
50. Dark, as a room
52. Troublesome
53. Baby raptor
55. Playing marbles
57. Radio dial
58. Below
59. "Quite contrary" gal
60. Was litigious

DOWN

1. Bangor's site
2. Lou Grant portrayer
3. Wrinkled dog
4. Gush forth
5. Western thief
6. Extraterrestrial
7. Debt security
8. Surrey slicker
9. Pulverizes
11. Bagel seed
12. British actor Michael
14. Brownish color
15. Get organized
17. Rash symptom
19. Bar mitzvah boy, for example
22. Canvas covers
24. Animal coats
25. Before today
26. Diner brew: slang
28. Scorches
30. — State, university in Ohio
32. Guitar cousin
33. Crooner Damone
34. Musical finale
35. — Island Red
36. Vexes: 2 wds.
37. Moore of film
39. Expunging aid
40. Does a dairy-farm chore
41. In vain
43. Full of smoldering passion
46. Mocking smile
47. Digging tool
48. Dished (out)
50. An arm bone
51. Greek symbols
54. Tooth holder
56. Safari creature

77

ACROSS

1. Tease: slang
5. "Pssst!"
8. Black avian
12. Shun
14. Cooking range
16. Place to live
17. Bart Simpson's mom
18. The whole — yards
19. Polish (text)
20. "Excuse me, mister…"
21. Fan favorite
23. Seizes by force
25. Inn resident
27. Frat letters
28. Print widths
29. Moves clumsily
32. Fizzy drinks
35. Locales
36. Exultant cry
38. Mimic
39. "The Martian" star
40. Twirl
41. Oil-field find
42. Major crook
43. "Rome — built in a day"
44. Breaks loose
46. Actor Kilmer
47. 8-Down from Holland
48. Cake dough
51. Collect; gather
54. Sugar stalk
55. Woodpile unit
57. Freudian topics
58. Hailing from Bangkok
60. Cheek makeup
62. Ballet costume
63. Window base
64. Alpine warble
65. Realizes
66. Urban rails
67. That girl's

DOWN

1. Pushes firmly
2. Benefit
3. Sword-wielding hero
4. Sharp-angled turn
5. Public esteem
6. Fiendish
7. Japanese coin
8. Dairy product
9. Curtain bars
10. Exclude
11. Dampens
13. Condescends (to)
15. Some anchors
22. — Moines
24. Barbecue staples
26. Costly
27. Don: 2 wds.
29. Fancy rides
30. Hits quickly
31. Below-the-knee area
32. "Wheels"
33. Howard role
34. Chicken drumsticks
35. Boston suburb
37. Pantry pest
39. Leaves
40. Sea extract
42. Become weaker
43. Diluted
45. Population count
46. Large vehicle
48. Helps (out)
49. Circumvent
50. "OK" via radio
51. Procures
52. Sick feeling
53. Fixed method
54. Cat chaser?
56. Salon substances
59. Hurry
61. Pleased sigh

78

ACROSS

1. Zenith
5. Christmas-poem beginner
9. Boars and bulls
14. Belt holder
15. "Yikes!": 2 wds.
16. Mrs. Bunker of TV
17. Goofing off
18. Lacking cash
19. Hash
20. Superman's "dressing room": 2 wds.
23. Bath cake
24. Hesitation noises
25. Spanish article
28. In an overly formal way
31. Sarcastic retort: slang
34. Wide-eyed
36. Adjective for Abner
37. — carotene
38. Restrained expressions
42. As required
43. Satisfied sighs
44. Start
45. CIA employee
46. Bruce Willis film: 2 wds.
49. Before, for a bard
50. Feel awful
51. Shoe parts
53. Stevenson classic: 2 wds.
60. Take turns?
61. Arctic barker
62. Butter sub
63. Funny O'Donnell
64. Different
65. Dabbling duck
66. Inquired (of)
67. Tinted (hair)
68. Hawk wares

DOWN

1. Touched down
2. Cipher system
3. Gangster's girl: slang
4. Fencing swords
5. Tails' accessory: 2 wds.
6. Ms. Goldberg
7. Shortly
8. Carrying a grudge
9. Recollection
10. "Farewell!"
11. Cloth fuzz
12. Impress distinctly
13. That maiden
21. Tricky riddle
22. Ball star?
25. Praises
26. Confess (to)
27. With regret
29. Camera adjunct
30. In good shape
31. Impenetrable
32. Pronounce
33. Big hurry
35. Piano button
37. Comic Stiller
39. Goes boating
40. "Remember — Alamo!"
41. Methods
46. Tuned in (a radio station)
47. Military command: 2 wds.
48. Irritated
50. Eagle's home
52. Coin openings
53. Low cards
54. Endanger
55. Brought into play
56. Depend
57. Helm heading
58. "Hud" actress
59. Toy for a tot
60. Song syllable

79

ACROSS

1. — saxophone
5. Ridicule
10. Leaning Tower site
14. In — of, instead of
15. Stockings fabric
16. Shoot dice
17. Adjusted too much
20. Clobber
21. Possesses
22. Canadian city
23. Sticks fast
25. A woodwind
26. Home: slang
27. Rubber boots
31. Slow mollusk
34. Vacation spot
35. Thurman of Hollywood
36. Soft mineral
37. Foot trails
38. Winter maladies
39. Greek letter
40. Soars singly
41. Garbage
42. Locale
44. China leader
45. Till bills
46. Skill for an identity thief
50. Hunting hound
53. Garage filler
54. Maiden-named
55. Hidden agendas: 2 wds.
58. Garden substance
59. African river
60. Ramble
61. Oppressed one
62. Sheen; luster
63. Storm centers

DOWN

1. Hilo hello
2. Enraged
3. Pearly whites
4. Your and my
5. Fell in flakes
6. Mass numbers?
7. Lofty peaks
8. Skier Tommy
9. Dignifies
10. Talks foolishly
11. Trifling amount
12. Vanquished (a dragon)
13. Dr. Pierce portrayer
18. — reef
19. Bar perch
24. Sweeping saga
25. Serious vows
27. Mounted: 2 wds.
28. Island dance
29. Feathered sprinters
30. Flashy accessory
31. Porch feature
32. Western alliance
33. Woeful wail
34. Saintly glows
37. Finger action
38. Pond hopper
40. Beef source
41. Occult deck
43. Reflexive pronoun
44. Tours by car
46. Vapors
47. Diplomatic representative
48. "Superman" star
49. Affirmative answers
50. Playful kiss
51. Fleshy lily plant
52. Begin to move
53. Mythic ship
56. Viscous fluid
57. Deep anger

80

ACROSS

1. Cool refreshers
6. Bhutan's continent
10. Flip through
14. Mature
15. Prime sunburn time
16. Cantina item
17. Guilty of wicked behavior
19. Bachelor of —
20. Smoked fish
21. Tartan sporter
22. Singer Nelson
24. Cottage-cheese component
25. Eight quarts
26. Pumps and clogs
28. Indicates the limits of: 2 wds.
32. Drives away
33. Birdie negator
34. Athlete Ripken
35. Laze (about)
36. Crispy side dish
37. Mr. Preminger
38. "Hail!": Latin
39. Sophia of film
40. Doze
41. Cowboy movies
43. Comes upon
44. Certain bills
45. Regrets
46. Cager Dennis
49. Defraud
50. Fanged snake
53. Biz bigshot
54. High spirits
57. Lugosi of horror
58. Foot surface
59. Birth-related
60. Piqued mood
61. Purchased
62. Soap target

DOWN

1. Except for
2. "Garfield" canine
3. Monotonous
4. "— right!"
5. Hiding places
6. Nettle
7. Chimney dirt
8. Debt note
9. Gave a reply
10. Celery units
11. Author Sagan
12. Dramatic beginning: 2 wds.
13. Human snout
18. Sweet treats
23. Gross: slang
24. Sweater yarn
25. Nonbeliever
26. Hard push
27. Golf goals
28. Burrowing pests
29. Four duos
30. Destinies
31. Broadway dud
32. Picnic fare
33. Farm shelters
36. Cause for a massage
37. Córdoba cheers
39. Funny Dunham
40. On the hunt for
42. Prowler in an alley
43. Think (over)
45. Made angry
46. Yankee foes, briefly
47. Plow pullers
48. Hero shop
49. Calf's father
50. Naysayer
51. Swindle: slang
52. Brazilian soccer star
55. Arena jeer
56. Hearing aid?

81

ACROSS

1. Nearly all
5. Routes
9. Lasagna base
14. In re: 2 wds.
15. Jai —, speedy sport
16. Stomach issue
17. Arkin or Cranston
18. Performances of a song
20. Recurring theme
22. Bump on a tree
23. Pal of Pooh
24. Lass
27. Shore bird
28. Elementary recitation
31. Viscous
32. Coronation sphere
33. Spoil; damage
34. Warm embraces
35. Sleek
38. Publicize
40. Like many supplements
41. Alpine athletes
42. Ringlet
43. Hose defect
44. — Jacinto
45. Indian abode
46. Rabbit mama
47. Immense
49. Mom and Dad
51. Investment option
52. Assigned portion
53. Mean feeling
57. Struggle
61. Keats pieces
62. Fall bloom
63. Bushy hairdo
64. Wield a scythe
65. Bowling button
66. Dark breads
67. Lenient

DOWN

1. Woman's title
2. Capital on a fiord
3. Numerical fact
4. Gin companion
5. Armed strife
6. Bar brew
7. New York squad
8. Actor Poitier
9. Green stroke
10. 1996 Olympics torch lighter
11. Stadium sight
12. General drift
13. Fiery felony
19. Electrically charged atom
21. Liner sounding
25. Oafs
26. Theater box
27. Horse's pace
28. Music magnifiers
29. Snap (at)
30. Bakery buys
32. Egg dishes
35. Raid signal
36. Wee combo
37. 38-Across sensationally
39. Deli purchase
40. Deceive
42. Vouch for
45. — sauce, seafood condiment
47. Church figure
48. Went skyward
49. Piping god
50. Future fern
52. Flippant
54. Conception
55. Herbal drinks
56. Detect
58. Gridiron gizmo
59. Raw metal
60. Flat refusals

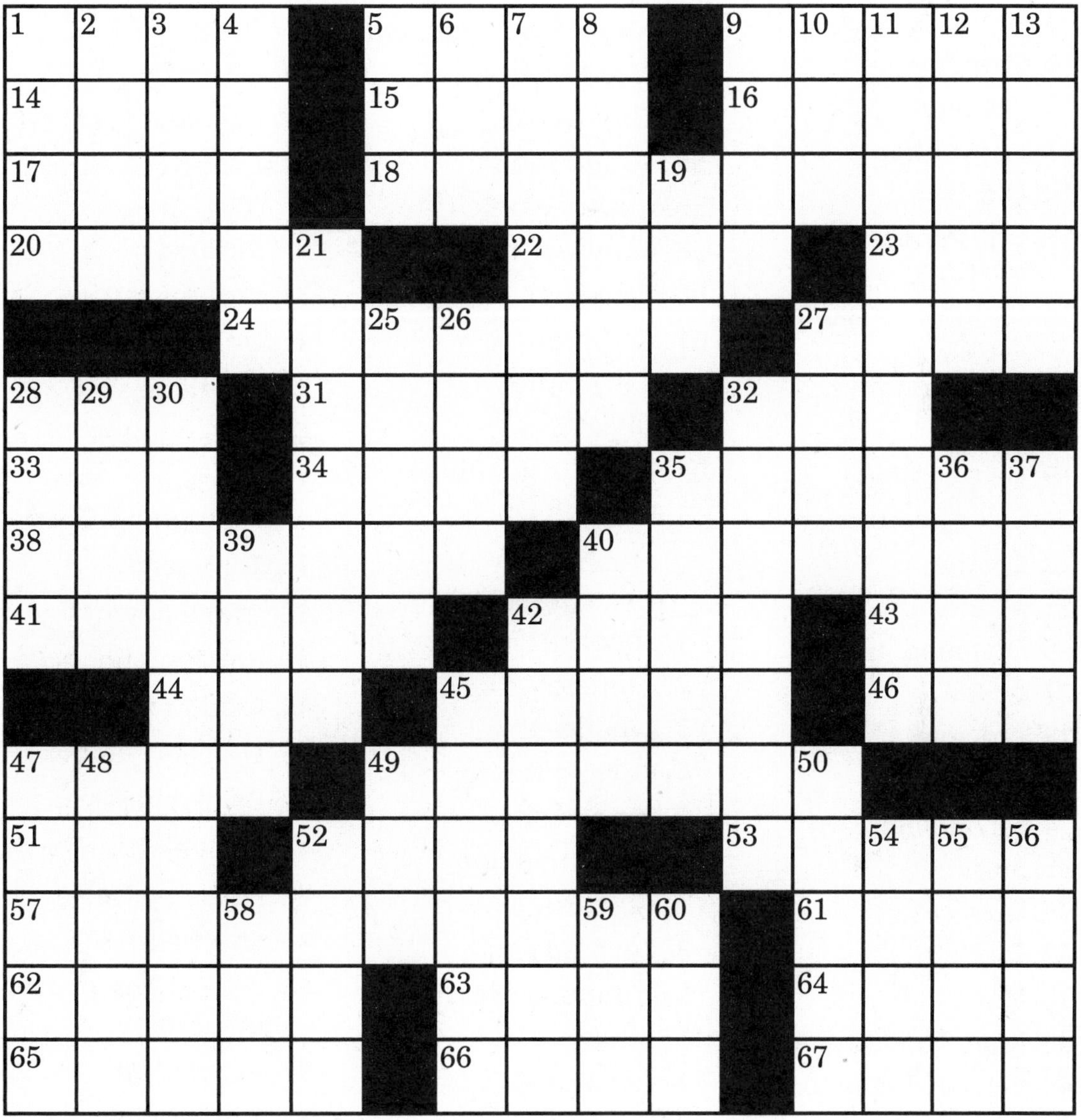

82

ACROSS

1. Bikini half
4. Tennis legend
8. Stratagem
12. "Misery" costar
13. Convention platform
14. Old
15. British noble's territory
16. Roughly speaking: 2 wds.
17. Prod along
18. Anger
19. Garr of films
21. Full of barbs
23. Loathe
25. Author Uris
26. Diamond judge
27. Only
28. Pro vote
31. Sparkled
34. Mr. Philbin
35. Stray
36. Duplicate
37. Dig find
38. Hook lure
39. Mary Todd's hubby
40. Earp of Tombstone
41. Clouded, as water
42. Hurler Guidry
43. Skirt lines
44. Tone after fa
45. Short cuts?
46. Trash
50. Fold down: hyph. wd.
53. A red Muppet
54. Clothes label
55. Boring tools
56. Austen work
58. Bond portrayer Daniel
60. Well-kept
61. Ambitions
62. Baby pinto
63. Objectives
64. Salad —, youth
65. Beanpole Olive

DOWN

1. Supports
2. Arena cry
3. Whenever
4. Be mad for
5. Indian robe
6. Towel marking
7. Abstruse
8. Covered cart
9. Composer Stravinsky
10. Lanky
11. Wind swirl
12. Smoke (bacon)
15. Sufficed
20. Psychic skill
22. Weed whackers
24. Itty-bitty
25. On the up and up: slang
27. Dissolves
28. Calendar span
29. Estrada of "CHiPs"
30. Aesthetically inclined
31. Wound vestige
32. Unkempt drifter
33. Boutique sign
34. Paper units
37. Sandwich component: 2 wds.
38. Tulip seed
40. "Slow down!"
41. Rabat's land
44. Frodo's friend
45. Defeats
46. Drink holder
47. Even a little: 2 wds.
48. Horse's pace
49. Soufflé base
50. Copenhagen inhabitant
51. Actor Clive
52. Tickled pink
53. TV prize
57. Olympian Hamm
59. Acuff of music

83

ACROSS

1. Doily fabric
5. Field section
9. Fades
13. Basic component
14. Tree material
15. Decree
17. Attacked vigorously
19. Narrow vessel
20. Swift
21. Class
23. Historic time
24. "— you serious?"
25. Listener's phrase: 2 wds.
27. Hard journey
28. Good friends
30. Chiding sound
31. Mr. Aykroyd
33. Kimono closer
34. Unctuous
35. Rome's nation
39. Gun (a motor)
40. Manipulate
41. June VIP
43. Cry of a cow
44. Put in office
46. Bait-shop buy
47. Lunch sack
48. Western power: abbr.
50. Pen fluid
51. Sinatra daughter
52. Johnny of film
55. Stun
57. Pulpy fruit
58. Biblical 59-Across
59. Female parent
60. Ceremony
63. "Ditto!": 2 wds.
65. Highlight
68. Ready to be drawn: 2 wds.
69. Presently
70. Sicily peak
71. Small child
72. Sidle
73. Tinting pro

DOWN

1. Science rooms
2. Above
3. Awaken: 2 wds.
4. Hot coals
5. Off
6. Atlantic fish
7. 6-Down eggs
8. Singer Vedder
9. Pack of cards
10. Lovely Lupino
11. Gold-rush figure
12. Garner points
16. Durable 14-Across
18. Beach cooler
22. Headed up
25. Cruise view
26. Clouds' site
27. Blasted stuff
28. Ponder (over)
29. A son of Adam
30. Scale tones
32. Staff helper
34. Inning enders
36. Aspect of innuendo
37. Money advance
38. Gym offering
41. Ridge of sand
42. Boat for Noah
45. Flour measure
46. Ms. Taylor, to the tabloids
49. Dither
51. Having noble rank
52. Audition tape
53. Happening
54. Trifling
56. Tickle
57. Pine relative
59. Be downcast
60. Philosopher Descartes
61. Poet Sexton
62. Tragic king
64. Mature acorn
66. Show approval
67. Pooch

84

ACROSS

1. Boisterous play
5. Present for approval
10. Leave-taking gesture
14. Declare firmly
15. Rhythmic throbbing
16. Exam variety
17. "Star Wars" knight
18. Clear (from memory)
19. Elevator man
20. Gone skyward
22. Parade venue in California
24. Nebraska metropolis
26. Short bark
27. Bub: slang
29. Inner beings
31. Flour sources
35. NHL great
36. Adjust, as a piano
37. Napping
38. Bride topper
40. Band platform
42. Roof edge
43. Complete
45. Vibrant hues
47. Snug chamber
48. Assurance: hyph. wd.
49. Fierce growl
50. Turner of CNN
51. Bakery treat
53. Georgia fruit
55. Silver stamp
59. Round shape
62. Famed canal
63. Color shades
65. Astounded
66. Some annexes
67. Call forth
68. Damp forecast
69. Domino specks
70. Made a quilt
71. Talking avian

DOWN

1. Indian ruler
2. Spanning
3. Ordinary state
4. Beam bender
5. Informal reception: 2 wds.
6. Canine coat
7. Envelope seal
8. School papers
9. Della of song
10. Hearth heap
11. Comic Johnson
12. Self-centered
13. "Born Free" cat
21. Dawn direction
23. Charity funds
25. Bee, to Opie
27. Changes homes
28. Area of conflict
30. Gain a skill
32. Be a guide: 3 wds.
33. River bank
34. Devote (time)
37. Spoke to
39. Lethargic
41. Tide descriptive
44. Meander about
46. Blatant insult
49. Tried hard
52. Has value
54. Beguile
55. Mind
56. Guthrie of folk
57. Pleasing accent
58. Be sure of
60. Leather strap
61. Literary Ferber
64. Portion (out)

85

ACROSS

1. Constant pain
5. Defame on paper
10. Throat-clearing sound
14. Pole or Czech
15. Arizona brick
16. Cause tedium
17. Mitchell plantation
18. Site for a spur: 2 wds.
20. Joining term
21. Small room
22. "I dropped it!"
23. Moccasin orb
25. Keep in touch?
27. Surrounded by
29. Deflected
32. Legal release
34. Boggy ground
35. Pouring edge
37. Paris airport
38. Martini extra
40. Eruption flow
41. Deceitful utterance
42. Stage signals
43. Of a 2-Down
45. Counsels
47. Fresh air: slang
48. Continuously
49. Male swine
50. Pasta choice
52. Find
54. Clio honorees
57. Club deliveries
60. Pack carefully
61. Diva Callas
62. Cuts of pork
63. Cuzco's country
64. Without life
65. Daft
66. Economist Smith

DOWN

1. Nora's dog
2. Kinship unit
3. Like some eggs: hyph. wd.
4. Topsy's friend
5. Tied (shoes)
6. Celebrity heartthrob
7. Soup holder
8. Abate
9. Zodiac symbol
10. Comedian Bud
11. Earring shape
12. God of love
13. Assembled
19. "— welcome!"
21. Canary coop
24. Jealous discontent
25. Tel follower
26. Cannes cap
27. Military baddie
28. Obsession
29. Faulty
30. Added details
31. Large couch
33. Excite
36. Lose color
39. Nasty look
40. Ms. Minnelli
42. Formally polite
44. Tree base
46. Nixed
49. Domineering
50. City sector
51. Indian of 63-Across
52. Deck division
53. Bottled (up)
55. Wee cartoon explorer
56. Done laps in the pool
57. Stylish 1960s youth
58. Antiquated
59. Sticky gunk
60. Posh getaway

86

ACROSS

1. Sluice gate
6. Casual wear
11. Easter blooms
12. Is in tune (with)
14. Environment
15. Vie (for)
17. Evaluated
18. "A mouse!"
20. Symbol of evil
21. Remote
22. French impressionist
24. Baron's peer
25. Dramatic Ryan
26. Ewes and cows
28. "— heard that!"
29. Took for granted
31. Blew off steam
33. Showing wear
34. Comedian Jay
35. Superficial coating
38. Traveling entertainer
42. Munched lunch
43. Kitchen alcove
45. Famous Gardner
46. Sea craft
48. Pearly white
49. Hefty piece
50. Prime-time hour
52. Winged hunter
53. Ralph — Emerson
54. Academic institutions
56. Before
58. Parlor sofa
59. Removed facial hair
60. Medical measures
61. Sealed (a box)

DOWN

1. Dating from a period long past
2. Change the fit of
3. Committed perjury
4. Plague
5. Well-respected
6. African scavenger
7. Id's partner
8. Upper limbs
9. Himalayan nation
10. "Get the job done!": 3 wds.
11. Laceless shoe
13. Go hungry
14. Sudden muscle pain
16. Completed
19. Old euphemism
22. Negative mark
23. — heaven
26. Welded
27. Feel strongly
30. Johnny Cash title name
32. Short refusal
34. Most minute
35. Flower urns
36. Moral principles
37. Whinnied
38. Cat comment
39. Made a comeback
40. Escaped from
41. Intense toil
44. Rope knots
47. Trip souvenir
49. Burn ointment
51. Small kiddies
53. Deli order
55. Director Spike
57. Yell of triumph

87

ACROSS

1. Eject (lava)
5. Slumps
9. 2009 Nobelist
14. Plus
15. Ninny
16. Marine
17. Jeopardize
18. Indian royal
19. Folklore figure
20. "Good golly!"
21. Showed over
22. Comb sweet
23. Attempted
25. Dancer Verdon
27. Enjoy ravioli
28. Shipboard jail
29. Fine trap
32. Oak's fruit
35. Daily drama: 2 wds.
37. Arizona native
38. Celeb West
39. Optical piece
40. Drives away (friends)
42. Dunces
43. 22-Across producer
44. Yale alums
45. Bawl

46. Yacht spot
47. Cut violently
51. Shoot for: 2 wds.
54. Following behind: 2 wds.
56. Dinghy blade
57. Loud noise
58. Wildlife parks
59. Enveloping mist
60. Certain Scandinavians
61. Ms. Sedgwick
62. "— it wonderful?"
63. Computer key
64. Religious branch
65. More or —

DOWN

1. Beetle Bailey's boss
2. Tissue layers
3. Track curves
4. Canton cooker
5. Map find
6. Contest prize
7. Actress Gershon
8. Dangerous fish
9. Busy: 3 wds.
10. Feudal lord
11. English river

12. Bull or ram
13. Trade partner
21. Gosling of film
24. Eagle's pad
26. Cleaning cloth
28. Canine treats
29. Bewail
30. Shore soarer
31. Quartet member
32. Melville captain
33. Cabbage relative
34. Andy Taylor's boy
35. Ridicules
36. Gimmicks
38. Curly 33-Down
41. Word of exclusion
42. Make sketches
45. Hanger's site
46. Out-of-date
47. Impassive
48. Abode
49. Brings home
50. Mild oaths
51. Puberty woe
52. Anemia remedy
53. Place of commerce
55. Stem joint
59. Feel queasy

88

ACROSS

1. Cloister inhabitant
4. Knob position
7. Slightly: 2 wds.
9. "To Sir With Love" singer
10. Big cats
12. Electric cords
13. Compensate in advance
15. In the distance, to Blake
16. Drained of color
18. Arraignment answer
20. 2012 Affleck movie
22. Art tablet
23. Substantial
24. Technical skill: hyph. wd.
26. Golfing feat
27. Ignited (a fuse)
28. Beach bronze
29. Shot the breeze
33. Spiritual medium
37. Estranged
38. Debt marker
39. Nice currency?
40. Mexican money
41. Ups and —
43. June preceder
44. Like Saturn
46. Edgar — Poe
48. Film genre: hyph. wd.
49. Grunt of pain
50. Pizzeria need
51. Oft-misspelled possessive
52. Before, in a sonnet

DOWN

1. Took a siesta
2. Driving maneuver: hyph. wd.
3. Christen
4. Group pronoun
5. Hound hounder
6. Worrywart
8. Neatly dressed
9. Dialect
11. Lunch choice
12. Tattered
14. Hard-to-believe sighting
15. Asian beast
17. "Hee —," old TV show
19. Capitol Hill vote
21. Nocturnal fledgling
23. Chop finely
25. Cached away
26. Small inlet
28. Destructive wave
29. Wee chasm
30. Impressionist
31. Fundamental theory
32. Rodeo mount
33. Explosive boom
34. Mortal being
35. Islamic land
36. Kittenish
38. Salt additive
41. Postpone
42. Coin groove
45. Contribute
47. Ditty syllables

89

ACROSS

1. Appends
5. Loose stitch
10. Election word
14. Defeat badly
15. Radii neighbors
16. Sheltered
17. Embedded things
19. "Hud" costar
20. The Jetsons' pooch
21. Heavy weight
22. Scents
23. Polar helper
25. Fleming of fame
27. Learned one
31. Least bright
35. New Mexican resort
36. Loafer
38. Seesaw
39. Marine eagle
40. Lungfuls of air
42. Shake a leg
43. Acid neutralizer
45. Metallic rock
46. Quaker William
47. Occult figures
49. Steel-plated, as a truck
51. Wild burros
53. Imbibe slowly
54. Fiery gems
57. Firm denials
59. Islam holy book
63. Casino offering
64. Rider described by Longfellow: 2 wds.
66. Dock rodents
67. Befuddled: 2 wds.
68. Revamp (text)
69. Sudsy drinks
70. All prepared
71. Towel bars

DOWN

1. Opera melody
2. Henley and Ho
3. Fine dirt
4. Audio systems
5. Yet
6. Came to earth
7. Prying person
8. Treated (hides)
9. Curve shape
10. Actor Dick: 2 wds.
11. Bagel topper
12. Shred (paper)
13. Snaky catches
18. Dice toss
22. Club carriers
24. Silk and satin
26. Collects
27. Sauna vapor
28. Singer Simon
29. Horn sounds
30. Experience remorse
32. Primitive anesthetic
33. Paris waterway
34. Vogue
37. Chinese revolutionary
40. Divine state
41. Choir syllable
44. Perplexed: 3 wds.
46. Puffy muffin
48. Capitol gang
50. Accessory for an emcee
52. March maven
54. Soup pods
55. Ring out
56. Kitty payment
58. Winter glider
60. Draft again
61. Like the Gobi
62. Tuna trappers
64. Average level
65. Sunshine beam

90

ACROSS

1. Map proportion
6. Lyrical lines
10. A court great
14. Was wearing: 2 wds.
15. Bread choice
16. Brutal hoodlum
17. Pop up
18. Quarantine purpose
20. Three Stooges member
21. Continued: 2 wds.
23. Convenes
24. Customs concern
26. Magic staff
27. Deli request
28. Burbank neighbor
32. Weighty work
35. Took a medical picture of: hyph. wd.
37. Candle stuff
38. Athenian character
40. Funny Sothern
41. Striped rock
43. Hand: slang
44. Lightly asleep
47. Caustic liquids
48. NBA team: 2 wds.
50. Cato's 13-Down
52. Joint ailment
53. Remedy
58. Prayer enders
60. — pigeon
61. Eye shutter?
62. Samuel Clemens: 2 wds.
64. Ski chalet
66. Garfield's buddy
67. Lotion add-in
68. Strange
69. Roll topper
70. Room fee
71. Forward-looking folks?

DOWN

1. Impostors
2. Bumper bounce
3. "Goodbye!"
4. — Lobos, band
5. Strength
6. Express a view
7. Planning bane
8. Collar style
9. Mineo of film
10. Be present
11. Drew back (from): 2 wds.
12. Pursue prey
13. Roe, basically
19. Blake of TV
22. Author Haley
25. Mr. Louganis
26. Minute
29. Singer Loretta
30. Long overdue
31. Former mates
32. Soy product
33. Drop
34. Small zoo
36. Josh: slang
39. Tinker with
42. Delighted
45. Feed grain
46. Head for: 2 wds.
49. Sounded a horn
51. Ritzy retreats
54. Musical group
55. Golden song?
56. Indian feline
57. Idyllic spots
58. Bible prophet
59. Established
60. Mall magnet
63. 1812 event
65. Bravo, in Barcelona

91

ACROSS

1. Overzealous
6. Close
10. Curl (around)
14. Without help
15. Ballet skirt
16. Rural road
17. Tortilla dip
18. Help (a crook)
19. Words of comprehension
20. At random: 3 wds.
22. Smile smugly
23. Put (down)
24. Cuts of beef
25. Behind with the bills: 2 wds.
28. Manhattan neighbor
30. Female deer
31. Lebanon city
33. Light tan
37. Far from watertight
39. Energy
40. The British —
41. A Fitzgerald
42. Midwest state
44. "For — thing…"
45. Making knots
47. Stock pro
49. Stuck around
52. Big snakes
53. Winter afflictions
54. Pregnancy unit
59. Unsupportive of
60. Afternoon hour
61. GI's vacation
62. Interpret
63. Was 25-Across
64. Nepal neighbor
65. Misjudges
66. Breaks off
67. Horse pen

DOWN

1. Poorly considered
2. Jai —, sport
3. Cloth roll
4. Shoe extra
5. Advice column: 2 wds.
6. Solemn
7. Wheel centers
8. Colorado natives
9. Sound of disapproval
10. Big finales
11. Caravan stop
12. Static
13. Soup bulbs
21. Wee critter
22. Certain heir
24. Decompose
25. Frivolous
26. Yule carol
27. Store bargain
28. Carry
29. Jamaican exports
32. Cruel tsar
34. Dolt
35. Artist Magritte
36. Person at a terminal
38. Noisy insects
40. Jerusalem inhabitants
42. Baby goat
43. Basic particle
46. "Totally!"
48. Agree (to)
49. Frighten
50. Copy-machine fluid
51. Church table
52. Eagles and hawks
54. Village
55. Regretted
56. "Look here!": hyph. wd.
57. Corrupt
58. True
60. Antagonist

92

ACROSS

1. Consumer advocate Ralph
6. Ms. McEntire
10. On the briny
14. Existing
15. Thespian Roberts
16. Federal agent: hyph. wd.
17. Mind products
18. Slant
19. Rattle off
20. Deep spoon
21. Moves
23. Cancel
25. In an impetuous way
26. Mozart work
29. Assigned job
31. Slightly: 2 wds.
32. — Antony
34. Golf feat
39. Lack of any
40. Fancy feather
42. Cozy niche
43. Honking flock
45. From the top
46. Neck scruff
47. Floppy —
49. Hams it up
51. Clears (a windshield)
55. Donkey call
56. Track event: 2 wds.
59. Like some voices
63. Large flower
64. Oodles: 2 wds.
65. Silly
66. Evergreen tree
67. Preceding nights
68. Tennis skill
69. Becomes fast
70. Lord's wife
71. Relinquishes

DOWN

1. Carpentry joiner
2. Talented Alan
3. Perished
4. Assesses
5. Chafe at
6. Popularly nostalgic
7. Iroquoian tribe
8. Bar tab
9. Stage performers
10. Reference book
11. Sword maker
12. Studio stand
13. Unable to sit still: slang
22. Tiered treat
24. Wet
26. Played the bass?
27. English-horn kin
28. Diamond squad
29. Luggage piece
30. Apex
33. Mournful cry
35. Exasperating thing
36. Milk producer
37. Easy run
38. Stretches (out)
41. Washstand jug
44. Nervous
48. Haifa's land
50. Zealous fan
51. Faucet leaks
52. Quite strange
53. Sparking rock
54. Fertile spots
55. Sewing Ross
57. Edison's middle name
58. Adjective for many dorms today
60. Pronounced
61. Writer Brontë
62. Mutton servings

93

ACROSS

1. Compete (for)
4. "What?"
7. Thieve
10. Heat source
11. Put to work
12. Merino moms
14. — energy
15. Fellow: slang
16. Bar of metal
18. May be found
19. Wee devil
21. Boxer Norton
23. Important age
24. Company consolidations
26. Group of puppies
28. Braying beast
29. Legal claims
31. Forcibly take
34. Medicinal salt
35. Tying product
39. Shoot (for)
40. Signified
41. Stun
42. Rise: 2 wds.
44. Canal locales
45. Deli offering
47. British peers
49. Scot's cap
50. Katie of TV
53. Lull
57. Creative pursuit
58. Tint (hair)
60. Log chopper
61. Timid
62. Songstress Page
64. Small boy
66. Loud conflict
68. Svelte
69. Tycoon Onassis, to pals
70. Level out
71. Toupee: slang
72. Do a slalom
73. Crooner Cole

DOWN

1. Less pleasant
2. Investment option
3. Most surreal
4. Camel features
5. Olympics chant
6. "Shucks!"
7. Control: 2 wds.
8. "To each his —!"
9. Generate
10. Golfing cry
13. Feeling pain
14. "Cheers" bartender
17. Asphalt kin
20. Wifely title
22. Pick (a pol)
25. Fuel for cars
27. Chiding sound
29. Fib tellers
30. Lodging spots
31. Move briskly
32. — Bravo
33. Outback bird
34. Ardor
36. Old horse
37. Have debt
38. Aviv preceder
40. Compassion
43. By order of
45. Some Yankees
46. Music booster
48. Assisting
49. Singer Ritter
50. Maximum
51. From the mouth
52. Give voice to
53. Arm bones
54. Tiny landmass
55. After that
56. Vision organ
59. Frat letters
63. Sigma follower
65. Clumsy boat
67. Famous Perón

94

ACROSS

1. Five minus five
5. Church benches
9. Film's Lugosi
13. Chopped down
14. Universally accepted statement
16. Uncork
17. Chilled
18. Bass violin
19. Burst
20. Gun (a motor)
21. Give work to
22. Ripe old age
24. Refined
26. Dish (out)
27. In days of yore
28. Summons silently
31. Purple fruits
34. Room dividers
35. French affirmative
37. Celtic land
38. Ms. O'Donnell
39. Hairdo
40. Writing tool
41. Subdues
42. Uncles' mates
43. Illegally seized
45. Broad container
46. Demolish

47. Loathes
51. Hit high
54. Casino city
55. Jazzy Tormé
56. Laos's locale
57. Woolly beast
59. "Goodbye!"
60. Map (out)
61. Klondike area
62. Virtuous gift
63. Affectation
64. Refined guy
65. Net fabric

DOWN

1. African river
2. Surpass
3. Actor Christopher
4. Unmatched
5. Al of movies
6. Put forth
7. Trick
8. Fa follower
9. Large Malay island
10. Thin sword
11. Church season
12. Art's Warhol
15. Dated item of eyewear
21. Caldron stirrers

23. Sorts; types
25. Fun contest
26. Meat shops
28. Premised (on)
29. Time of day
30. "— yourself!"
31. Animation
32. Place
33. Footed vases
34. Many adults
36. Suppositions
38. With haste
39. Sugar unit
41. Bona fide
42. Garage filler
44. Suave
45. Lease party
47. Cruel person
48. Grin broadly
49. Jets and Nets
50. Splash about
51. Kola Peninsula dweller
52. Cold capital
53. Preference
54. Toolshed find
58. Haul around
59. Engine rod

95

ACROSS

1. Gun noise
5. Island nation
10. Some: 2 wds.
14. Puerto —
15. Move slowly
16. King of rhyme
17. Opinion pieces
19. Bothers
20. Moines leader
21. Pour out
22. Most bizarre
24. Gleeful cries
25. Salad veggie
26. Boston suburb
28. Take abruptly
29. Cut roughly
32. Airport tool
33. Headline site: 2 wds.
35. Anemia remedy
36. Reduces speed
37. Precipice
38. Untruth
40. Flour measure
41. "This is for — birds!"
42. Scary fate
43. Newly hatched fish
44. Less crazy
46. Author Uris
47. Spa treatment
49. Pursue
50. Decide (to)
53. At any point
54. To one's eyes
57. Distinct pitch
58. Lead to
59. Over
60. Kitchen pests
61. Ceased
62. Church VIP

DOWN

1. Brought up
2. School worker
3. Mark Harmon series
4. Came into
5. Shrill shriek
6. Zodiac ram
7. Feminine title
8. Hooting flier
9. Losers: hyph. wd.
10. Etching chemicals
11. Be an omen of
12. Horned beasts
13. Toward sunset
18. Alternative
23. Money owed
24. Alda and Ladd
25. Large throng
26. Isaac's mom
27. Teenager
28. Stable worker
30. Spur: 2 wds.
31. Sob loudly
32. Split
33. Flabbergast
34. Oval nut
36. Sneaker tie
39. Writer Ferber
40. Gave a talk
43. Fume: 2 wds.
45. Buenos —
46. Rent
47. Salty cheese
48. English county
49. Idaho export
50. German king
51. Plunk (down)
52. Category
55. Cake vessel
56. Kindergarten event

96

ACROSS

1. Travel by yacht
5. Fed up
10. Gossip tidbit
14. Western pact
15. Actor David
16. Flowing cloak
17. Shah's realm
18. Arches across
19. Leave the room
20. D.C. vet: slang
21. Appropriate
22. Song words
24. Whine tearfully
26. Bedlam
28. Dollar part
29. Impose (a tax)
30. Mouse foe
33. Friendship
35. Minor role
36. Created by us
37. Jerk: slang
38. Wearied (of)
39. Heal
40. Before, in odes
41. Dressy fabric
42. Deck out
43. "— Misérables," Hugo novel
44. Music symbol
45. Coin receiver
46. Like old bread
47. Embosses
50. Louisa May —, writer
53. Argument side
54. Food scrap
55. Lone flight
56. Spry; nimble
59. Pita stuffer
60. Trudge
61. Enticed: 2 wds.
62. Like: 2 wds.
63. Simon —, game
64. Bring glee to
65. Meat option

DOWN

1. Cuts (a thread)
2. Home-run great
3. Prints at a slant
4. Mr. Chaney
5. Disparage
6. Ready to eat
7. Famed Gardner
8. One plus nine
9. Subjugated
10. Cake pros
11. Airport car
12. Grand movie
13. Phillies rival
21. Refute
23. Vary: hyph. wd.
25. Nix
26. Explain
27. Strong guys: hyph. wd.
30. Trial locale
31. Inner glow
32. Playing card
33. Eve's second
34. Plea from Oliver
35. Referred to
38. Dubious yarn: 2 wds.
39. Nile dweller, briefly
41. Dundee native
42. Choral voice
45. Pacific
46. States of mind
48. Funny Kovacs
49. Office group
50. Scary snakes
51. Girl in a Kinks title
52. Satiate
53. Story outline
57. Hair product
58. Ms. Lupino
59. Indenting key

97

ACROSS

1. Star, for short
6. Improvised line: hyph. wd.
11. Porch rug
14. Fragrance
15. Reunion attendee
16. It can be bruised
17. Flooded with sun
19. Neighbor on "The Simpsons"
20. Dickens lass
21. Rembrandt works
22. Zoo beast
24. Flu symptom
26. Main ideas
27. Social class
30. Assurance
32. — pole, carved tower
33. Pretty flower
34. Brightened (up)
37. "Goodness!"
38. Pet name?
39. Window piece
40. Close chum
41. Toys with strings
42. Islamic city
43. Bank exec, sometimes
45. Russian liquors
46. Revered
48. Ms. Moore
49. Steak option: hyph. wd.
50. — grapes
52. Havana's country
56. Satisfied sighs
57. Animation classics: 2 wds.
60. Fated outcome
61. Pass (a law)
62. From Dublin
63. Hesitation sounds
64. Nitwits
65. Minor

DOWN

1. Son of Adam
2. Author Stanley Gardner
3. Laze (about)
4. Copied
5. "Pow!" kin
6. Musical with orphans
7. Oven knob
8. Allows
9. Ache soother
10. Sleep chamber
11. Will Smith film: 3 wds.
12. Insurance pro
13. Fusses: hyph. wd.
18. Debt notes
23. That king
25. Chewy stuff
26. Sneaky trick
27. Pace length
28. Roman robe
29. No matter what: 3 wds.
30. Change
31. Poker purses
33. Chomp on
35. Early Andean
36. Morning brews
38. Noted pirate
39. Nail service
41. Struck a humble pose
42. Tattoo favorite
44. Coastal eagle
45. Quite
46. Shopworn
47. Really hate
48. Songs for couples
50. Dirt fighter
51. Formerly
53. Motel rental
54. Most valued
55. Gray
58. Warbling Yoko
59. Diner bonus

98

ACROSS

1. Fictional Karenina
5. Double agent
9. Musical piece
13. Blood sucker
15. Zenith
16. In the sack
17. Chatter away
18. Arizona city
19. Irk
20. Make wet
21. Curved bones
23. Quiet as a —
25. Signal "Hi!"
26. Sty critters
27. Pointless
30. Car option
33. Upright: 2 wds.
34. Native abode
35. Damage slightly
37. Some: 2 wds.
38. Military unit
39. Turkish money
40. "— Abner"
41. Flavorful
42. Ruin
43. Person at large
45. Employs again
46. Moisture-free
47. "Come again?"
48. "Wonderful!"
50. Huge melee
51. Greek letter
54. Yale grads
55. Cancún cheers
57. Revered folks
59. See 51-Across
60. Jump
61. Subway coin
62. Cave dweller
63. Wee swallows
64. Small lizard

DOWN

1. Swiss mountains
2. Roman emperor
3. Moderate tide
4. Assume a role
5. Perchance
6. Numbered work
7. NASA craft
8. Inspects
9. Tenor Enrico
10. Kimono sashes
11. Edit out
12. Beach cooler
14. Court messenger
22. "— never gone there!"
24. Feisty giant
25. Coil (around)
26. Young dog
27. Barn baby
28. Turn loose
29. Wild ducks
30. Suit fabric
31. Leaves out
32. Broad comedy
34. Like fit muscles
36. Stadium roars
38. Buildings for state legislation
39. Rude guy
41. Skater Lipinski
42. "Get lost!": 2 wds. (slang)
44. Historic Julius
45. See 51-Across
47. Hair strands
48. Sheer delight
49. Ms. Coolidge
50. Gain, as rewards
51. Nudge
52. Large amount
53. Common contraction
54. Decline
56. Hula necklace
58. Actor Cheadle

99

ACROSS

1. Fizzy drink
5. Acted without words
10. Children
14. Nose offender
15. Be wild about
16. Adams of song
17. Swingy tune
18. Work hard
19. To shelter
20. Samson's betrayer
22. Musical groups
24. Spot's pal?
25. Papal name
26. Coarsely textured
29. Lack of bias
34. Pound fraction
35. Fool
36. Ring legend
37. Push
38. "Thou — not kill"
39. Sports number
40. — Friday
41. Reads quickly
42. Mr. McQueen
43. Highly charged
45. Porcupine quills
46. Issa of comedy
47. Handle roughly
48. Hogwash: slang
52. Confessed: 2 wds.
56. Margarine
57. Madcap: slang
59. Tiny tot
60. Pious fellow
61. Favored few
62. Driving aids
63. Good Queen —, English monarch
64. Style scheme
65. About: 2 wds.

DOWN

1. Auction cry
2. "Garfield" dog
3. Toy figurine
4. Clever deception
5. Sickness
6. Potato source
7. Riotous crowd
8. Winged god
9. Abandoned
10. Funny Diane
11. Far from busy
12. Food plan
13. Realizes
21. Bus route
23. Fringe benefit
26. Chisel (out)
27. Bucolic
28. Viewpoint
29. Pre-euro coin
30. Is indisposed
31. Already consumed
32. Toil (away)
33. Building lots
35. Asian cuisine
38. Filtered
39. Small dagger
41. Jazzy Getz
42. Pirouetted
44. Criminals
45. Twain hero
47. Slogan relative
48. Big flop
49. Salve ingredient
50. Telescope piece
51. Winter holiday
53. Tinting pro
54. Small guitars
55. Mexican currency
58. Facial contraction

100

ACROSS

1. Sedans and convertibles
5. Uncertain
9. Endures
14. Length times width
15. Artist Salvador
16. Extreme
17. Yule hanging
19. Earn
20. Cookout sites
21. Drink (up)
23. Had lunch
24. Sphere
25. Fish sticks?
27. Bowled over
28. Land measure
30. Jar top
31. Busy airport
33. Greek letter
34. Ms. Leigh
36. Burn (milk)
40. Attila the —
41. Double curve
42. Outrage
44. Graceful deer
45. Urged (on)
47. Rarin' to go
49. Rummy game
50. Through
52. Bother
53. Tree house?
54. Escape
57. Wharf
59. Male kid
60. Remiss
61. Legendary slugger Mel
62. Main arteries
65. "Goodbye!"
67. From one corner to the other
70. Vends
71. Bagel feature
72. Poker stake
73. Genuflected
74. Sagacious 34-Down
75. 365 days

DOWN

1. Tenting site
2. Opera ditty
3. Freshening up
4. Funny spoof
5. Midmonth date
6. Chubby
7. "Alice" role
8. Cede
9. Piece of coal
10. Brewery quaff
11. Dried fodder
12. Banal
13. Glutted
18. Tennis ploy
22. Gray hue
25. Wash lightly
26. Loving lines
27. D lead-in
28. Dull pain
29. Drink quickly
30. Vegas intro
32. Exploitative sort
34. "Star Wars" knight
35. Striped cat
37. Buenos Aires native
38. "Hi & —," comic strip
39. Can defect
43. Tyrannosaurus —
46. Biblical mom
48. Ancient greeting
51. Likely (to)
53. Scandinavian land
54. Lab bottle
55. Burdened
56. Banish
58. Like hives
59. Call for aid
61. Eject
62. On the waves
63. "The Thin Man" dog
64. Omen pro
66. Building annex
68. Pal of Pooh
69. Archaic

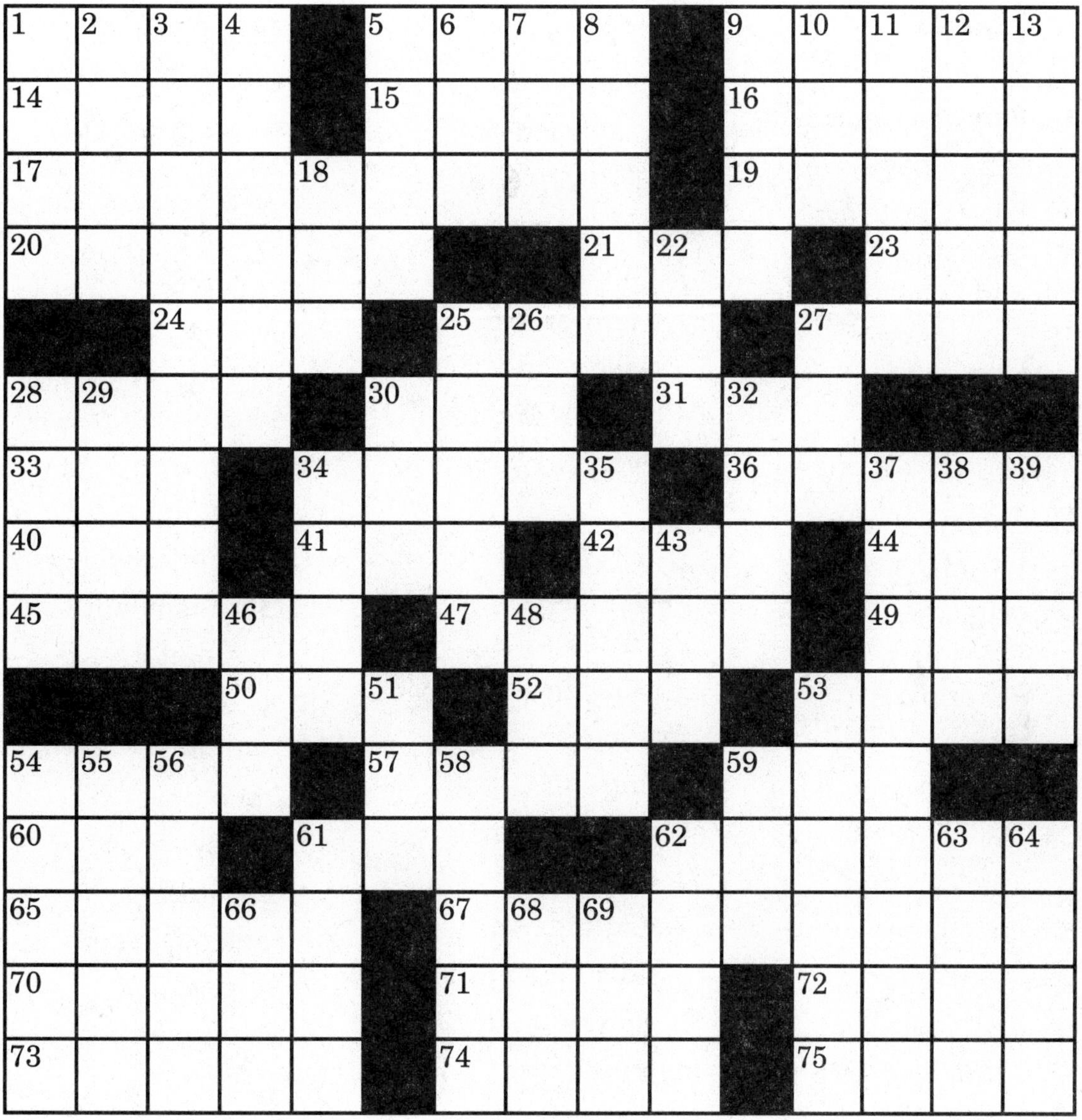
1
2
3
4
5
6
7
8
9
10
11
12
13
14
15
16
17
18
19
20
21
22
23
24
25
26
27
28
29
30
31
32
33
34
35
36
37
38
39
40
41
42
43
44
45
46
47
48
49
50
51
52
53
54
55
56
57
58
59
60
61
62
63
64
65
66
67
68
69
70
71
72
73
74
75

101

ACROSS

1. Stop sleeping
6. Rip up
11. Near the stern
14. Public persona
15. Ms. Linney
16. For each
17. Stephen Sondheim and Cole Porter
19. Compensate
20. Pieces (out)
21. Experts
22. Discontinues
24. Chiding cluck
25. Most irate
26. With 48-Across, rustic sack
30. Poker ploys
32. Wan
33. Great sadness
34. "You —?!"
37. Enjoy poetry
38. Cake raiser
39. Bit of swordplay
40. Psychic skill
41. *Santa* —, 1492 ship
42. Speed trials
43. Drenched
45. An Anderson
46. Oak fruits
48. See 26-Across
49. Computer adjunct
50. Goad (on)
52. Of mouths
56. Luau food
57. With vigilance
60. Author Harper
61. Imbibed
62. Merit award
63. Asner and Sheeran
64. Accrues (interest)
65. Everyday language

DOWN

1. Learned
2. Berserk
3. "Citizen —," movie
4. Coop finds
5. Current
6. Very smooth
7. Detest
8. Regrets
9. Commit a mistake
10. Leave quickly: 2 wds.
11. Fruit dessert
12. Brave deeds
13. Clandestine meeting
18. Rough file
23. Cry from Fido
24. Earth tone
25. Animal fat
26. Plain
27. Wields
28. Tunes of tribute
29. Conducted
30. Pigtail kin
31. Funny Kudrow
33. "Chicago" star
35. Be dizzy
36. "Frozen" princess
38. Asian oxen
39. Block (up)
41. Synthetic: hyph. wd.
42. Cloth remnant
44. Base metal
45. Section
46. Plenty
47. Aped doves
48. Narrow beds
50. Cast header
51. Famed Quaker
52. Beyond
53. Modernize (a kitchen)
54. Pained sigh
55. Country's Lovett
58. Refrain start
59. Little devil

102

ACROSS

1. "Who was that masked —?"
4. Thesaurus guy
6. Thin, protective layers
8. Coffee: slang
9. Impediments to studying
11. Crooner Damone
12. Office skill
14. Popular vacation island
17. Lacking slack
19. Nickname for Coolidge
20. Blew a horn
23. Skin (an apple)
25. Certain primate
26. Danny's twins?
27. He wrote "The Gold Bug"
29. Brazilian resort
30. Griffin of TV lore
32. Directs (a car)
34. Hibernation spot
35. Former Asian kingdom
37. Ropes on boxers
39. Sets up
42. Succor
43. Eastern university
44. Methods
46. Ballet pros
48. Sacred hymn
49. Refuse to renew

DOWN

1. "— Lisa," Nat King Cole hit
2. Grow gray
3. Far from wealthy
4. Speed (up)
5. Journey
6. Move out of (a home)
7. Minor fit
8. Singer Morrison
10. Bite (at)
11. Ms. Harper
12. Create lace
13. Wary
14. Jests
15. Charged particles
16. Business estimate
18. Strives (to)
19. Machinery wheel
21. Fencing weapon
22. David Copperfield's spouse
24. Hundreds of years
28. School compositions
31. Fluctuate
33. Chicago transports
36. Honey beverage
38. That boy's
40. Show approval
41. Under strain
44. Join with heat
45. Fortify for war
47. "I — do it!"

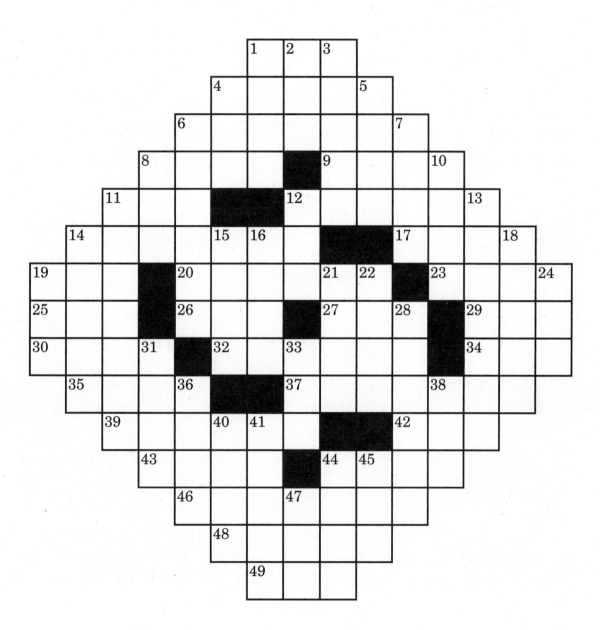

103

ACROSS
1. Special skill
6. Cold capital
10. Eruption flow
14. Proportion
15. Moab's site
16. Stupefies
17. Sticky stuff
18. Wee jazz band
19. Bean: slang
20. Sewing aid
21. Allied (with)
23. Socks
24. Home to Adam
26. Auto gear
27. A Turner
28. Game animal
30. Supplement
32. Arrest
35. Hair-raising
38. Ms. Ferber
39. The Flintstones' pet
40. Lack of guile
42. Situates
44. British queen
45. Diner dish
47. Dog's tether
48. Understand
49. Immense
50. Popular tree
51. Pub feature

52. "What a shame!"
54. Brings to court
58. Oscar winner Streep
61. La Scala's city
63. Athlete Bando
64. Loads: 2 wds.
65. Admonish
66. Degrade
68. Aid for Holmes
69. Mental conception
70. Called by beeper
71. Has breakfast
72. Famed Fed Eliot
73. Loses fur

DOWN
1. Thin pancake
2. Swift
3. Turn away from sin
4. Remedy
5. Playthings
6. Surpass
7. Scattered
8. Deposited
9. "I found it!"
10. Intertwined
11. Missing GI
12. Express anger
13. Seeks answers
22. Class
23. Restful spot

25. Gall
27. Fabric mishap
29. Harsh cleanser
31. Be sure of
32. Ship of 1492
33. Aardvark meal
34. Twaddle
35. Entangle
36. Sugar source
37. Informal negative
38. Slippery fish
39. Judges
41. Russian title
43. Unwell
46. Dresses up
49. Kilmer with parts
50. Greek letter
51. Digital storage units
53. Arm bones
55. Habit
56. Let (up)
57. January 5-Down
58. Swung weapon
59. Jazzy Fitzgerald
60. Defeat badly
61. Built
62. Siestas
65. Taste victory
67. Sneering cry

104

ACROSS

1. Musical Miles
6. "Try — best!"
10. Malevolence
14. Oust
15. For: poetic
16. Shuttle servicer
17. Bothersome
18. Stage hints
19. Frenzied
20. Scrap of food
21. British coats
23. Deserved
25. Russian VIP of old
27. "SOS" performers
28. Craving
29. Artist with a chisel
33. Spoil: 2 wds.
36. Pour water on
37. "Uncle Tom's Cabin" girl
38. U.K. river
39. Dirt
40. Donkey sound
41. Styling goo
42. Noisy fight
43. Sad cries
44. Busy mounds
46. Little bit
47. Bible book
48. Tile designs
52. Rabbit shelter
55. "I'm hurt!"
56. Pine fluid
57. Tel —
58. Signs: slang
60. Occur next
62. A shoe size
63. Lobe locales
64. Wake up
65. High-strung
66. Legal delay
67. Feisty mount

DOWN

1. Train stop
2. Announces
3. Outlook
4. "Gross!"
5. Thwarted
6. Desert growth
7. Full burden
8. Colorado native
9. Flowering plant
10. Cover
11. Self-centered
12. Skye or Capri
13. "Shane" star Alan
22. Raggedy —, doll
24. See 61-Down
26. TV host Seacrest
27. Very serious
29. Foot bottoms
30. Polo on screens
31. Watermelon shape
32. Light beams
33. Loopy: slang
34. Hot spot?
35. Cloth measure
36. Sour pickles
39. Rap-sheet entries
40. Polish cake
42. Silent performer
43. Laundromat machines
45. Cinematic Keitel
46. Pal of Sleepy
48. Rumpled
49. Debate topic
50. Bring about
51. Celerity
52. Diminish
53. Ardent, as a fan
54. Boxing space
55. Soup veggie
59. Insurrectionist Turner
61. With 24-Down, incompetent

105

ACROSS

1. Made by us
4. — Moines
7. Get ready
9. Clock readout
10. TV-show advertiser
13. Bawl out
16. Contains
17. Pedicure target
19. Six minus four
20. "Will there be anything —?"
22. Rude looks
23. Require
24. Tone down
26. Considerably
27. Shift abruptly
28. Bill of fare
30. Family symbols
32. Sloping entryway
34. Melody
35. Cover completely
37. Popular pear
39. Animal protein
40. Bald Brynner
42. Catty comment?
44. — Scouts
45. Food fish
47. Plant support
49. Tycoon Onassis, informally
50. God, to some
52. Paving stuff
53. Direct route
55. Charms
57. Claylike sediment
58. Ireland, in poetry
59. Aviv lead-in
60. Week segment

DOWN

1. Tree marsupial
2. Catering vessel
3. Chill out
4. Radio knob
5. Print measures
6. Small sofas
8. Basement game
9. Alternative to that
10. Personal pronoun
11. Miami growth
12. Coral ledge
13. Treat for a horse
14. Bedstand vessel
15. Sign of approval
18. Well-kept
21. Unending
23. Foes
25. Ordain
27. Snake extract
29. Ms. Thurman
31. Bath spot
33. Human mind
35. Most spine-tingling
36. Amsterdam dollar
38. Soft
39. Soggy patch
41. Ballad theme
43. Sport
44. Talk a lot
45. Put in the mail
46. Hamlet, for example
48. Address for a wife
50. Jack's partner in a rhyme
51. Firm
54. Tell fibs
56. Talented Farrow

106

ACROSS

1. Buddhism branch
4. Curtain-call event
7. Welding device
9. Dubuque resident
11. Pretty blooms
13. Improved over time
15. Flock daddy
16. Speak falsely of
18. 15-Across's mate
19. Leave out
21. Pharmaceutical products
22. Cauldron concoction
23. Undemocratic person
25. Individual
26. Bar serving
27. Collects
29. Heavy breeze
30. Emulated 22-Down
31. Of two minds
32. Jeans ornament
33. Smoothed, as wood
35. Pasture din
36. — Beta Kappa
37. "Watch your —!"
39. Stand up to
40. Fairway selections
42. Field cover
44. Cereal grain
45. Left quickly
47. Legal charge
48. Voted in
50. Most morose
52. Mean smile
53. Thick pipes
54. Clique
55. "I agree!"

DOWN

1. Moving fast
2. Coastal eagle
3. Long-running CBS series
4. Clumsy clod
5. Barn resident
6. Vacillated
7. Pairs (up)
8. Contained
9. Folksy Burl
10. Less stale
11. For
12. Island dress
13. Inch (along)
14. Dawn moisture
17. Pious sisters
20. Writer Leo
22. Crooner Tony
24. Boyfriends, quaintly
26. Feathered creatures
28. "Bonnie — Clyde," 1967 movie
29. Failed to lose
31. Sullies
32. Tones down
33. "Beat it!"
34. Is too loud for
35. Daily trio
36. Push
38. Squeeze tightly
39. Female bunny
40. Frosting expert
41. Sewn juncture
43. Vet client
45. Editorial direction
46. 6/6/44: hyph. wd.
49. Mediocre mark
51. Fade away

107

ACROSS

1. Shrill barks
5. Closet wood
10. Leg joint
14. Name hidden in "peerless"
15. Tickle
16. Handy
17. African plant
18. Wild uprisings
19. Likewise
20. Expert: slang
22. Tiny waves
24. Aspiration
25. Volcanic peaks
26. Grumpy look
29. Some ammo
30. Neighbor of Tonga
34. Little shaver
35. Smell
37. Motorized vehicle: hyph. wd.
38. Puts in
40. "Encore!"
42. Joshes
43. Abounded
45. Paint messily
47. Last letter
48. Err
49. Err
50. Met offering
52. Caused: 2 wds.
54. Audience reaction
55. Clinton daughter
58. Apple variety
62. Bunny kin
63. Raise (dogs)
65. Folk legend
66. Charity funds
67. Christopher of film
68. Lobbing Lendl
69. 29-Down extract
70. Inquired
71. Dollar part

DOWN

1. "Right!"
2. A Guthrie
3. Flower bed
4. Vary
5. Billiards bounce
6. Throw off
7. Third of a sextet
8. Texas team
9. Varnish base
10. Burden for a hiker
11. Entertainer Carter
12. Deftness
13. Love god
21. Hawaiian city
23. Mexican bill
25. Semi set: 2 wds.
26. Sports data
27. Army student
28. More offbeat
29. Swampy tract
31. Corn
32. Menu request
33. Cruising: 2 wds.
36. Soccer coach, maybe
37. African beast
39. Least large
41. Author Fleming
44. Scrutinizes
46. Good thing
49. Gazes intently
51. Written in verse
53. Messing of TV
54. Was patient
55. Fellow
56. Fit
57. Funny Bombeck
58. "Now — done it!"
59. Put aside
60. Actor Rickman
61. Cooped (up)
64. Cry of fright

108

ACROSS

1. Early Peruvian
5. Without equal
10. Lost traction
14. Bluish green
15. Peaceful protest: hyph. wd.
16. Jedi Master
17. Great Lake port
18. Winds around
19. Chimney ash
20. Violent storms
22. Irritate
24. "— settled!"
25. Be furious
26. Last exams
30. Popular craft
34. Each
35. Diced, as carrots
36. Expected now
37. Dwell (at)
38. Cantered
39. British farewell: hyph. wd.
40. Flower loop
41. Exposure to harm
42. Boring: hyph. wd.
43. Stated positively
45. Bed awning
46. Minus
47. Pro's foe
48. Metal combos
51. Board of —
56. Embroidery frame
57. Sophia of classic movies
59. Hose shade
60. Eye rudely
61. Bungling
62. Fraudulent
63. Floor votes
64. Frost and Poe
65. Chuck

DOWN

1. News article
2. Mean Roman
3. Bible brother
4. Happy-hour trayful
5. Wide ties
6. Maned cats
7. Redding of soul
8. Zip
9. Trapped
10. Set procedure
11. Pillage
12. Screen fave
13. Chewy fruit
21. Too smooth
23. "By Jove!"
25. Fight back
26. Guy
27. They creep
28. Caribbean island
29. Exist
30. Roman god
31. Western state
32. Chop: 2 wds.
33. Sordid
35. Pear parts
38. Blurts out: 2 wds.
39. Weight measure
41. Hunt victim
42. — Christian Andersen
44. Marries secretly
45. Says "1, 2, 3..."
47. Snuck around
48. Nautical greeting
49. Theater area
50. "Damn Yankees" vamp
51. Cedar, for example
52. Try out
53. Bounced sound
54. Epochs
55. Totals
58. Noted Yoko

109

ACROSS

1. Golfer John
5. Bitter-tasting
10. Cut covering
14. Mayberry boy
15. Valerie Harper sitcom
16. The old you?
17. Dexterous
18. Sailing craft
20. Pindar piece
21. Rowing poles
22. Art great
23. Cheap bar: slang
25. Czech or Pole
27. Give power to
29. Raised road
33. Cantina snack
34. Formal dances
35. Like: 2 wds.
36. Walk a trail
37. Fend off
38. Move
39. Hymn starter
40. Dueling steps
41. Dastardly demon
42. Computer systems
44. San Diego team
45. Pol Long

46. Group leader
47. Cereal seed
50. Closet closer
51. Fitting
54. Far from direct
57. Lot (of)
58. Take home
59. Mum Marx
60. — bargaining
61. Dull color
62. Benefits
63. Some snakes

DOWN

1. Fuddy-duddy
2. Mimicked
3. Protective vest: 2 wds.
4. Up until now
5. Esoteric
6. Marine map
7. Breaks down
8. Film's Lupino
9. River barrier
10. Tried hard
11. Action star Jackie
12. Super: 2 wds.
13. Arrest
19. Gather

21. Rich paints
24. Clarinet kin
25. — rep
26. Calm period
27. Mr. Hawke
28. Artless
29. Hooded cloaks
30. River outlets, maybe
31. Straighten
32. Houses' plots
34. Tom Sawyer's gal
37. Partly raw
38. Box section
40. Stray-dog pen
41. Lovely
43. Horse noise
44. Album inserts
46. Car style
47. Biggest Brady brother
48. Traffic din
49. Inner glow
50. Awkward kid: slang
52. Hatchery cry
53. Poetic contraction
55. Satisfied sighs
56. Cote call
57. Sauna site

110

ACROSS

1. Dark brown
6. Heroic Parks
10. Heavenly aura
14. Old anesthetic
15. Carved gem
16. — Khayyám
17. Hard to move?
18. Ade fruit
19. — bean
20. School dances
21. Untidy fellow
22. Army award
23. Mr. McGraw
25. Heroine of "A Doll's House"
27. Lou Grant player: 2 wds.
31. Most luxurious
36. Apple color
37. Senate votes
39. Without density
40. High poker pair
42. Arrive at
44. Crackle
45. Spiced meat
47. Egg center
49. Small guitar
50. Refined
52. Gods
54. Flu symptom
56. Swine's abode
57. Stable worker
61. Wiping cloths
63. Lacerates
67. Corker: slang
68. Start the pot
69. Farmyard fowl
70. March date
71. Horse guide
72. Escapade
73. Defeat
74. Coastal flier
75. Baking ingredient

DOWN

1. Fuse together
2. German king
3. Cut of lamb
4. Bank robberies: slang
5. Circle piece
6. See 7-Down
7. With 6-Down, savory bun
8. , &, or $
9. Wood chopper
10. Bagel center
11. Mingling with
12. Buddhist monk
13. College exam
21. Rubbing grease on
22. Bran mixture
24. Lodging spot
26. Cruel
27. Delete
28. Car sticker
29. "Hello" singer
30. Hearty bread
32. The guy's
33. Boredom
34. Allay (a thirst)
35. Varieties
38. Mention
41. Hang loosely
43. Mild fish
46. Polite address
48. First-aid set
51. Rocker Tina
53. Power of film
55. Dine at home: 2 wds.
57. Smooth-spoken
58. Uncouth
59. Cancún cheers
60. Supplant
62. Trait carrier
64. Smidgen
65. Greek letters
66. Religious branch
68. "— we agreed?"
69. Full of mirth

111

ACROSS

1. African land
5. Some summer babies
9. "Arrivederci, —"
13. Study method
14. V-shaped indentation
15. Fictional captain
16. Per person: 2 wds. (slang)
17. Striped stone
18. Mr. Porter
19. Zodiac sign
21. Looked (for)
23. Perm result
25. Jazz group
26. Caves
30. Nosy person
33. Kettle tops
34. British spa
36. Deli purchase
38. Out-of-date
39. Mind products
41. — low, hide
42. From Cardiff
45. Glut
46. Kennel cry
47. Writer Thomas
49. The Velvet Fog: 2 wds.
51. Name hidden in "limerick"
53. Snow craft
54. They plot
58. Strength
62. Loads: 2 wds.
63. Not as ugly
65. Folk stories
66. Knowing
67. Utopian spots
68. Polish (text)
69. Went fast
70. Fashions a frock
71. Singer Lovato

DOWN

1. Jutting rock
2. Intense desire
3. Elemental bit
4. Portrays
5. Woodpile item
6. Frat letters
7. Singing collective
8. Cutting tools
9. Garbage-can bandit
10. "Here comes trouble!": hyph. wd.
11. Stag or bull
12. Retired
14. Kenya's capital
20. Edible seed
22. Hockey area
24. Is in first
26. Shine softly
27. Agitated
28. In a weird way
29. — engine
31. Edmonton pro
32. Ancient hymn
35. Abhors
37. Promote
40. Merchants
43. Poured icily
44. Impair
46. Vocalized across the Alps
48. Family-reunion array
50. Brunch time
52. Uncouth
54. Familiar adages
55. Trim (nails)
56. Hydrant hook-up
57. Souplike meal
59. Was driven
60. Serious
61. Sasquatch kin
64. Limits of nylon?

112

ACROSS

1. Chocolate — cookie
5. They honk
10. Cry of triumph: hyph. wd.
14. Brand symbol
15. Be helpful
16. Demonic
17. Minor prophet
18. Parisian subway
19. Incense
20. Relates (to)
22. Sewing tool
24. Some jokes
25. Becomes older
26. Mighty
29. Mischievous person
33. Was inclined
34. Thin openings
35. Bent pipe
36. Playwright William
37. — Island
38. Art great
39. Alphabet chunk
40. Retains
41. Made progress
42. Inner natures
44. Night flight: hyph. wd. (slang)
45. Denote
46. Dweeb kin: slang
47. Scattered
50. Vacation purchase
54. Pathetic
55. Snitches
57. Run fast
58. Very eager
59. Favored class
60. Thames school
61. Set price
62. Certain coins
63. Accomplished

DOWN

1. Show approval
2. Living space
3. Frankenstein's aide
4. Defer
5. Casino pastime
6. Becomes level
7. Nibbles on
8. Manly address
9. Draw out
10. Mother —
11. Rapacious
12. Pickle flavor
13. Sheltered
21. Pa's sister
23. Thin fish
25. Etching chemicals
26. Pizza serving
27. Looks after
28. Expresses anger
29. Food for pigs
30. Interlace
31. Back street
32. Flow smoothly
34. Luster
37. Took back
38. Shook
40. Had awareness of
41. Griffin of old TV
43. Come to light
44. Employs again
46. Actor Nick
47. Sail support
48. Forum garment
49. Cheer (for)
50. Meager
51. Defense group
52. Holy image
53. Russo of film
56. Hebrew priest

113

ACROSS

1. Bang (a toe)
5. Rajah's wife
9. Cornered: 2 wds.
14. Bistro list
15. Water vessel
16. Temporary peace
17. Turning point
18. Flower holder
19. Auburn dye
20. Meowing pet
21. Affected ways
22. Pistol: slang
23. Worked, as dough
25. Pronounced
26. Crow squawk
27. Cutting tool
31. Beguile
34. Milk measure
35. Yes, to Yves
36. City division
37. Tows
38. Chooses (to)
39. Vigoda on TV
40. Bankrupt
41. — bar
42. Kin of canoes
44. Make a doily
45. Italian volcano
46. Popular pizza topping
50. Empty (cases)
53. Monk's hood
54. "Bonanza" dad
55. Compass point
56. Informed
57. Rear
58. Revue host
59. Will figure
60. Garfield foil
61. Antlered beasts
62. Wind swirl
63. Garden bane

DOWN

1. Noisy slap
2. Austin native
3. Come together
4. Tour vehicle
5. Critique
6. Coveted prize
7. Loch — monster
8. Fierce anger
9. Religion avoider
10. Tire grooves
11. Batting move
12. Skin woe
13. 365-day unit
21. First name?
22. Head strands
24. Bit of land
25. Climb
27. Pouts
28. "My bad!"
29. Bible woman
30. Acapulco assent: 2 wds.
31. Russian ruler
32. Unkempt drifter
33. From scratch
34. Fixed share
37. Playful joke
38. Inning sextet
40. Screws up
41. Writer Bellow
43. Kitchen gadget
44. Cheap and showy
46. Dependable
47. Stay
48. Magic being
49. Wrapped up
50. Second-hand
51. Alaskan port
52. Purplish hue
53. College girl
56. "She's — one!"
57. Query word

114

ACROSS

1. Form
6. Cab cost
10. Dating from: 2 wds.
14. Like some cigars
15. Missing GI
16. Give (out)
17. Paying attention
18. The Pilgrims' ship
20. Nonsense: slang
22. Mr. Welles
23. Placed (down)
24. Dime or penny
26. Koran reader
29. Send
33. Colorado resort
34. Head cooks
35. Even a little
36. A Collins
37. "Blue Suede —"
38. Deli order
39. Athlete Dawson
40. Healthy
41. Bangor's site
42. Building
44. Turned into mush
45. Unwieldy vessel
46. Profuse
47. Edgar — Poe
50. Allotted meagerly
54. Grew: 2 wds.
57. Hanker for
58. Trading center
59. Rocker Lovett
60. Moore's TV costar
61. Folks
62. Boat section
63. Find out

DOWN

1. Con: slang
2. Island dance
3. Genesis son
4. — lines
5. Get on a railroad car
6. Noted
7. Elsewhere
8. Singer Clark
9. Impish being
10. Decorates
11. Farm beasts
12. Bagel topper
13. Common houseplant
19. Pork cuts
21. Ms. Novak
24. 2015 boxing movie
25. Big lugs
26. Tapped tree
27. Bring (in)
28. Backbone
29. Leather strap
30. Nobelist Curie
31. Silly
32. Pecked at a keyboard
34. Large piece
37. Garden dirt
38. Battle steed
40. Crazy feat
41. "Cats," for example
43. Intones
44. Deposited
46. Jacket flap
47. Arsenal stock: slang
48. Bank deal
49. Attract
50. Be the king
51. "Peter Pan" dog
52. Continuously
53. Cinematic Laura
55. Game animal
56. Lose the gray?

115

ACROSS

1. Modern memo: hyph. wd.
6. Quote
10. Sports judges
14. Ms. Messing
15. Disturb
16. Ark guy
17. VIP
18. Astounded
19. Volcano fluid
20. Actor Cumming
21. — Today
22. Expressed a view
24. Runs into
26. London native
27. Risky
30. College group
31. Supporting
34. Speckled steeds
35. Intoxicating
36. Pouring edge
37. Precious metal
38. D.J.'s milieu
39. Jargon
40. Track shape
41. Air again
42. Asset for a model
43. Briny zone
44. Dwell (on)
45. Sold
46. Meddling
47. Rackets
48. Texas city: 2 wds.
51. Refrain start
52. One on-line
56. Rare desert forecast
57. Houston institution
59. Buddy
60. Forthright
61. Waxed cheese
62. Ice chunks
63. Nimble
64. David Copperfield's spouse
65. Salad veggie

DOWN

1. Writer Ferber
2. Milled stuff
3. Swedish pop group
4. Severe control: 2 wds.
5. Dog breed
6. In bad taste
7. Midwest state
8. Create bows
9. Legendary place of riches: 2 wds.
10. Dark
11. Ghostly cry
12. Make smooth
13. Roe source
21. Colorado tribesman
23. Feel bad for
25. Suppositions
26. Thinking organ
27. Forces onward
28. Rope snare
29. Chip dip
30. Exasperated: 2 wds.
31. Kilt pattern
32. Wash out
33. Decided (to)
35. Wizard Potter
38. Applied logic
39. — Reports, magazine
41. Greek letters
42. — pal
45. Itinerary term
46. Kid watcher
47. Serious story
48. Love god
49. Certain Scandinavian
50. Area to unload
51. Old Russian title
53. Father
54. Coop crop
55. Noted Betsy
58. Hoopla
59. Early trio

116

ACROSS

1. Comical folks
5. Green stones
10. Slender stalk
14. Common metal
15. Coral island
16. Small child
17. See 38-Across
18. Shrewd
19. Copycat
20. Blondie's husband
22. Far from terse
24. Boxing blow
25. Danger
26. Mechanical worker
29. Hair knot
30. Office tables
34. Prized steed
35. Chatter
36. Toady: 2 wds. (slang)
37. Harsh; cruel
38. With 17-Across, Jimmy Fallon predecessor
39. "Who — that?"
40. Absorbed
41. Defeats
43. Canyon border
44. Noted canal
45. Boa or asp
46. Big truck
47. Spud, quaintly
48. Miffed
50. In honor of
51. Gets going: 2 wds.
54. Ends: 2 wds.
58. College grad
59. Matt of movies
61. Audition aim
62. Garden beauty
63. Honshu city
64. Kin of vases
65. Deficiency
66. Girder material
67. Deli purchase

DOWN

1. Reckless
2. — rug
3. Dinner bell
4. Bit of trickery: 2 wds. (slang)
5. Esau's brother
6. Some: 2 wds.
7. Furry pal
8. Six plus five
9. More cunning
10. Horse barns
11. Editorial bane
12. Pieces (out)
13. Lowly; humble
21. Bran source
23. Midway sights
25. Local tavern
26. Train tracks
27. Acrylic fiber
28. Buoyant wood
29. Port location
31. Brainy
32. Journalist Couric
33. Show contempt
35. Stove fuel
36. Starchy root
38. Mocks
39. Disguise part
42. Read quickly
43. Relieve (of)
44. Auditory membrane
46. Meal
47. Coal amount
49. Praise
50. Last
51. Caution
52. Healing plant
53. Deceptive scheme
54. Roused
55. Painful
56. Arm bone
57. Gnat or rat
60. Ms. West

117

ACROSS

1. Scary reptiles
5. Vamoose: slang
10. Desk topper
14. Film spool
15. "Toy Story" sheriff
16. Australian export
17. Funny Garr
18. 24-Across, to sailors
19. Executive refusal
20. Customs foe
22. Listened to
24. "Stop!"
25. Definite favoritism
26. Cavern
29. Is a hit
33. Gray soldier, for short
34. Cager Patrick
36. Nun's outfit
37. Scored well on
39. Wading bird
41. Bull, to Luis
42. Lazy —
44. Fencing picks
46. Contemporary
47. Insurance charges
49. Companions to fauns

51. Landers and Patchett
52. Move a bit
53. An evergreen
56. Darkening period
60. Writer Waugh
61. High nest
63. Fuzzy image
64. Male suitor
65. Goes bad
66. Lot find
67. Invites
68. Prepared to beg
69. In case

DOWN

1. College major
2. Appear
3. Cuzco's land
4. Insignificant
5. Sky swoopers
6. Envy
7. Stadium sound
8. Paid promos
9. Legendary
10. Sofa kin: 2 wds.
11. Parroted
12. Domestic partner

13. Trudge
21. Fence door
23. A pop
25. "Taps" tooter
26. Hold
27. Happen again
28. Portly
29. Uses shears
30. Dark wood
31. More disastrous
32. Loads cargo
35. Separate units
38. Syrian city
40. Least patient
43. Noted caravel
45. Glide (by)
48. Reveal
50. Of a clan
52. Fudge —, ice-cream flavor
53. Ali —
54. Pub wares
55. Pipe fault
56. Substantiated
57. Crafts supply
58. Grass homes
59. Bring (out)
62. Long period

118

ACROSS

1. Scottish affirmative
4. On top of
9. Green Jedi
13. Has creditors
14. Beautiful Sophia
15. Highest point
16. Aired out
18. Ten minus one
19. Take stock of
20. Jacket parts
22. Vichyssoise veggie
24. Caviar source
25. Uses up
29. Odors
33. Car shaft
34. 18-Across's square root
36. — Baba
37. Sigma follower
38. Most risqué
40. Dusty hue
41. Shade tree
42. Grate residue
43. Climax
44. Guides (a boat)
46. Asian vehicle
49. Cruise garland
50. Tidal term
51. Technologically enhanced humans
55. Needing iron
59. Lasso circle
60. Very short time
63. Club wielder
64. Fill with joy
65. Young kids
66. Fastened
67. They must be paid
68. Box-office letters

DOWN

1. Flabbergasts
2. Strong urges
3. Getty of "The Golden Girls"
4. Ready: 2 wds.
5. Crushing snake
6. Treat for Fido
7. Louis-Dreyfus comedy
8. Sanctions
9. Mickey Mantle, for example
10. Aunt Bee's grandnephew
11. Can dimple
12. Cutting tools
13. Germ cells
17. "Aha!": 2 wds.
21. Celestial streaker
23. Sailing vessel
25. Fruitcake ingredients
26. Praise
27. Ornamental feather
28. More bashful
30. Gate fastener
31. Pack animal
32. Strength
35. Pine product
38. Less plentiful
39. — seats
43. Sides
45. Wed secretly
47. Quits
48. Movie role for Orson Welles
51. Thick lump
52. Cartoon bear
53. Dreary person
54. Retail transaction
56. British heath
57. "— the Woods," musical
58. LP successors
61. Arrest
62. Giant legend Mel

119

ACROSS

1. Spoken exams
6. Cry of relief
10. Voiced a tune
14. Film
15. Pisa dough?
16. Shah's realm, once
17. Adored ones
18. Voluminous coif
19. Madame Bovary
20. X
21. Oppressed person
23. Good quality
24. Ventilated
25. Shrivel up
27. Begin a computer session: 2 wds.
29. Break (a law)
32. Compare
33. Actor Glover
34. Ms. Gardner
36. "Holy cow!"
37. River edges
38. Call up
39. Hardly bold
40. Farm shelters
41. Wards (off)
42. Russian empress
44. Aegean isle
45. Squeak cures
46. Skating jump
47. Divvy up
50. Wheel centers
51. Confess to
54. Be at hand
55. "Goodbye!"
57. Boise's state
59. Famous Alan
60. Start of a play: 2 wds.
61. Macabre
62. Soup veggies
63. Bird abode
64. Pauses

DOWN

1. Overlook
2. Tormented
3. U.K. river
4. "— Abner," comic strip
5. Therapy unit
6. Ready for bed
7. Snit
8. Flub
9. Try to win the love of
10. Afternoon nap
11. Sofa parts
12. Zach, Zane, or Zelda
13. Small pest
22. Marine raptor
23. Side (with)
24. Old
25. Flirtatious signals
26. Charged atoms
27. Buoyant
28. Approves
29. White of "Wheel of Fortune"
30. Poison
31. Dodge
32. Guitarist Paul
33. Mends
35. Roker and Pacino
37. — out, assist
38. Exploit
40. French cheese
41. Kelsey Grammer sitcom
43. Major arteries
44. Tiger baby
46. Tossed ring
47. Trade
48. Feeling great
49. Popular opera
50. Chapeaux
51. Regatta tools
52. Smidgen
53. Dissenting replies
55. Recycled item
56. Frosty cubes
58. Grand finale?

120

ACROSS

1. Roman robe
5. Land (a fish)
10. Hidden valley
14. Gloating cries
15. Midwest metropolis
16. Long car
17. Cheerful tune
18. Oxen harnesses
19. Flashy bloom
20. Some sodas
22. Scarlet
23. Weaken
24. Roam idly
27. Bill of the NBA
31. Flew
36. Sick
37. Tin, once
38. Talk in church?
39. Tour of duty
40. Helms and Begley
41. Ambition
42. Money on the table?
43. Begonia beginning
44. Dawdle
45. Pullman car
47. Demented
48. Be in pain
50. Let
54. Jewelry buy
55. Slant
60. Point of —
61. Ms. Midler
63. Pushed (out)
64. Roundish
65. More austere
66. Diver Louganis
67. Marries
68. Nap noisily
69. Behalf

DOWN

1. Bath powder
2. Akron's state
3. Effrontery
4. Whodunit dog
5. Reticent
6. Lacking ethics
7. Accepted
8. Hard cheeses
9. Suffers from
10. Flippant
11. Turkish money
12. Give off
13. Poke (around)
21. Refine, as 37-Across
23. "Exodus" hero
25. Pipe fitting
26. Funny Arden
27. Oxidizes
28. Up to
29. Steal: slang
30. Intuit
32. 720 hours in spring
33. Uninspired
34. Roof rims
35. Batik pros
37. Eccentric
40. From Denmark or Greece
41. Showers love (on)
43. Plead
44. Gossip guru Smith
46. Furry "foot"
47. Freezin' season
49. TNT kin
50. Announce
51. Bait description
52. Direct
53. They hoot
56. Tripod trio
57. Gumbo staple
58. Look slyly
59. Inches (in)
61. Toy ammo
62. Poetic adverb

121

ACROSS

1. Footwear item
5. Guns (a motor)
9. Great warmth
13. Improve, as text
15. Much: 2 wds.
16. Without interest
17. Wild fight
18. Greek letter
19. Pickle seasoning
20. Smart
23. Ballet prop?
24. "Behold!": hyph. wd.
25. Gentle breeze
27. Chest of drawers
31. Walks up to
33. Kin of 18-Across
34. Hacking quest
36. Actress Loy
40. Acid humor
42. Saves
44. Clip (wool)
45. Mama's guy
47. Engage
48. Oater group
50. A Jackson
52. Secret plot
55. Vex
57. Golf gadget
58. Secure vehicles: 2 wds.
64. Vocalist Fitzgerald
66. Passport stamp
67. Flight path?
68. Charity funds
69. British school
70. Thespian Nick
71. Forfeiture
72. Gourmet shop
73. Have a bawl?

DOWN

1. Big truck
2. Bad sign
3. Ancient European
4. Leg bender
5. Fanatic
6. Quite refined
7. Ballot
8. Verse part
9. Secreted
10. Archie Bunker's wife
11. Metal mix
12. The 10th U.S. President
14. River deposit
21. Extols
22. Periods in office
26. Cupid's love
27. First Lady Truman
28. Western state
29. Beef order
30. Get out
32. O.K. Corral figure
35. Concert gear
37. Devastate
38. Dull sort: slang
39. To the ocean
41. Pleasant odor
43. Coin bird
46. Spray-can propellant
49. "Dinner is —!"
51. Enticed: 2 wds.
52. Amazing bargain
53. Violin cousin
54. Ship tillers
56. Person of Esfahán
59. Wee critter
60. Boast
61. Competent
62. Customary practice
63. Porch feature
65. It may bray

122

ACROSS

1. Badminton necessity
4. — Plaines, Illinois
7. Greek letter
10. Grinding tooth
12. Shrill cry
13. Eased (in)
14. Punch: slang
15. Big number
16. Hilo dance
17. Yoko of pop
18. Knitting fiber
20. Mexican bill
21. In
22. Cab cost
24. King, for one
26. Made broader
29. Diet dish
30. Pan pal?
31. Pair
33. Against
34. Legal claims
35. Spot
36. "— do I care!"
37. Oozes
38. Fish basket
39. In a snide way
41. Kid
42. Fill (up)
43. Lip, ship, or hip
44. Plunk down
46. Actor Sean
47. Definite article
50. Bit of paper
51. Teem
53. Bend to pray
55. Camera glass
56. Jason's craft
57. Units of time
58. Tibetan ox
59. Address for a wife
60. Emma's twins?

DOWN

1. Midday hour
2. Red Muppet
3. Faucet
4. Thespian Laura
5. A Manning
6. Classy resort
7. +
8. Farm tower
9. Author Tarbell
10. Barn sound
11. Wrote 43-Across's clue?
12. Play area
13. Gloss
19. Ambience
20. Hunt quest
21. Jai follower
22. Some Europeans
23. Interjects
24. Continued: 2 wds.
25. Excessive
26. Tearful
27. Detroit dud
28. Fooled
29. — Mateo
30. Handle (a tool)
32. Animated Olive
34. Sci-fi royal
35. Waltons girl
37. End
38. Far from slim
40. Pig food
41. See 33-Across
43. Sleuth Wolfe
44. Strong request
45. Connect
46. Cute dogs
47. Yoked oxen
48. Of that lass
49. Chicago trains
50. Devious
51. Dawber of TV
52. Athlete Bobby
54. Originally named

123

ACROSS

1. Bossy Stooge
4. Bran mixture
8. Intersect
12. In the open
13. Audio effect
14. Gung-ho
16. Garage tools
18. Dull hums
20. Risqué
21. Sharp pang
23. A
24. Cuban dance
26. Funny Kudrow
27. Prepare tea
28. Asian sashes
29. A lot
30. Flower urns
31. "— to worry!"
32. Stadium suite
33. Vegas verb
34. Lock slit
36. Get advice from
40. Mound insect
41. Buffoon
42. Presently
43. Test result
46. In a trance
47. Sicilian volcano
48. Exited
49. Theater award
50. Ice masses
51. Totality
52. Metallic element
53. Bantu language
54. Set down
56. Chicago suburb
60. Vacant look
61. Let
62. Color tone
63. Love god
64. Visualizes
65. Mr. Caesar

DOWN

1. Cut (a lawn)
2. "— Town," play
3. Limitless time
4. Islamic city
5. Feeling sore
6. That mare
7. Shelter for travelers
8. News sources
9. Work hard for
10. Alter —
11. Some singers
15. Ms. Zellweger
17. Old horses
19. Wraps (up)
22. Blond shade
24. Hit on the head: slang
25. Bassoon kin
26. Olympics sled
27. Night flyers
29. Lose plumage
30. Release (anger)
32. Isolated
33. Door fastener
35. Stag
36. Facsimile
37. Lies
38. Extended
39. Poetic contraction
41. Ballet pros
43. Palm blow
44. Jail rooms
45. Recently: 2 wds.
46. Reagan son
47. Reef critters
49. Shore surges
50. Batting ploys
52. Six minus six
53. Novelist Grey
55. Train part
57. Civic center?
58. French affirmative
59. Actor Beatty

124

ACROSS

1. Hissing sound
6. Neck region
10. Hawk
14. Prone to chatter
15. Actor Clive
16. Fresh thought
17. Improvise: hyph. wd.
18. Musical stage
20. "Why not?"
21. Depend
23. Desert rover
24. Flood barrier
25. After that
27. Surrounded by
30. At large
31. Cricket judge
34. Surfeits
35. Religious brother
36. Diver's milieu
37. Was deceitful
38. Rug's place
39. Box tops
40. Ms. Longoria
41. Bed boards
42. Mimicking birds
43. A Williams
44. — and mighty
45. Hair knot
46. Popular tunes
47. Flirty girl
48. Author Wilde
51. "— Soup," Marx Brothers classic
52. Office holder: slang
55. Storage place
58. Ryan or Dunne
60. Be hidden
61. Graduate
62. Dorothy, to Em
63. Keats tributes
64. Tense
65. Gives (out)

DOWN

1. Collar insert
2. Walk through a creek
3. Misfortunes
4. — patrol
5. Some cars
6. Lofty
7. Elsewhere
8. Farm enclosure
9. Finalize
10. Suppress: 2 wds.
11. Dutch cheese
12. Singer Horne
13. Alan of film
19. Smile snidely
22. Scrape (out)
24. Expired
25. Small bands
26. Catch wind of
27. Tiny landmass
28. Unsophisticated
29. Lieu
30. Foamy stuff
31. Employing
32. Olympics prize
33. Out of fashion
35. Loses strength
38. Dart quickly
39. Canadian predator
41. Avoid (work)
42. People
45. Nervous twitch
46. Chops roughly
47. Pyramid find
48. Christiania, today
49. Belt ornament
50. Heart
51. Football's Flutie
52. Pare
53. Grimm intro
54. Wine dregs
56. Charlotte of TV
57. Obsolete
59. Brazil resort

125

ACROSS

1. Searches (for)
6. Minor tiff
10. Death notice
14. Concur
15. Top-quality: 2 wds.
16. Musical end
17. Southern farm
19. Placid
20. Vet patient
21. Refrain syllable
22. Essential characters
24. Turn down
27. Funny fellow
28. Held the front position
29. Rocking Diamond
31. Disparity
34. God of love
37. Yearly event in Dallas, Texas: 2 wds.
39. Fundamental particle
40. Five times eight
41. Arsenal stock: slang
42. Cellular linings
44. Salad green
45. Strange knack
46. In addition
47. Rivers of the NBA
48. Elevator innovator
50. Fast-food faves
54. Refused
57. "What happened next?"
58. Merino mom
60. Clever
61. U.N. employee
64. Map speck
65. Lose zing
66. Flynn of early films
67. The Say Hey Kid
68. Chooses (to)
69. Tea go-with

DOWN

1. Certain Scandinavian
2. Made eyes at
3. Be bombastic
4. Author Kesey
5. Colonized
6. Evil overlord
7. Polynesian staple
8. In a bit
9. Perseverance
10. Transpire
11. Rainy-day fun: 2 wds.
12. Useless
13. Scottish caps
18. Boring
23. Grimm work
25. Go up
26. Main courses
30. Gobbles down
32. Purposes
33. Golf teachers
34. Arrived
35. Plains tribe
36. With a self-important manner
37. Mamas' boys?
38. Broad comedy
40. High voice
43. Pull (in)
44. Treats gently
47. Rackets
49. Shade givers
51. Country paths
52. Vintage, as clothing
53. Faint
54. Glide through the Atlantic
55. Tower city
56. Trickle
59. Writer Stanley Gardner
62. Gallery acquisition
63. Circle chunk

126

ACROSS

1. Cons: slang
6. Manual work
11. Theater sign
14. Pol Cuomo
15. Banish
16. Greek letter
17. Mysterious
19. The thing's
20. Flowed
21. Spoken pauses
22. Gem side
24. Press down
27. Grazing mob
29. Scared yell
30. Singles-bar fun
33. Building wing
36. Tendency
37. Sound catcher
38. Polite address
39. Went skyward
40. Site of China
41. Hairpin curve
42. Light stroke
43. With competence
44. Least unfashionable
46. Author Burrows
47. Small pieces
48. Sin
52. Rapper West
54. Young fellow
55. Bustle
56. Bar beverage
57. Erased
62. "Viva — Vegas!"
63. Photo holder
64. Due (to)
65. Donny's duo?
66. Phone messages?
67. Highly-strung

DOWN

1. Blue cartoon character
2. Ear feature
3. Sports hall
4. Varied group
5. Become wet
6. Come to know
7. WWII alliance
8. Coal canister
9. Spanish shout
10. "Truth" star
11. Most problematical
12. Have merit
13. Evict
18. Soup veggie
23. Play portion
25. Abound
26. Singer Ritter
27. Muscular tissue
28. Pencil mark
30. Crop hazard
31. Iron spike
32. Drab color
33. Pious ending
34. Shuttle launcher
35. Mean quality
36. Bind
39. Territory
40. Imitated
42. Chomp on: 2 wds.
43. Tummy muscles, briefly
45. Bauble
46. Legal helper
48. Ship officers
49. Dine at home: 2 wds.
50. Paradises
51. Quickly evade
52. Hearty greens
53. Funny King
54. Clock reading
58. Lingerie buy
59. Loose
60. Go bad
61. Fearful respect

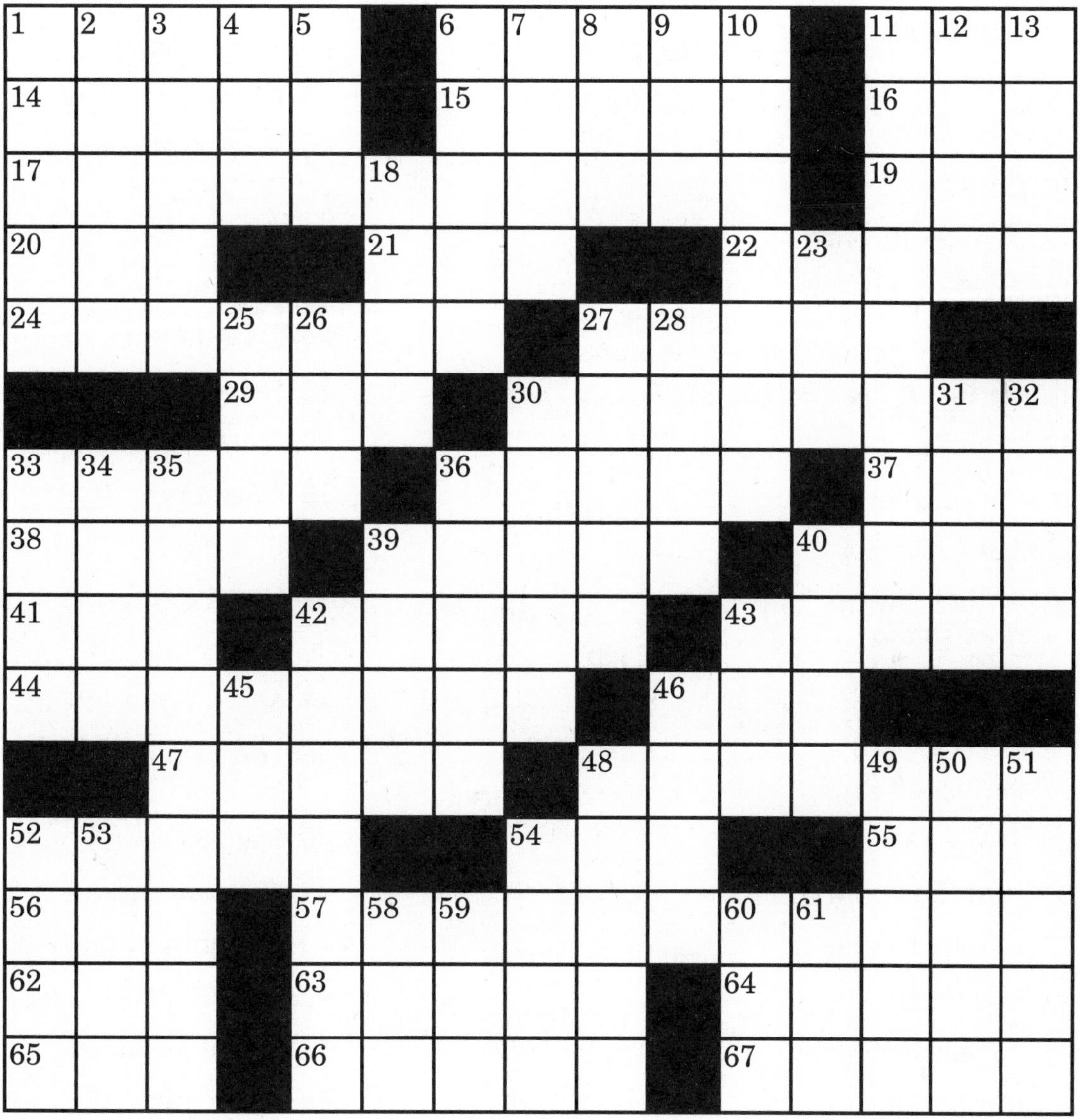
1 2 3 4 5 6 7 8 9 10 11 12 13
14 15 16
17 18 19
20 21 22 23
24 25 26 27 28
29 30 31 32
33 34 35 36 37
38 39 40
41 42 43
44 45 46
47 48 49 50 51
52 53 54 55
56 57 58 59 60 61
62 63 64
65 66 67

127

ACROSS

1. Vacation option
4. Word with "bone"
7. Pang relative
8. Is behind
10. Do a January task
12. Avoids reticence
14. Far from dense
15. Absorb
17. Designer hue
19. "I — you!"
20. Concern for a CEO
22. See 23-Across
23. With 22-Across, poor rating
24. See 2-Down
26. Watch
27. Pernicious soul
29. 16 on a board
31. Nasty confrontation
32. Music marking
33. Sub bases?
35. 16-Down orders
37. Ms. Kazan
39. Household problem
41. Depot pickup
44. Funny Scott
46. Smart
47. Hem adjunct
48. Magnet duo
50. Sour stuff
51. Wasn't apathetic
52. Answer
54. Tiara inserts
56. Like Action Comics #1
57. Smelting focus
58. Ran
59. "Granted!"

DOWN

1. Keep
2. Update some 24-Across
3. Pitcher Alvarez
4. "— to it!"
5. Floors
6. Daily trio
7. Displayed magnanimity
9. Sails (through)
10. Pond presence
11. Get
12. Too dear
13. Legal term
14. Kerfuffle
16. See 35-Across
18. Bardic preposition
20. Patricia Highsmith output
21. — the obvious
24. Unimpressive
25. Change one's mind
28. Farm resident
30. Pull in
33. Coupe pro
34. Bad guy?
35. Northwest array
36. Drives (away)
37. Shock noise: slang
38. Locker-room feature?
40. See 28-Down
42. First-rate workers
43. Hyacinth home
45. Bismuth, e.g.
47. Kin of 24-Across
49. Inevitable
51. Pith
53. Florid
55. Flirt (with)

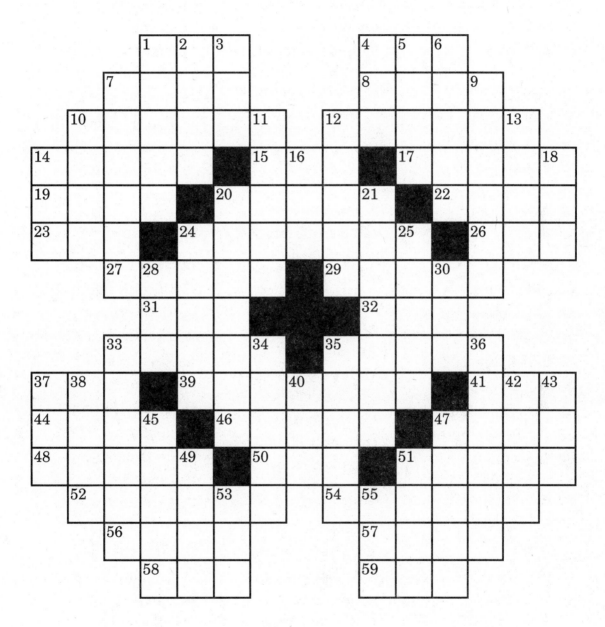

128

ACROSS

1. Photo defect
5. Flat bone
10. Big brass
14. Succeed
15. Made overt
16. — house
17. Cruising
18. Con catcher: slang
19. Very chic: slang
20. Protective sheet
21. Treat hay
22. Blog mention
24. Ideal juror
26. Overflowed
27. Says firmly
29. Option option?
30. Far from bombastic
33. Do a farm chore
34. Exercised a preference
35. Clover cousin
36. Survey rudely
37. A Walker
38. Writer O'Casey
39. Shell find
40. Break intake
41. Vivacity
42. Both Begleys
43. Gardening verb
44. Absorb
45. Audition rejects: slang
46. Manse expanse
47. Bistro supply
49. Road —
50. Flourish
54. Take off
55. Vex a tad
57. Big motivator
58. Barre move
59. Fare fan?
60. Square
61. Fabric buy
62. Trim
63. Chrome mar

DOWN

1. Recalcitrant lad
2. Leslie of sports
3. Warranty beneficiary
4. Keep manifesting
5. Moistens, in a way
6. Physics unit
7. Beyond sere
8. Study, perhaps
9. Laterally
10. Tribal icon
11. Covering
12. Caved
13. Word with "thing"
23. Spray holder
25. Be off
26. Really impact
27. Winning
28. Turns around
29. Luxuriant
30. Fishing implement
31. Actor George
32. Attention getter
33. Uncultivated fruit
34. Tight groups
37. Zingy
38. Key adjective?
40. Lie across
41. Create shirring
44. Pub array
45. Engaged
46. Doesn't cut it
47. Soft purchase
48. Wee margin
49. Vendetta fuel
51. Gad about
52. Cafe fixture
53. Split
54. Plant in a plant?
56. Drum site

129

ACROSS

1. Processed fuel
5. Sounded out
9. Hard knock
13. Sloop salute
14. Ragged on
15. Contract signer
16. Writing guides
18. Parent, often: 2 wds.
20. Indolent sort
22. Sticky spot
23. Bolt down
24. Goblin Valley locale
26. Ditch ledge
28. Suite bits
32. — exhaust
36. Shocked scream
37. Breaks open
39. Mobile home
40. Harm; loss
42. Soil creepers
44. Small lake
45. Bent braces
47. Gelid region
49. Disencumber
50. Agora pro
52. Lowest points
54. Hyperbolic comments
56. Disposition
57. Muscle relaxant
60. Energy sources?
62. Typewriter roller
66. Casual cover
69. Chalk mark
70. Flute range
71. Bonito kin
72. Blue hue
73. Mental climate
74. Go (out)
75. Excited: slang

DOWN

1. Brief sojourn
2. Where Athens is
3. Hawaiian brew center
4. Lulu: slang
5. Sports great
6. Word with "leg"
7. Wing it: hyph. wd.
8. Regarded wryly
9. "¿Quién?"
10. Birding blind
11. Math product
12. Tenderize?
17. Drink fixings
19. Due honor
21. Pilot aid
25. Bayou sight
27. Deal (with)
28. Small bundles
29. Swiss flower
30. Studio need
31. Submit (to)
33. Lean
34. Uncanny
35. Makes an advance?
38. Toss about
41. Distinguish (between)
43. Damage (gears)
46. Ocean snare
48. Rises of sorts
51. Starts, perhaps
53. Gradual slope
55. Gargoyle, for example
57. Unreal?
58. Mounted fun
59. Air polluter
61. Balanced
63. Rent
64. Hibernia, to Yeats
65. 25-Down creation
67. Yard patch
68. Heel plate

130

ACROSS

1. Ocean catch
5. Cafe supply
9. *Eux*
13. Hall sign
14. Underway
15. Be peripatetic
16. Judy Garland, e.g.
17. Itinerary datum
18. Does
19. Turn (to)
21. Vet visitors
23. Dressage exhibition
25. Close well
26. Rap-sheet list
30. Light show?
33. Roomies, often
34. Revival venue
36. Surpass
38. First-rate
39. Condescend
41. Nursery buy
42. Bold appraisals
45. — hand
46. Wet pole?
47. Music degrees
49. Short bios
51. Title encumbrance
53. Clinical administration
54. Planning aid
58. Cracking challenge
62. Environs
63. Acknowledges
65. Consider
66. Etui contents
67. Bun locales
68. Empowered
69. Mollify
70. Pung kin
71. Clears

DOWN

1. Abide
2. Wheelbarrow part
3. Holds court
4. Funny foils
5. Curious craft, for short
6. Conquer
7. They're taken
8. Den installation
9. Road hog?
10. Morale booster
11. Word with "how"
12. Base meal
14. Bohemian group
20. Recurred
22. Transfixed
24. Losses for babes
26. Ring insert
27. Mugs
28. Like cheetahs
29. Detective, maybe
31. Of the sticks
32. Beguile
35. Rocker bookings
37. Is affectionate with
40. Treat
43. Legal document
44. — doctor
46. Artery user
48. Comfy carriers
50. Buff
52. Maritime
54. Atlas designation
55. Cantata segment
56. Pince-nez element
57. Length for a gaucho
59. Rude remark
60. Blend
61. Floors
64. Fuse firmly

131

ACROSS

1. Border defenses
6. Imposter
10. Very rich
14. Lit great
15. Give (out)
16. Fallow
17. Room (at)
18. Slippery shaders
19. Trunk covering
20. Aix article
21. Thane kin
23. Is striking
25. Aimless jaunt
26. Praise
27. Park perambulation
30. Intimates
34. Antisocial act
35. Has interest
36. Cote call
37. Lose coherence
38. Breakfast nooks?
39. Catch
40. Maven
41. Foul haunts
42. Tight
43. Is productive
45. Bows to
46. Hose woes
47. Trough filler
48. Yearn (after)
51. Vegas pools?
52. Testy tiff
55. Sallow
56. Rapids din
58. Hot spot?
60. Meaningful indication
61. Rework (a work)
62. Sidles (in)
63. Free of charge?
64. Fail to accept
65. Done in

DOWN

1. "Get —"
2. Soap extra
3. They might be flipped
4. Record of sorts
5. Village high point?
6. Adamant
7. Cycling challenge
8. Passing ability
9. Prophetic tidings
10. Break
11. Lovely site
12. More
13. Favored group
22. Need nursing
24. Sticks close to
25. A fraction
26. Pulls in
27. See 28-Down
28. Wee vestige
29. Ohio, e.g.
30. Jewelry boxes?
31. Unpleasant display
32. Dinner proposal?
33. Saddle —
35. Grows detached
38. Monopolized
39. Be aware of
41. Watch mark
42. Gussies up (for)
44. Familiar
45. Contract
47. Court score
48. Footless creature
49. Word with "self"
50. Bar request?
51. Cause anguish to
52. A Kennedy
53. See 58-Across
54. Wild chaser?
57. Staid lines
59. Use

132

ACROSS

1. Strike
5. — stitch
10. Where Aymara is heard
14. Order from Mom
15. Besides
16. Bible guy
17. Spanish pronoun
18. Heated
19. Building pick
20. Season abroad
21. Seed container
22. Annual event
24. Linen option
26. Musical aunt
27. Toby fill
28. Carte order
32. Pursue grimly
35. Wise lawgiver
36. Word with "child"
37. Exaction
38. Opera hire
39. Now
40. Reef find
41. Pleiades enumeration
42. Designer hue
43. Strove
45. Match endings: slang
46. Slip area
47. Record list
51. Bon mot, perhaps
54. Healing plant
55. Coaster kin
56. Way to run
57. Pond visitor
59. Sprig holder
60. Trident third
61. Like sheep
62. Film dog
63. Colleen handle
64. 2008 candidate for Prez
65. Rivals to us?

DOWN

1. Big win
2. Ruin
3. Mum cousin
4. Common article
5. A King
6. Really fit
7. Glitzy affair
8. Extend
9. Valiant effort
10. Grid figure
11. Throw off
12. Mindless performance
13. Manual student?
21. Foil
23. "I concur!"
25. Designate
26. Picnic treat
28. Fish descriptive
29. Went on?
30. Skirt insert
31. Flawless spot
32. Stop: slang
33. Pressure unit
34. Nautical term
35. Bisect
38. Pledge generator
39. Fashion buy
41. Recipe verb
42. It's handed down
44. Declaimed
45. Coins of Norway
47. Sans a hand?
48. Great success
49. Experience
50. Energy
51. Count
52. Muslim notable
53. Author Morrison
54. Quite dull
58. Stowe girl
59. Plant vessel

133

ACROSS

1. Racked grazer
5. Far from loud
10. Sinai dangers
14. "Bloom County" bird
15. Fatuous
16. Shock
17. Frontier outcrop
18. Niamey locale
19. Lombok neighbor
20. Deduces (from)
22. Supply base
23. Hack command
24. Elate
26. Sweated (over)
30. Brushed
34. Garish
35. Scales, in a way
36. Cut off
37. Rested (on)
38. Royal permits
39. Suave
40. — du Diable
41. Pens: slang
42. Shakespeare heroine
43. Uninformed
45. Foremost
46. Harness part
47. Fatima's spouse
48. Reactor woe
51. Like crepe
56. Line touchers
57. Dress defect
59. Tap tube
60. Mine entrance
61. Put on
62. Deal prelude
63. Bête noire
64. See 1-Down
65. Proximal

DOWN

1. Word with "room"
2. Pointy end
3. Car trouble
4. Historic royal
5. Took baby steps?
6. Coalesce
7. Some IDs
8. Compass point
9. Bern article
10. Sacred sites
11. Manual sound
12. — shirt
13. "M*A*S*H" star
21. Went downhill
22. Hutch habitués
24. Costly bonds
25. Java jars
26. Iced
27. Veil netting
28. Eastern natives
29. Emcee asset
30. Plot
31. Bohemian affair
32. Remote punishment
33. Prevent
35. Fishing aid
38. Arise (from)
39. Fizz extra
41. Mongkut's realm
42. Fruitless
44. Not racy at all
45. Pane covers
47. Sign of spring?
48. Penetrate
49. Score closer
50. Pony checker
51. Talented Irene
52. Turkish inn
53. Isolated
54. Peruvian pronoun
55. 1-Across, e.g.
57. Plant pouch
58. Up to

134

ACROSS

1. Harbor sight
5. Russian range
10. Yoke units
14. Perfect
15. TV demo
16. Mississippi feeder
17. Assay subjects
18. — *Gay*
19. Determination
20. Medicine for hand cramps?: 2 wds.
23. Bad: French
24. "Deep Space Nine" role
25. Goes on foot
27. A Page
29. Spring spots
32. Animated
33. Watch word?
36. Native of Japan
37. Medicine for astronauts?: 2 wds.
40. Lode locale
41. Unmarketed: 2 wds.
42. Forest find
43. Meet assignment
44. Twangy
48. Rip off: slang

50. Bible king
52. Aunt: Spanish
53. Medicine for 4:00 a.m.?: 5 wds.
58. HRE ruler
59. "25" singer
60. Author Wiesel
61. Person with a list?
62. Restless sort
63. Bold survey
64. Shore visitor
65. Smoothness
66. Trips

DOWN

1. "Prove it!": 2 wds.
2. Oater venue
3. 1936 Nobelist
4. Siting point
5. Overturn
6. A Starr
7. Scads: 2 wds.
8. Performer Falana
9. Shiv thrust
10. Fortress, often
11. Excuse, perhaps: 2 wds.
12. Shiny garb

13. Coin of Peru
21. Column style
22. Base band: abbr.
26. Actor Erwin
28. Red-rinded round
29. Set forth
30. Soft fare
31. Further
34. Ms. Rowlands
35. Era rep
36. 2006 Emmy winner
37. Unpalatable mouthful
38. Where Urdu is heard
39. Body parts
40. Coded call
43. Sign above
45. Less novel
46. More delicate
47. Court squad
49. Buzz
50. Work with keys?
51. Gives off
54. Unique taste
55. Dear figure
56. Fish of film
57. Striking order
58. Lines of credit?

135

ACROSS

1. Attic access
9. Tonsured
15. Shot shooter: 2 wds.
16. Notorious 20th-century figure
17. Zipped
18. Rich ensemble
19. It adds interest
20. Far from oblivious
22. Norway haul
23. Woodland haunters
24. Tanzanian flower
25. Buoy extra
26. Bottle refuse
27. Actress Best
28. Soft marten
29. Alberta native
30. They wander
31. Evergreen extract
35. Stops fretting
36. Covent Garden spectacles
37. Character builder?
38. Churlish chap
39. Crocus cousin
40. Tries (for)
44. Hoof shaper
45. Diagnostic tool
46. Unexpected help
47. Wing of sorts
48. Real beast
49. Boots
50. Rang (up)
52. Enemies of nature
54. Graceland, e.g.
55. Wood source: 2 wds.
56. Was upset
57. Laid hands on

DOWN

1. Drape adjunct
2. Emulate muscles
3. Pop up
4. Cut items
5. Participates at the table
6. Constantly, once
7. Toxic shrub
8. Pressed quaff: 2 wds.
9. Rustle (up)
10. Shrink from
11. Spot on
12. Noise maker?: 2 wds.
13. Base volunteer
14. Gratuitous
21. After: 2 wds.
25. Light cake
27. Desire sparker
28. Iron face
29. Speckled trout
30. Farm array
31. Intimates
32. Bee expert
33. 42-Down sharer
34. Warm up
35. Lapp resource
37. A Walton
39. Slay: slang
40. Jumps across
41. Mag fallout?
42. See 33-Down
43. Wised off
45. Went (with)
46. Silk pattern
48. Charity event
51. Bar topic
53. Considerably

136

ACROSS

1. Words of praise
10. Cash —
15. Draw into folds
16. Neglected beast
17. Perspicacious: hyph. wd.
18. Spray glycol on: hyph. wd.
19. Opposite of depress
20. Abrupt noise
22. — one
23. Iris, e.g.
24. Taken, slangily
27. Valuable diamond?
28. Give trouble to
29. 1950s fad
30. Far from pale
31. Asian capital
32. /
34. Set array
37. Led
38. Ancient catapult
39. Music term
40. Author Radcliffe
41. Leashes, basically
43. Reticent
46. Shad delicacy
47. Bit of progress
48. Barn locks?
49. Shiny knob
51. Talented Elliott
52. Earth, in sci-fi
53. Domestic hangovers?
55. Population stats
58. DC Comics superhero
59. Focus of a Syracuse, New York museum: 2 wds.
60. Cloth intro
61. Register pro

DOWN

1. Draw attention to
2. 48-Across place
3. Smooth
4. Wax pompous
5. Bring in
6. Be senescent
7. March segment
8. Super-long
9. Lot merchandise
10. "Let me just —…"
11. Ills
12. Political operative
13. Low-calorie snack: 2 wds.
14. Intensified
21. Chow source?: 2 wds.
24. Jazz venues
25. Bad load
26. Postal gizmos
29. Manuscript marks
31. Hogshead kin
33. Ant adjective
34. Most déclassé
35. Provide explanations for
36. Pull strings
37. Cast off
39. Foolish fancy
42. Sports-news subjects
43. Slip locale
44. Like some books
45. Small
48. Heavy stuff?
50. December 24 octet
52. Demonstrations of anxiety
54. Surreptitious
56. Low score
57. Take in

137

ACROSS

1. Epic
8. Walks of life
15. Make vulnerable
16. *Très* chic
17. Ignored a diet?
18. World metropolis
19. Mint values
20. Best
22. Classic ride
23. Demonstrates curiosity
24. Shore flock
25. Striking sound
26. Con basis
27. Pro with a sword
28. Drafted
29. Wee shaver
30. Fill a hold
31. Low-fat fare
32. Float follower
34. Storied being
37. Gridlock sight
38. Chanted delivery
41. Aids for colliers
42. Bad instructors
43. Bible priest
44. Event marker, perhaps
45. Snagging points
46. Quiet
47. Hypocritical show
48. Disgust
49. Special flavors
50. Black Sea neighbor
52. Environmentalism concern
54. Clouted
55. Unidentifiable sort
56. Odd groups?
57. More inexorable

DOWN

1. Dub in error
2. Soap ailment
3. Moved apace
4. Unorthodox bands
5. Gets to
6. Fight
7. Place of great abundance: 2 wds.
8. Décor object
9. Labors on
10. Long lunch?
11. Diva display
12. Lost it: 2 wds.
13. Diplomatic brokering
14. Comic victims
21. Shading of a sort
24. Pick up
25. Staunch
27. Scribe mishaps
28. African ravines
31. Pit wailers
32. Duplication ace
33. Insouciant
34. Music great
35. Smart sensation?
36. Gentrification target
38. Campus happening
39. Spent: 2 wds.
40. Bar order
42. Humans, e.g.
45. Faith component
46. Surgical tool
48. Quite ready
49. Weighty read
51. Quick
53. Turn

138

ACROSS

1. Whiny ones
9. Super psyched
15. Progressing nicely: 2 wds.
16. Honey flavor
17. Patisserie words
18. Tropical mammals
19. Fall breaker
20. Minor
21. Settle in, in a way
22. Line —
24. Music genre
26. Needle case
27. Public approval
29. Holy order
30. "Nebraska" star
31. Bardic ploys
33. Address spot
35. Frosting solution
36. Far from glowing
38. Adds (up)
40. Farm butter?
43. Historic pueblo
45. Divine quaff
49. Fleet ride
51. Pol Paul
53. See 50-Down
54. Off the hook
55. Like each end of a magnet
57. Stray lock
58. Button down
60. Very eager
62. Clingy fruit
63. Insignificant
64. Nail polish?
66. Escape route
67. Says again
68. Late rumbles
69. Nursery plots

DOWN

1. Less flat
2. Get out of a jamb?
3. Slow and deliberate
4. Animal pouch
5. Hyde Park wheels?
6. Cruel fellows
7. Tank beauties
8. Made resolute
9. Motivated movement
10. Creamy treat
11. Hung loosely
12. Soared
13. Moonless orb
14. Novelist Caldwell
23. Cry from a tyke
25. Fitzgerald métier
28. Erudition gauge
32. Stilton quality
34. Vex endlessly
37. Flake: hyph. wd. (slang)
39. Wide-beamed craft
40. Charity events
41. Accuse of wrongs
42. Consummate artist
44. Spicy cylinders
46. Protection money
47. Undoubted
48. Keep down
50. Converse of 53-Across
52. Wipe out
56. He is endowed
59. More
61. Wrap around
65. Crane perch

139

ACROSS

1. Things to dump
8. Canadian river
15. Ocean fish
16. Occupies
17. Storied band: 3 wds.
19. Abate
20. Illustrious
21. Staff symbol
22. "Yes!"
23. C sharp: 2 wds.
24. Pedigree mentions
25. Was a bellwether
26. Mark before a series
27. Bid figures
28. Designer hue
29. Pacific
30. Defendant descriptive
33. Has trouble standing
34. Cycle parts
35. Protracted span
36. They can get to you!
37. With gusto
38. Mean sort
41. Snappish?
42. Agora attire
43. Almanac heading
44. Replicating pro
45. Column style
46. Composing great
47. Truly wants: 4 wds.
50. Sites for groundskeepers
51. Author Caldwell
52. 1940 Oscar winner
53. Tricked out

DOWN

1. Like novas
2. Bit of intrigue
3. Cast down
4. Thorough
5. Pointed end
6. Zip
7. Acted blue
8. Court sport?
9. Mooring spot
10. Earned some wrinkles
11. Fall open
12. Plays the rabble-rouser
13. Old army unit
14. Ponders well
18. Kite feature
23. Cote array
24. Feat triggers
26. Docket list
27. Litigate anew
28. Stiff, perhaps
29. Decides irrevocably
30. Sates
31. Least dear
32. Small container
33. Impartial
35. Ashram notables
37. Sans guile
38. Musical Mayfield
39. Quite perturbed
40. Checked
42. Cosmetic buy
43. Reflexive moves
45. Wee amount
46. Mantel piece
48. Piece of wisdom
49. Slip

140

ACROSS

1. Mind-opening sites
11. Moves (along)
15. Closing act: 2 wds.
16. Profess
17. — of Austria
18. Rail position
19. Offspring
20. Relieved (of)
22. Ear-cuff shape
23. Collie concern
24. Regatta yell
27. Field for Fragonard
28. New World claimer
29. Job antagonist
31. Ill-humored response
35. Set
36. Phial fillers
37. Infers (from)
38. Pierces
39. Like many a 42-Across
40. Flip back
41. February complaints
42. See 39-Across
43. Fusses (over)
45. Soft sheepskin
49. Descriptor for 29-Across
50. Vague
51. — shark
52. Be pliant
54. Lose momentum
58. Out of a gale
59. Played evenly?
60. Handout in 1-Across
61. Antic nonsense

DOWN

1. Fail at harmony
2. Prop for Ivanhoe
3. Kinetic
4. Held
5. Beef cut
6. Flow freely
7. Vein pursuit?
8. Meal leaving
9. Prison presence
10. Arab honorific
11. Bridge locale
12. Serving as a hint (of)
13. Bears
14. Endearing term
21. Shows cupidity
24. Draws (out)
25. Beach pickups?
26. Cargo carrier
28. Wore
30. Organic dye
31. Harbor sight
32. Lacking growth potential
33. They're present
34. Arch support
35. Drives (off)
37. Relief effort?
39. Wee one
41. Revive: 2 wds.
44. Nucleus
45. Quiet, perhaps
46. Stump loudly
47. Old British auto
48. Busted flat
51. Film fish
53. Sooner or later
55. Machine part
56. Elrond, e.g.
57. Papal moniker

141

ACROSS

1. Fashion fright
5. Seared dish
10. Breathy sound
14. Word with "stem"
15. Viable
16. Talk (over)
17. Solid patch
18. Pantheist, for one
19. Contrary chap
20. Private retreat
22. Pleasure trip
24. Table scrap
25. Hair —
27. Plush cloth
30. Cry of surprise
31. Firm denial
35. A Gardner
36. Offer as a plea
39. Factless report
40. Dealt (with)
41. Role model, often
42. Born
44. Nice period?
45. Flat boat
47. "You —"
49. Fine trim
50. Sky holder
52. Aesthetic passion
53. Wild warnings
55. Daring deed
57. Faldo aid
58. Take down
61. Was out on a limb?
65. Vivacity
66. Besides
69. Recap, e.g.
70. Pug paw?
71. Rolls up
72. Parallel (to)
73. Avon adieu: hyph. wd.
74. Kin of 41-Across
75. Use charge

DOWN

1. Group vats
2. Passé Maltese coin
3. Spread out
4. Harbor sight
5. Ruined: slang
6. Actor Jack
7. Significant
8. Tiny cells
9. Film yapper
10. Spooky shade
11. Skein measure
12. Madrid pronoun
13. Least amount
21. 69-Across feature
23. Java pot
25. *Ella*
26. Hickory tree
27. Grassy plain
28. Ward off
29. Brazil port
30. Trite: 2 wds. (slang)
32. Spotted carnivore
33. River denizen
34. Stimulates
37. Cadiz article
38. Sargasso catch
43. Yard tool
46. Rich hue
48. Soil extract
51. Coral —
54. Sweet stuff
56. Muddle: slang
57. Overwrought
58. Skillful
59. Mr. Kazan
60. Aerial holder
61. Bore: slang
62. Hoist (up)
63. Hibernia, to some
64. Body damage
67. Earp tote
68. Compass mark

142

ACROSS

1. Kind handout
5. Recipe verb
10. Head: slang
14. Gridlock alert
15. Old pronoun
16. Liner route
17. Pervasive quality
18. Went off
19. Bible book
20. Down East growth: 2 wds.
22. Destroys
24. Zip
25. Tiny opening
26. Port sights
29. Ship part
30. Hardly forward
33. Strikes
34. More than toasts
35. Runner Sebastian
36. Wrench acknowledgment?
37. Resounding sounds
38. Astral observance
39. Rebuke intro
40. Hearing locale
41. Less crude
42. Focus getter
43. Skein kin
44. Fleet band
45. Wet film
46. Dearth
47. Patron, perhaps
50. Nursery buy
54. Crew addition
55. In a pet
57. Tuneful Guthrie
58. Send out
59. Central hub
60. On a big scale
61. — up
62. Meshed things
63. Cote dwellers

DOWN

1. Surmounting
2. Italian city
3. Realm of Selene
4. Rallying show
5. Spots for tillers
6. Word with "fold"
7. Old country handle
8. Donkey, in Dijon
9. Officious sorts
10. Ball: slang
11. Per capita
12. Playing amount
13. Topographical feature
21. Low ten
23. Purposes
25. Launch
26. Eatery fixture
27. Occupy well
28. A Martin
29. Expert: slang
30. Tea go-with
31. Fly in place
32. Orbit measures
34. Include
37. Hot pursuit?
38. Slim or Tex
40. Yak: slang
41. It might be red!
44. Untwists
45. Experiences
46. Following
47. Toque wearer
48. Designer hue
49. Greek deity
50. Flow to avoid
51. Bout result
52. Further
53. Polar sea
56. Ms. Dawn Chong

143

ACROSS

1. Sleeve inserts?
5. Overt tease
10. Mother of Apollo
14. Farm building
15. Sleek serpent
16. Polecat trail
17. Signaled loudly
18. List closer
19. Widespread
20. Eye
22. Driving force
24. See 57-Down
25. Set in motion
26. Unreserved
29. Especial
30. Traded (in)
34. Austere stretch
35. Campaign ammo?
36. Certain salt
37. Person: slang
38. Artless
40. Back
41. Green
43. Curb; restraint
44. Cast off
45. Prie-dieu resters
46. Character aspect
47. Composer Ernest
48. Foolish folks
50. Cargo space
51. Resolves (differences)
54. Celtic spirit
58. Garden mix
59. "What I — was …"
61. Siouan tribe
62. Color quality
63. Real innocent
64. Staggers
65. Bellicose deity
66. In dire straits
67. Warm haunt

DOWN

1. Lea plot
2. Beguile
3. Lab lamp
4. Share
5. Kelp shoot
6. Unsatisfactory
7. Rare gems: slang
8. Social order
9. Long march
10. Rhine beauty
11. Censor, in a way
12. Bland stuff
13. Vein fillers
21. Publicity: slang
23. Clutch, e.g.
25. Humor
26. Tiny patch
27. Lear kin
28. Word with "right"
29. Plate call
31. Bowie's last stand
32. Math branch
33. Old pledge
35. Cow tummy
36. Languishing
38. They smell!
39. Home to Cariocas
42. Vegan fare
44. Blissful
46. Arcane mystic
47. Proscribe
49. Ira Allen's bro
50. Very much
51. Utah resort
52. Opportunity, figuratively
53. Grey lass
54. Cultured
55. Sports great
56. 14-Across denizens
57. With 24-Across, London area
60. Time interval

144

ACROSS

1. Nursery buy
5. Word with "side"
10. Nave neighbor
14. Beef intro
15. Old coin
16. Joe source
17. Smacked duo?
18. Rolling rises
19. A Guthrie
20. Crack
21. Brief cite
22. Distributes
24. Justly win
26. 1958 Pulitzer recipient
27. Big —
28. Dispatched, in a way: 2 wds.
32. Acknowledge as true
35. "— why…"
36. Move apace
37. Advance of sorts
38. Saint of Wales
39. Bad list?
40. Galley item
41. Confused mix
42. Vamp locales
43. Greatly reduced
45. 20th-century leader
46. Fold members
47. Cheeky pair?
51. Exit
54. Hand (out)
55. Period to study
56. Shoat sire
57. Try to gall
59. Like a kiwi
60. Recipe verb
61. Organic chemical
62. Staff symbol
63. Seasonal ride
64. Saga subjects
65. Little couple?

DOWN

1. Carte offering
2. A Walker
3. Shows shock
4. Driving challenge
5. Rebuke to imps
6. Stir up
7. Rudely scan
8. Quite
9. Composed
10. Humiliated
11. Paita site
12. Rep coup
13. Son of Seth
21. Field visitor
23. Wanes
25. Harrow rival
26. Digs on high
28. Soiree time
29. Mississippi feeder
30. Magnum fill
31. Promontory
32. World range
33. Mien
34. In arrears
35. Glowing rings
38. Couldn't abide
39. Place for a keeper
41. Common gulls
42. Corresponding
44. Emulated a cad
45. Band at a meet
47. Treated, perhaps
48. Current checker
49. Take out
50. Lab compounds
51. Decreases
52. Sports climax
53. Casino find
54. See
58. Spanish pronoun
59. Ant prize

145

ACROSS

1. Breach
4. Crude crew
8. Sliced thin
14. Had
15. Vaudeville act
16. Lovely Rita
17. Edible seed
19. Looks
20. Refer
21. Singular
23. Go south
24. Forum salute
25. Cracking aid
26. Simple
27. Racer Scheckter
29. Mixer attendee, maybe
30. Fed up, perhaps
31. Stand order
32. Spelling need?
33. Stole stuff
34. Left thing?
36. Check
40. Bio datum
41. Word with "room"
42. Stowe girl
43. Wolfish bands
46. Far from bad
47. Blue plant
48. Sports great
49. Con talk: slang
50. Take out
51. Olympics chant
52. *Ici*
53. Moves apace
56. Order member
58. Witty exchange
60. Bible book
61. Painful woe
62. Weighty time
63. Quite hard
64. Runs out
65. Indistinct

DOWN

1. Crazy: slang
2. Tiny bit: 2 wds.
3. Saturates fully
4. Bear in a Shel Silverstein poem
5. Clan figure
6. Conical topper
7. Famous
8. Flip
9. Trendy pair
10. Art notable
11. Swung around
12. It might follow a hand
13. Swiss adjective
18. Collection
22. Then again
25. Perfect
26. Goods seller
27. Pickle
28. Lines of credit
29. Aviary item
30. Jettison
32. Droll sorts
33. "Heads up!"
35. Behalf
36. Soft-shoe prop
37. Caved
38. Some germ cells
39. Sans care
41. Branch off
43. Obeys a comma
44. Promote
45. Beyond prim
46. Forest find
47. Stampede cause
49. A Hall
50. Quiet disrupters
52. Pump part
53. Eyed food
54. Ms. Russell
55. Joining sign?
57. *Las*
59. Protracted span

146

ACROSS

1. Pithy wisdom
5. Antilles native
10. Jab and feint
14. Sandstone find
15. Keen
16. Balmy: slang
17. Antonia Fraser, for one
18. Mrs. Gorbachev
19. Bun option
20. Assayed load
21. Possessive pronoun
22. 65-Across, e.g.
24. Ocean passes
26. More blanched
27. Familiar contraction
28. Rigged vessel
29. Rely (on)
32. Err
35. Glass limit
36. Have cold feet
37. Voiced
38. Some pole climbers
39. Measured clip
40. Pea poker
41. — Timor
42. Gym block
43. Deplorable
44. Sires

45. See 32-Across
46. Parrots, often
48. Flat people
52. Waylay
54. 28-Across vet
55. Biting
56. Bank claim
57. Prior to
59. Asian aristocrat
60. Card game
61. Nenes, for example
62. Gets nosy
63. Dory array
64. Rain runnel
65. Base spread

DOWN

1. Ballet highlights
2. Notwithstanding
3. Marsh denizen
4. Captious
5. Text additions
6. Culture media
7. Social reformer Jacob
8. They: French
9. Pack heat: 2 wds.
10. Vail view
11. Rare omnivore: 2 wds.

12. Experts
13. Etymology concern
21. Writer Shere
23. Yosemite bugler
25. Church egress
26. Use rouge on
28. Gall
30. Roadside sign
31. Blood chart
32. Heaps
33. Recital piece
34. Chinese treasure: 2 wds.
35. Wee bubbles
36. Anterior
38. Warm greetings
42. Intimation
44. — Plaines
45. Market figure
47. River craft
48. Stud play
49. Axe
50. Human classes
51. Dotted fabric
52. Further
53. Translucent mineral
54. Heavy dish
58. Society-page word
59. Bump into

147

ACROSS

1. Polar explorer
5. Harmony disrupters
10. Hinduism book
14. Got off
15. Central point
16. Word with "how"
17. Soft snack
18. Sans assistance
19. Foolscap quantity
20. By and by
22. Without luck
24. Scuttlebut, maybe
25. Fiefdom figure
26. Spanish city
29. Trimmed to the max
33. Equal
34. Get louder
36. Ring response?
37. Relent
39. Out state
41. Crisp side
42. Stuff
44. Oman neighbor
46. Threshold
47. Certain show
49. Put on
51. Type-A display
52. Can
53. Wrangling contest
56. Cutting yield
60. Taxing test
61. Less dated
63. Setting selector
64. Psychic study?
65. Clientele
66. Thespian Raines
67. Two in a queue?
68. Gist
69. Quite grave

DOWN

1. Transfixed
2. Table stick
3. Realm of King Mongkut
4. Advanced boldly
5. Prey of kestrels
6. Conduct
7. Swear
8. Hold holding
9. A Tyler
10. Vets well
11. Exact
12. Shady thing?
13. Huge body
21. Clears (of)
23. Cunning
25. Willamette River hub
26. Silent
27. Wax lyrically
28. Plumbing aid
29. Moving apace
30. Pretty Page
31. 25-Across, e.g.
32. Like some wrecks
35. "Family Ties" mom
38. Gifts for Taurines
40. Stock list
43. Ousting order
45. Behavior guide
48. Subs, perhaps
50. Key
52. Sustains
53. Bowl feature
54. Poetic land
55. Club booking
56. Pond visitor
57. View from Aswan
58. Bit of 24-Across
59. Duel trigger
62. Poetic palindrome

148

ACROSS

1. Evening, quaintly
5. Frame feature
9. Suit option
14. Norse god
15. Skin treatment
16. Olympics array
17. Sweetie kin
18. Pea chaser
19. Cedes
20. Very little: 4 wds.
23. Certainly: 2 wds.
24. Exhume: 2 wds.
28. Audiophile stack
29. Atlantic diver
31. Truth alternative?
32. Pleased sigh
35. Skater Michael
37. Squeals: slang
38. Little bit: 4 wds.
41. Clarify?
42. French commune
43. Radiator racket
44. Lowdown
45. Urban rides
46. Graze?
48. Less novel
50. Paint dispenser
54. Offering little interest: 4 wds.
57. Sun block?
60. Riant sound: hyph. wd.
61. Mohave rise
62. Sniffle prelude
63. Actor Novello
64. Square
65. Swells (with)
66. Malt dryer
67. O'Brien follower

DOWN

1. A Ryan
2. Nampa locale
3. Pusillanimous
4. United: 2 wds.
5. Putter Peter
6. Thermal-buoyed
7. Biblical land
8. Lyon monster
9. Music notation
10. Serialized
11. Amp (up)
12. Guess start?
13. Guess end?
21. Bavarian king
22. River craft
25. Fails: slang
26. Pleads for
27. Grubs, e.g.
29. Razed ruins
30. Suited (to)
32. — Ababa
33. Common contraction
34. Labor leader
36. "— do!"
37. Stitched line
39. Hustler haunt
40. Admiral Nelson player
45. Lake raptor
47. Beat
49. Franc replacements
50. Greek mount
51. Dig implement
52. Metropolis redhead
53. Texas county
55. Home to Miamisburg
56. Leghorn legume
57. Big basin
58. Slay: slang
59. *Lei*

149

ACROSS

1. Customers
6. Overflowed
10. Souvenir of Mumbai
14. Black snake
15. Retinal cell
16. Went on?
17. Old medical administration
18. Turns, in a way
19. Carte offering
20. Hold off: 4 wds.
23. — fire
24. Almanac list
25. Lightheaded group?
28. Confounded cry
29. Tannin source
30. Small amount
34. Act bemused: 3 wds.
39. Ocean denizen: 2 wds.
40. Writer Beattie
41. Meadow visitor
42. Herbal stuff: 2 wds.
46. Order locales
49. A Sherman

50. "Hospital Sketches" author: 3 wds.
55. Graph reference
56. Tailoring piece
57. Mai-tai sipping spot
58. Blend
59. Freudian force
60. Wrongly seize
61. Book entries
62. Elated: slang
63. Plaguing sorts

DOWN

1. Tough slog
2. Matter
3. Stitch kin
4. Intensify
5. Thing to run
6. Gets lost?: slang
7. Like a copse
8. Unallied with
9. Fare sharer
10. River of Dixie
11. Broker, often
12. Add up to
13. Does zip

21. Start of today?
22. Bar topics
25. Important pol
26. Holey bolt
27. Palatable pod
28. Nap disturber
30. Word with "pie"
31. Drink descriptive
32. Rattan stem
33. Thespian Best
35. Service no-shows?
36. Busing aids
37. Sprays to wear
38. Shade
42. Least frank
43. After: 2 wds.
44. Famed statistician
45. Sheathe
46. Texan tree
47. Sought a title?
48. Establish
49. Bible guy
51. Unsated demand
52. Blame
53. Patisserie buy
54. Input from pros

150

ACROSS

1. Versatile ride
9. Head count
15. Baggage handler?
16. Momentarily
17. Citation mark
18. Certain organs
19. Iron source: 2 wds.
20. Like some eyes: hyph. wd.
21. Tart stuff
22. Vengeful antihero of fiction
24. Tank beauty
25. Soft shoes
28. Great —
30. Cellar filler
31. Battle swag
33. NFLer Lorenzo
35. Forage crop
36. Abets, perhaps: 2 wds.
39. Dust collector
42. Tropical plant
43. Simple chords
47. Soft-finned swimmers
49. Comes together
51. Stand out
52. Lie lack
54. Trial judge?
56. Shiloh high priest
57. Office scramble: 2 wds. (slang)
59. Discredited
62. Enemy of Rome
63. Produce
64. He works with staves
65. Unusual pet
66. Explorer Shackleton
67. Tremulous

DOWN

1. Luxor amulets
2. Backed off: 2 wds.
3. Geometric style: 2 wds.
4. Pushkin product
5. Lead on
6. Elephant modifier
7. Stacked closely
8. Light leather
9. Spread unchecked
10. Forest youngster
11. Spooky apparitions
12. Oater emblem: 2 wds.
13. Advanced
14. Explain, maybe
20. Charity, often
23. Repair hatch
26. Calf hide
27. Vent cousin
29. Cardinal point
32. He's alone
34. Bygone coins
37. Shirt cloth
38. Water spirit
39. Go back over
40. Aquarium device
41. Unsated sort
44. Film material
45. Axes
46. Fast-food noshes
48. Pin chaser
50. High-ranking
53. Forces to go
55. Regular fees
58. Ox haul
60. Verse bits
61. Russian river
63. Toothy fish

151

ACROSS

1. Wrenched (off)
8. See 16-Across
15. More perspicacious
16. Like an 8-Across
17. In an exact manner
18. Caves
19. Unevenly edged
20. Lively fling
21. Travel tote
22. Turf measure
23. Cactus nesters
25. Poppet cry
26. Act badly: slang
27. Grapple with
28. Dunk pro: slang
29. Cruise booking
31. Strip (of)
32. Infamous hotel
34. Toss about
37. Solid conviction
41. Responds to 1-Down
42. Economy boosters, often
43. Opportune
44. Inventor Elisha
45. Cancels out
46. Syrian nosh
47. Shabby-looking
48. Earth movers
49. Indispensable
50. Certain steed
52. Fleshy gastropod
54. Bound (to): 2 wds.
55. Seasoned stuff
56. Does some cobbling
57. Roman magistrate

DOWN

1. They're hilarious
2. Locks changer?
3. Wolf down
4. Mulling need
5. Midway thrill
6. Jellied buy
7. Wine modifier
8. *Très* tranquil
9. Canada folk
10. Barnacle host?
11. Horace piece
12. Close affinity
13. On and off: 2 wds.
14. Computer verb
20. Ruling voidances
23. Fierce choler
24. See 23-Down
25. Expert in his mind
27. Knob material
28. Alludes to
30. Some trophies
31. Provokes
33. Easy mark
34. War horse
35. Crisis connection: 2 wds.
36. Sortie chaps
38. Shining example
39. Far from nice
40. Least green
42. Nappy goods
45. Nick of note
46. Indian dish
48. Fish harvest
49. Lush hollow
51. Show of scorn
52. Fang flasher
53. Sand strand

152

ACROSS

1. Draws on a board
11. Boy band?
15. Old number
16. Disembarked
17. Navel base?: 2 wds.
18. Court figure
19. Cast off: 2 wds.
20. Man: slang
22. Social happening
23. Faddish duo?
24. Famed guerrilla
27. Icon of Egypt
28. Drudges
29. Trace
31. In a pecuniary way
35. Purple flier
36. South African natives
37. Give aid to
38. Street —
39. Under arrest
40. Group on the go
41. Ill-gotten gains
42. Rite occasion
43. Makes start
45. Friendly exchange
49. Chinese-zodiac member
50. Be off
51. Exclaim loudly
52. See 27-Across
54. Fills with fondness
58. Protector of salts
59. Mythical menace: 2 wds.
60. Handful for a bed
61. Annual event: 2 wds.

DOWN

1. Call to account
2. Word with "score"
3. Having wings
4. Is unsated, perhaps
5. Thus: Latin
6. A Howard
7. Heading sternward
8. Rocky rise
9. Sets up
10. Rep ruiner
11. Envelop
12. Skin descriptive
13. Brandy, e.g.
14. Grew greater
21. Plumb
24. Soft buys
25. Afflicts
26. Machiavellian
28. White toy
30. Cantata element
31. School sites
32. Quite stoic
33. It's free!: 2 wds.
34. Witty sort
35. Softens
37. Con
39. Purr of endearment
41. Kalimantan locale
44. Drop of water, often
45. Contrives quickly
46. Effigy adjective
47. Sphere for war
48. Snappish
51. Sound of Scotland
53. Nursery stock
55. Very fertile
56. Pyre product
57. Curling target

153

ACROSS

1. Whatever
5. Barrel attachments
11. Resistive unit
14. Mentally adroit
15. Yellow companion
16. Clover cousin
17. Ramble: 5 wds.
20. — Island
21. Contingency plan
22. Turned stoic
24. Horse chaser
25. Varnishes plane wings
27. Modus operandi
30. Wizard
33. — plum, African shrub
35. D.C. transport
36. Interior cavity
38. Art great
40. Fly swatter?
41. Leaf sections
43. — clam
45. Stable
46. Alpine challenge
48. Font feature
50. Fondue grips
52. Divert (from)
56. Cable precursors
59. Kid
60. Fanciful response: 2 wds.
62. Clumsy chap
63. Proscriptions
64. Hand over (to)
65. Damask hue
66. Ballot groups
67. Expatriate, perhaps

DOWN

1. Respected ones
2. Wolf-pack member: hyph. wd.
3. In the ballpark
4. Picked up
5. Bridge need: 2 wds.
6. Singer Janis
7. Boxer warning
8. Shrinks from
9. Wee amounts
10. Good, to satisfactory
11. Offenbach specialties
12. Certain lobsters
13. Tanker official
18. Major con
19. Glove insert
23. Dissuade (from)
26. Complex tales
28. Ohio borderer
29. Emulate some birds
30. Saddler tools
31. Together
32. Under siege
34. Was indolent
37. Contradicts
39. Crabby trait
42. Petrarch products
44. Solemn practices
47. Domestic servant
49. Wall decoration
51. Carnival dance
53. Last word?
54. Plow targets
55. Shared belief
56. Remotely
57. Mane locale
58. Primer pup
61. Bass of tomorrow?

154

ACROSS

1. Lead base
9. Extensive spreads
15. One with the goods?
16. Exhort: 2 wds.
17. Caribbean keys
18. Ragged range
19. Performances by doubles
20. Very embroiled: hyph. wd.
22. They may get cracked!
23. Disappeared
24. Time out
25. Word with "dog"
26. Zebra feature
27. Move like a caster
29. Prescribed procedure
30. Courting sort
31. By and large: 3 wds.
35. Saints, often
36. Gorp bits
37. Callao site
38. Some accords
39. Storied trio
40. Audio range
44. Big-egg layer
45. Home, to Cristian
46. Silently seen
47. Military missions
50. Recent
51. Abalone, e.g.: 2 wds.
52. Prone to anger
54. Steep slope
55. Gives help to
56. Smart trends
57. Crab display

DOWN

1. Realizes
2. Pad, perhaps
3. Make agree
4. In distress
5. Dagger sections
6. Lament list
7. Capital of Thailand?
8. A Caldwell
9. Knit well
10. View from Ashtabula
11. Red descriptive
12. Goal of a meditator
13. Erstwhile caped figure
14. Edible catch
21. Alumna adjective
23. Blog detail
26. Wire measures
27. Life coach, maybe
28. Animated
29. Recurs
30. Indian souvenir
31. Slakes
32. Most sordid
33. Unerring exhibition
34. Cheese fan?
35. Huge
37. Fast-lane group?
39. Unearthing aid
40. Flooring strip
41. Participating
42. Galley items
43. Source of woe
45. Allied band
46. Creature with a snout
48. Treatment
49. Beyond odd
50. Pip: slang
53. Classic wheels

155

ACROSS

1. Open participant
4. Speculative risk
7. Room mate?
9. Court figures
11. Mart objective
13. Tries to hit
15. Fine stuff?
16. Line extensions
18. Teased surface
19. They get the yoke
21. Shadow
22. Grand revelry
23. Deliberate
25. Evil
26. See 4-Down
27. Contend (against)
29. Word with "position"
30. Treated coat
31. Burden for Jack
32. Grants
33. Visit: 2 wds.
35. Hot stuff?
36. Public mover
37. Bamboozle: slang
39. Shortened by
40. Sports prize
42. Cut off
44. Rolled morsel
45. Some ads
47. Tinge
48. Leave: 2 wds.
50. Hudson activity
52. Haughty look
53. Disburse
54. Hunkered down
55. Dip

DOWN

1. Major access
2. Jazzy opus
3. Voiced
4. 26-Across features
5. Macaroon need
6. Juvenile, maybe
7. Strips
8. Fades away
9. Commons, for example
10. Far from exciting
11. Cricket implement
12. Endemic
13. Show partner
14. Generous tub
17. Landscape dent
20. Nurtures lovingly
22. Capacity quantities
24. Process words?
26. They twist
28. Instinctive forces
29. Intimate
31. Montana options
32. Heeds advice
33. Brusque
34. Vacuum filler
35. Thrilling demonstration
36. Head piece?
38. Duel damage
39. Argentine article
40. Discharge profusely
41. Measured periods
43. Small dowel
45. Rimbaud, for one
46. Wee samples
49. Tendril-bearing plant
51. Bardic field

156

ACROSS

1. Got going
5. Art great
10. Exploited hire
14. Lily of Africa
15. Break out
16. Press
17. Cracking aid
18. Jibe
19. Journalist Logan
20. Suspect account
21. Retirement locale?: hyph. wd.
23. Key on a map
25. Hindu deity
26. Dare to
28. Queue pair
31. Cleared
35. Ancient letter
36. List makers?
38. Less passé
39. Black stuff
41. Dickens protagonist
43. Riled
44. Writer Michael
46. — mix
48. Popular
49. Rock projections
51. Manx tongue
52. Gung-ho reply
53. Bubbly descriptive
55. Manor worker
57. Frank
62. Midwest river
65. Score part
66. Word with "card"
67. Braces
68. Title cloud
69. Huge success
70. David of "Rhoda"
71. Insurance concern
72. Rude displays
73. Existence, to Nero

DOWN

1. Like a jabot
2. Singer Henderson
3. Dandy buy: 3 wds.
4. Texting fans
5. Blew away with a racket?
6. Hence: Latin
7. Ashram figure
8. Unoriginal band
9. Be a meddler: 2 wds.
10. Quivers
11. QED part
12. Mean guy
13. Akin
22. Bistro find
24. Set the pace
26. Newton of football
27. Square things
29. Sewing fold
30. REM disturber
32. Framing pile: 3 wds.
33. Quite curious
34. Cask bits
37. Kite
40. Dungeon staples: 2 wds.
42. Minority opinions
45. Minute fractions, familiarly
47. Shelter
50. Trilogy piece
54. Thick sort
56. Mountainous sector
57. Occur
58. Hodgepodge
59. Colorado natives
60. Wing: French
61. Garrulous guffaw
63. Coaxes
64. Sports great

157

ACROSS

1. Commercial flow
5. Back-fence exchanges
10. Boring
14. Flute range
15. Mixology bit
16. Fissure filler
17. Acute
18. Keep on the track
19. Early herder
20. Business damages
22. Pledged underling
24. Delphic VIP
25. Gridiron play
26. Party lists
29. California river: 2 wds.
33. Was disposed to
34. Mitered corners
35. Storage option
36. Petulant
37. Perambulates
38. Donne, for one
39. Waste away
40. Rend
41. Peace prelude
42. Switched lanes?
44. Rubs the wrong way
45. Snappish
46. Get a rise out of
47. After-dinner selection
50. 22-Across trait
54. Equine hue
55. Common saw
57. Court term
58. Differently
59. Turn to junk: slang
60. Lea lopers
61. Nettle,for example
62. Aids for a 56-Down
63. Spring (up)

DOWN

1. Encrust
2. "Madagascar" lion
3. Word with "foot"
4. "Come on!"
5. Chucks
6. Evolve, perhaps
7. 5-Across, often
8. Threshold
9. Pages, e.g.
10. Russia neighbor
11. Holds up
12. Creative kernel
13. Wee depression
21. Dearth
23. Shticky skits
25. More lucid
26. Certify (to)
27. Hogan cousin
28. Twist drill
29. Bailed out
30. Circa
31. Blood kin
32. Deal costs
34. Hunger after
37. Convents, as a rule
38. Gushed idly
40. Seeks redress
41. Minor combo
43. Cut the ribbon of
44. They rap
46. Triggered
47. Athletic pursuit on campus
48. Mouse escape
49. Adroitness
50. Ledger info
51. Home to Hoover
52. Surmounting
53. Limb cradle?
56. Clinic moniker

158

ACROSS

1. Tiny amount
5. Feud fuel
9. Square —
13. African plant
14. Soft buys
15. Unsated feeling
16. Word with "book"
17. Soldering devices
18. Duel trigger
19. Firmly avows
21. Panache
22. Vat sediment
24. Prompt
25. Diamond base
29. Forsakes
34. Vast quantity
35. Split
36. Animation
37. Was a blowhard
39. Clearly evince
42. Port, e.g.
43. Addled trio?
45. Dichotomize
46. Too forward
49. Escaped
50. Tile protector
51. Untaken
53. It may be slippery

56. Well-off: slang
60. Hailed thing
61. Farm supply
64. Milieu
66. In any manner
67. Tends (to)
68. Grinding device
69. Bay part
70. Extract
71. Lime segment

DOWN

1. Beyond reserved
2. Firm answers
3. Raptor feature
4. Meadow visitor
5. Team member?
6. Brouhaha
7. Hose choice
8. Head of state?
9. Sat back
10. But
11. Like litchis
12. Nature
14. Singer of myth
20. On its way
21. Realm of Apollo
23. Combo element
24. Ms. Blanchett

25. Native of Asia
26. Survey quantities
27. Registers
28. Seize
30. Tries
31. Prismatic purchases
32. Game show?
33. Zip
35. Xanadu
38. Tweak, perhaps
40. Bistro store
41. Scale tones
44. Driving force, often
47. Rules maven
48. Ms. Whitman
49. Litter racket
52. Party platform
53. Pas
54. Flow to shun
55. Draft group
57. Far from arid
58. Soprano Mills
59. Proof notation
61. Arch
62. Caddy cache
63. Incurred
65. "That's —!"

159

ACROSS

1. Ousting cry
5. Zippy
10. Poll query
14. Soft stuff
15. Sans peers
16. Rugby rival
17. Writer Paton
18. Silent signals
19. Was accepted
20. Moan from a tween
21. — count
22. Blows
24. Digestion, e.g.
26. Formal function
27. Trendy buy
28. In disarray
32. It detects
35. Sylvan finds
36. Kerfuffle
37. — door
38. Hamlike?
39. Visible trace
40. Stout relative
41. Lament list
42. Mow store
43. Put back
45. Elapsed
46. Score part
47. Some fee recipients
51. Concocting aid
54. Fail: slang
55. Envelop
56. Cut periods?
57. Film-archive stock
59. Court term
60. Piquancy
61. Take out
62. Links event
63. Word with "bed"
64. Showed pluck
65. Give in

DOWN

1. Puckish sort
2. Artistic application
3. Twisted tree
4. Moleskin kin
5. Least trained
6. Con assumption
7. Heron hangout
8. Blot maker
9. Left
10. Hiring help
11. Straddling
12. Sulky puller
13. Abolishes
21. Try
23. Goes south
25. Easy confab
26. Oriel elements
28. Lifeless
29. Marsh native
30. Advantage
31. Oxford band
32. Elevate
33. Hot-rod component
34. Losing proposition?
35. 51-Across verb
38. Rode smoothly
39. See 4-Down
41. Silo fill
42. Party in a casino
44. In concert
45. Did a salon task
47. Unsubstantiated
48. Miss a shower?
49. Shiny black
50. Wear out
51. Historic force, for short
52. Thespian Falco
53. Case mention
54. Spree: slang
58. Prime time?
59. See 59-Across

ACROSS

1. Gaff, for example
5. Shape a (topiary)
9. Bit of progress
13. Word separation
14. Aquatic grass
15. Buck box
16. Hay stabbers
17. Sweet libations
18. Thereto
19. Absorbed
20. Seal bunches
22. Spread halite
24. Fix
26. Genealogy designation
27. Half of eleven?
28. Deemed
32. Lacking heat?
35. Catches with a saw
36. Forum salute
37. Promising
38. Offers
39. Blood chart
40. Torah chest
41. Skin treatment
42. Vile brute
43. Takes a plunge
45. Tropic root

46. Closes
47. Shrinks from
51. File (past)
54. Frame section
55. Pump part
56. Exercises
57. Bewitched
59. Emulate King
61. Factor of 162
62. Cleveland sight
63. Toned down
64. Knots lace
65. Snug havens
66. Holy domains

DOWN

1. Rancor
2. Flat sheets
3. Clean serve
4. Be affected
5. Profession
6. Clears (of)
7. Tundra array
8. Semaphore sendings
9. Less novel
10. Rake
11. In other situations
12. Trudge
13. General emblem

21. Claim harvest
23. Grave exhalation
25. Stylish: slang
26. Physics unit
28. Gets promoted
29. "I — you!"
30. Constant
31. Safe paper
32. Eccentric fastener
33. Ancient wisdom
34. Goes fishing?
35. Junk —
38. Reflected
39. "Stop working on the test!"
41. Lead (to)
42. Gets
44. Checks
45. "*Mais oui!*"
47. Takes out
48. Civic power
49. Schleps
50. Word with "bird"
51. Gridiron verb
52. Georgia locale
53. Tore off
54. Twist (facts)
58. Happen
60. Bitter herb

ACROSS

1. It's gravity-driven
5. Appreciates
10. Sunken sites
14. Cut down
15. Love abroad?
16. Bailiwick
17. Bass delivery
18. Conveys
19. Larder stash
20. Pacific port: 2 wds.
22. See-through pair?: slang
24. Leave behind
25. Famed person
26. Intense spell
29. Greetings to hams
30. French-wine descriptive
33. Title encumbrances
34. Vegan staples
35. Stock value
36. Nautical term
37. Enjoys a log?
38. Final result
39. Dry (hay)
40. Blue display
41. Some bays
42. Social introduction?
43. Gorp bits
44. Hot spot
45. With 50-Down, thinner
46. Soupçon
47. Rio Grande hub: 2 wds.
50. Wanted to know
54. Word with "cloth"
55. Focusing problem
57. Killer of Britannicus
58. Wolf intro
59. Clan dignitary
60. Polish prose
61. Iowa city
62. Epic subjects
63. Ward figures: slang

DOWN

1. Vacation options
2. Superman's mom
3. Poetic land
4. Procrastination challenge
5. Last
6. Conception
7. "The Mikado" role
8. Odic preposition
9. Regular appointments
10. Sermon topic
11. Jejune
12. Wee legacy
13. Cheeky reply
21. Lab specks
23. "Bonanza" son
25. Oppresses
26. Designer hue
27. Accumulations
28. Fen finds
29. Yields
30. Free
31. Gourmand, e.g.
32. Big moment
34. Overcomes
37. Sound
38. Far from loose
40. Lowly ten?
41. Reform
44. Gala guests
45. Dash strips
46. Wet (down)
47. Ms. Raines
48. Impend
49. Sylvan scent
50. See 45-Across
51. Adjust
52. Norse VIP
53. Times symbols
56. Valencia support

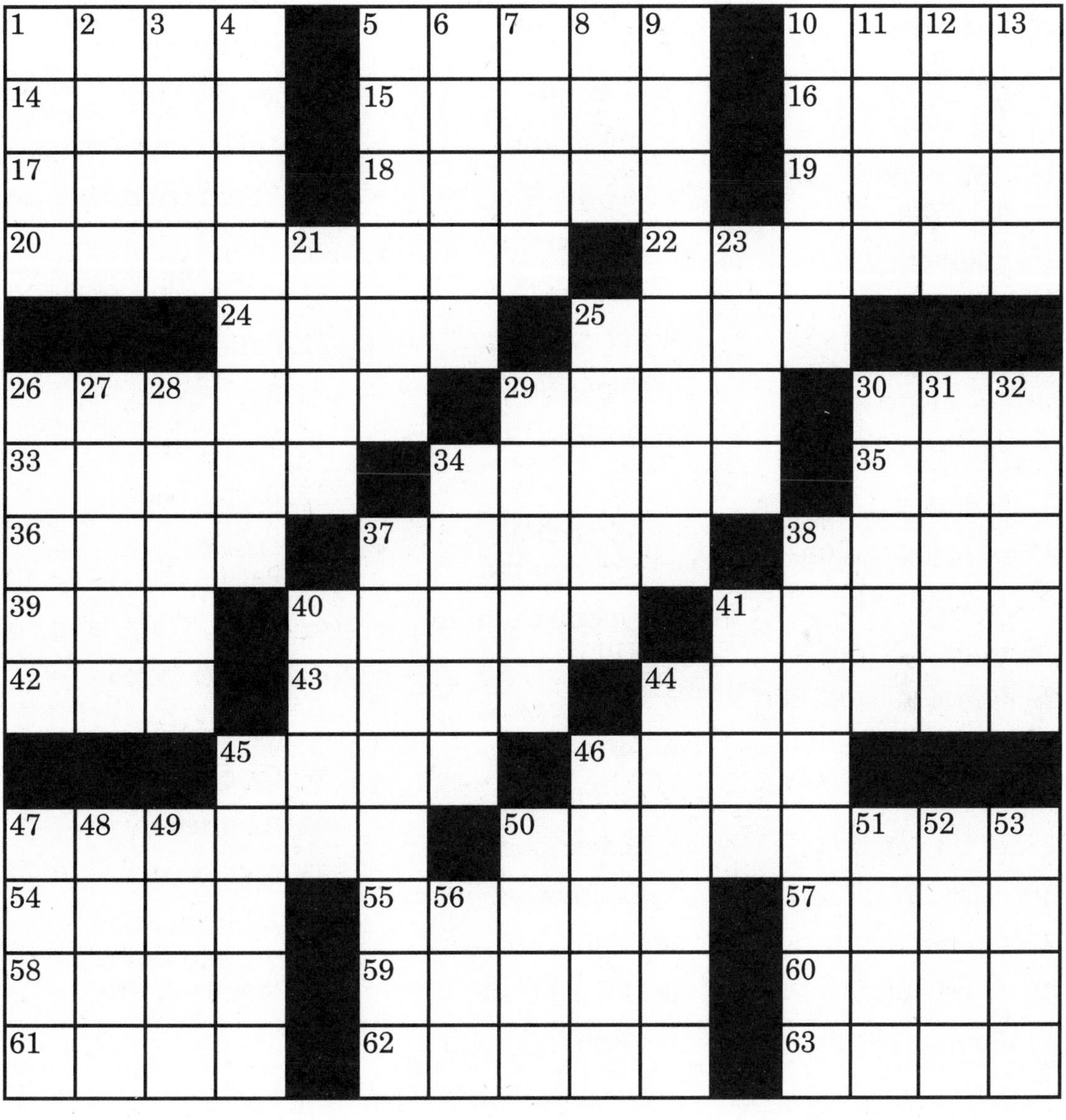

162

ACROSS

1. Lapping motion
5. In advance
10. Talk prelude?
14. Square block
15. Appreciative avowal, in Arles
16. Beguile
17. Thin brace
18. Certain Celts
19. Genius Turing
20. HILO: 2 wds.
23. Miters, e.g.
24. Love expression
25. Temple array
28. Hanker after
30. Prince Valiant's son
33. Flashy display
34. Toledo title
35. NFLer Lemon
36. FLORENCE: 4 wds.
39. Offend proboscises?
40. Overhaul
41. Composer Luigi
42. Like some socks
43. Choice for 35-Across
44. Court figure
45. Stripling

46. Acoustic unit
47. VENICE: 4 wds.
53. Cast material
54. — dome
55. A Romanov
57. Cry uncle
58. Jail facer
59. Not mint
60. Seeing things?
61. Rare Derby winner
62. Novelist Gerritsen

DOWN

1. Represented
2. Woody Guthrie's scion
3. Parch
4. Auto style
5. Bounds
6. Lea croppers
7. Exploration notable
8. Church accounts
9. Sink adjunct
10. Running group
11. Dance with gestures
12. Uttered
13. Holding space
21. Western republic

22. Libido cousins
25. Old-fashioned
26. Hurt badly
27. Meld (into)
28. They come and go
29. Recon collectible
30. Tilting
31. Hockey pro Dylan
32. Formal reply: 2 wds.
34. Food extras
35. Terminates: 2 wds.
37. Better barter: hyph. wd.
38. Pacific deity
43. Crash site?: slang
44. Rocker Rotten
45. Water systems
46. Dairy perch
47. Raucous cry
48. Gallivant
49. Apartment on a ground floor, maybe: 2 wds.
50. Satiate
51. More
52. Long time
53. Sweet treat
56. Paper inserts

163

ACROSS

1. Backdoor
7. Well schooled
15. Beach-bound
16. Vanity object
17. Word with "cookie"
18. "Tootsie" thespian: 2 wds.
19. Escape: slang
20. 1692 hot spot
22. Arkansas River hub
23. Tiny change
25. Type flourish
27. Hammer piece
28. Spring locale
30. Goes off?
32. Major choice
33. Be an escort to
35. Pond visitors
37. Experiment with: 2 wds.
39. Souvenirs of Sonora
43. Frames for trams
45. Verb from the pulpit
46. Repeatedly, to bards
49. Joint part
51. Show pain
52. Spread tales
54. Edging device
56. Low stretch
57. A Brown
59. Lab element
61. Enfold
62. Slowly fade
64. Make operable again
66. Selling tactic: 2 wds.
67. Trendy topics
68. Span supports
69. Sans guile

DOWN

1. Junk, for one
2. Intensify
3. Reaction seekers?
4. Pilfer
5. Greek deity
6. Cowgirl Hall of Fame site
7. Presently: 2 wds.
8. Details
9. Craggy rise
10. Give forth
11. Contrive: 2 wds.
12. Nursery buy
13. More clipped
14. Roving
21. Bossed around
24. Virtuous conduct
26. Less plentiful
29. Face
31. Disperse thickly
34. Court guests
36. Quite tasty
38. Cuttlefish feature
40. Put at a disadvantage
41. Surrounded territories
42. Most precipitous
44. Livery boarders
46. End
47. Palate pleaser
48. Cantina order
50. Quaff that may be laced
53. Acquiesces
55. Pad amenity
58. Hutterites, e.g.
60. Relative of Claudius
63. Athlete Bando
65. Artery user

164

ACROSS

1. Paint spreaders
9. In need: 2 wds.
15. Water
16. Panacea
17. Coral or sponge
18. "Casino" costar: 2 wds.
19. Meat source
20. Amalgamate
22. Web sparkler
23. Household moniker
24. Aspen regular: 2 wds.
26. Western capital
27. Walk all over
28. Door adjective
29. Word with "bull"
30. Carped at
32. Hinge (on)
33. Control
34. Organic quality
35. Demur
38. Habitués
42. Lacking respect
43. Asian palm
44. GPS alternative
45. Big motivator
46. False demeanor
47. Club hireling
48. Cap prelude
49. Cliffhanger element
50. Son of Agrippina
51. Klutzy chap: slang
53. Like some old platters
56. Nutritive
57. Roast staple
58. Gainsays
59. Well-versed

DOWN

1. Judges: 2 wds.
2. Bond of sorts
3. Incites
4. Light blows
5. Appalled cry
6. Arrange (tile)
7. Brought about
8. Sowing site
9. Obscure
10. QB Smith
11. Ear splitter?
12. Weather, in a way
13. Train stokers
14. Naughty
21. Vile remarks
24. Verbose power
25. Gold standard?
26. Nancy on the links
29. Cover with 21-Down
31. Cited folks
32. Enjoyed repasts
34. Not to mention: 2 wds.
35. Constrained
36. Luxury material
37. Field event
38. — point
39. Fancy butterfly
40. Recite
41. Twined, as wire
43. Sand strand
46. Lawn parties
49. Linear measure
50. "David," e.g.
52. Honshu tie
54. Tax term
55. Pose

ACROSS

1. Text piece
8. Turns self-conscious
15. Aardvark cafe?
16. Athletic sculpture?: hyph. wd.(slang)
17. Soda flavoring
18. Sans doubt
19. Transpire
20. Pines aloud
21. Nickname on "The Love Boat"
22. Geometry form
23. Saxon emperor
24. Enormous
25. Injures by injustice
28. Calendar keepsake?
29. Winter planting
30. Take in
31. Trunk covers
32. Certain thieves
34. Check out
37. Disgust with excess
38. Bind together
41. "Stifle it!"
42. Bar mitzvah, for example
44. Put to rights
45. Retitle?
46. Hellenic letter
47. Chem-class concern
48. Arctic loper
49. Paving aid
51. Senate paper
53. LPGA founder Hagge
54. Steamed eats
55. Regional hallmarks
56. Driver Jackie
57. Absolutely (against): 2 wds.

DOWN

1. Track lapper: 2 wds.
2. Partial resemblance
3. Mystifying
4. Girdle, e.g.
5. Tries (for)
6. Buoyant mood
7. Main fitting
8. Round caps
9. "The Hobbit" character
10. Sends packing
11. Rare spring
12. Ossifies
13. Pastoral poem
14. O'Hare employees
20. Make way: 2 wds.
23. Almondish?
24. Forget (a date)
26. March celebrants
27. Sargasso denizens
28. Muses (over)
31. Hand (out)
32. Mouse, often
33. Sea churner
34. Generous plays?
35. Go for: 2 wds.
36. Lineage indicator
38. Seasonal duds
39. Summit product?
40. Least economical
42. Most basic
43. Performed a farm task
45. Provision for a fee
48. Lanai wiggle?
49. Swift stream
50. Blackfish
52. Fancy marble
53. *Très* unwise

ACROSS

1. H feature
9. Mesa cliff
15. Thing with a nose
16. Gaslit object
17. Effuses
18. Entomology specimen
19. Give preference
20. Wire measure
22. Nest alert
23. Court reprieve
24. Fiddling aid
26. Computer command
27. Coin of Peru
28. Refined to a fault
30. Strain
31. Figures (out): slang
32. Consequence
34. Secures anew
37. Vamooses
38. Hamper
39. Install again
40. Zip
41. Made hard
43. Word with "hole"

46. Horned herd
48. Storied band
49. Mumbai souvenir
50. Shore flock
52. Fortune
53. Bony sort
54. Namibia neighbor
56. Manumit
58. Cold spot
59. Old ring VIP
60. Flat-fee payer
61. Food fish

DOWN

1. Coo go-with
2. Theater district
3. It's grueling
4. Ragout descriptive
5. Louver piece
6. Night swooper
7. Nursery buys
8. Shows intransigence
9. Lessen
10. Tallow source
11. Groups for coxswains

12. Fan of termites?
13. Germane
14. False fronts
21. Grift basis
24. Well sated
25. Challenging foes
28. Urges on
29. Bounded
31. End of childhood?
33. Coaster kin
34. Raccoon, e.g.
35. Celebrity
36. Ostentatious displays
37. Editorial process
39. Seditious events
42. Building detail
43. Show off
44. Expert spellbinder
45. Natives of Asia
47. Cliquish clan
49. Brief extract
51. Uncultivated fruit
53. Percolate
55. Get rid of
57. Support system?

167

ACROSS

1. Avoid
5. A pop?
9. Party lead-in
14. Essay form
16. Satirical work
17. Certain USPO transfer: 2 wds.
19. Subscribed (to)
20. Improves
21. Contemporary
22. Noble title
23. Heavy steels
26. Desolate
30. Posh growth
31. Badgered
32. Green upright
33. Ardent archer?
34. Treated with viands
35. Lent item
36. Used a flint
37. Plays with bones
38. Sweet and low, musically
39. Fizzled out
41. Kicked up
42. Doughnut adjective
43. Loses vigor
44. Having magnitude only
47. Cinema passage
51. Approach: 4 wds.
53. Compensate (for)
54. Pain-free state
55. Decompression periods
56. Chicago neighbor
57. Good pair at Reno

DOWN

1. Huge
2. Monthly event, to Nero
3. Church topic
4. Rakes more
5. Real heaps: slang
6. Garage can
7. Thespian Diane
8. Bitter stuff
9. Like derbies
10. Bank moorings
11. Hot spot?
12. Cheddar base
13. Pitch controls
15. Petulant
18. Had a bias
22. Passes (out)
23. Beguiling influence
24. Raptor abode
25. Fires
26. Well-ruled?
27. Libra rocks
28. Walk daintily
29. Broke off
31. Almost mashed
34. Bread
35. Garfield, e.g.: 2 wds.
37. Life segments
38. Links kink
40. Unvoiced
41. In an indiscreet manner
43. Long-necked lute
44. Lasting flaw
45. Pigeon place?
46. Entrepreneur Wally
47. Author Sewell
48. Discerning
49. Closely tied (to)
50. Bill passers?
52. Laugh inducer

168

ACROSS

1. Steams up: 2 wds. (slang)
8. Emptied by bailing
15. Landward
16. Vaudeville legend
17. Caved
18. Reads back
19. Troop concern
20. Motel supply
21. Animated
22. Be a huge fan of
23. Blows away: slang
24. Indian Ocean isle
25. Sidewalk establishment
27. Hockey frames
28. Cupel load
29. Groundhog, e.g.
30. Increased by 200%
35. Craft
36. Loan adjective
37. Nape find
38. Extremely zealous
39. Seasonal spells: 2 wds.
45. Fashion buy
46. Flavor, as cider
47. Tank swimmer
48. Prize for Pizarro
49. Lauded sort
50. Batting pick
51. Audited stock
53. Enthralled
54. Minor descriptive
55. Bright flock
56. Convinces
57. Dorm hanging

DOWN

1. Bar none: 3 wds.
2. Make cryptic
3. Undelivered deed, often
4. Fleecing pair
5. Quite a lot
6. Word with "style"
7. Stoked
8. Very calculating
9. Mixer band, perhaps
10. Good excuses: slang
11. Extolling work
12. Sacks
13. Sparks
14. Aversive feeling
20. Tough tissue
23. City section
24. Designer hue
26. Drove obliquely
27. Pen dweller: slang
29. Cheesy layer
30. Hollywood stalwart
31. Rule experts
32. Chapters
33. A Starr
34. Extend
35. Richly detailed
37. — tie
39. Afflicts
40. Pop over: 2 wds.
41. Lading weight: 2 wds.
42. Invader of Gaul
43. Evidenced
44. Least muddled
46. Artery verb
49. Grant
50. "Should I —?"
52. Uncommon pet
53. Nab: slang

ANSWERS

CROSSWORD 1

```
S K I _ A L S _ P A D _
P A I N _ S I N _ L I E S
W O U N D _ I D O _ A D U L T
A R C _ E R A _ B U N _ C U E
S T E R E O _ _ R E V E R E
_ _ I D O L _ A N T I _
S L A B _ F I L L S _ A R M S
E E L _ _ L E O _ _ O A K
W E E K _ S A I N T _ V E R Y
_ _ E R I C _ G A P E _
S W A Y E D _ _ P E T A L S
A A H _ N E T _ F E D _ D O T
T R E A T _ O W L _ A G O N Y
_ S A V E _ W O E _ L O R E
_ D A D _ N O D _ S O N
```

CROSSWORD 2

```
A D O _ T I M _ _ J A B
W A D E _ C H R I S _ S A N E
E V E N _ A R E N T _ T I N T
_ E S T A T E _ T A M A L E
_ E S S A Y _ R U B _
A I R S _ T O E _ G L E E
F U S S E S _ D A M _ E A V E
I T S _ T A P E R E D _ T E D
B O U T _ G E L _ L I K E N S
_ S E A T _ G E M _ V E N T
_ N U T _ D I N E R _
H A N G A R _ N O R M A L
P A C E _ R I L E S _ I R A N
A V I D _ S T O R Y _ T I N A
R E D _ _ A S S _ _ D A B
```

CROSSWORD 3

```
S C A B _ _ G A L _ A L S O
A I L E D _ A L L Y _ T I L L
S T A G E _ H O L E _ L O U D
H E N _ C R A B _ _ H A N G
_ _ R A Y _ E L V E S _
_ W H A L E _ A I M _ S H Y
D R A G _ R I C E _ _ T O O
R O T S _ C O N E S _ T O U R
A T E _ _ H A N D _ W O R K
B E D _ Y E S _ S L I P S
_ W O R T H _ H O G _
P E R U _ O L E O _ T A G
R A V E _ C A P E _ M A R C O
O P E N _ A G E D _ S N A R L
B A S S _ N O S _ _ D Y E D
```

CROSSWORD 4

```
S L A P _ _ C A B _ F E E
M E M O S _ P A L E _ D O L L
U N I T E _ R I P E _ R I S K
G O D _ T H E N _ _ P O L E
_ _ S T A Y _ S H O O _
_ P S A L M _ S K I P P E D
T R A C E _ S W I S S _ E R R
O I N K _ S P U D S _ T R I O
M E T _ C O I N S _ D A I L Y
_ S A I L I N G _ P A N E L
_ R O L E _ L E N S _
F L A G _ G O N G _ J E T
B A I T _ B L A B _ E L U D E
A C M E _ O O Z E _ R A N G E
Y E A _ O W E _ _ S E E N
```

CROSSWORD 5

B	I	G		S	T	E	P		A	L	D	A
A	C	E		A	H	O	Y		G	O	I	N	G
T	E	N		L	I	N	T		R	A	D	I	O	S
		T	H	A	N		H	O	E	D		M	O	P
P	I	L	E	D		M	O	D	E		C	A	S	E
A	V	E	R		P	O	N	D		R	I	L	E	D
G	A	S		S	O	B	S		N	O	T			
E	N	T	R	E	E	S		N	E	W	Y	O	R	K
		E	L	M		M	I	S	S		V	A	N	
S	N	I	F	F		H	U	N	T		W	E	R	E
T	O	N	S		W	I	S	E		T	H	R	E	E
A	S	H		K	A	T	E		B	O	O	T		
B	E	A	T	E	R		U	N	I	T		I	M	P
	S	L	E	P	T		M	A	T	E		M	O	O
	E	A	T	S		S	T	E	M		E	W	E	

CROSSWORD 6

T	O	T	S		A	J	A	R			P	R	O
I	O	W	A	N		P	O	S	E	S		L	A	W
P	H	O	N	E		T	H	I	G	H		A	R	E
		D	E	W		N	A	R	R	A	T	E	D	
	S	P	A	D	E	S		N	E	A	T	E	R	
S	K	I	L	L	E	T	S		T	N	T			
A	I	L		E	D	I	T	S		K	I	T	T	Y
G	L	O	W		S	N	A	P	S		C	A	R	E
A	L	T	A	R		G	R	A	T	E		C	O	N
		S	A	M		E	N	O	R	M	O	U	S	
	R	A	P	P	E	D		S	O	R	E	S	T	
C	O	N	S	I	D	E	R		L	O	T			
R	U	N		D	A	V	I	S		R	A	C	E	D
E	G	O		S	L	I	C	E		S	L	A	V	E
W	H	Y			S	L	O	T			S	W	A	N

CROSSWORD 7

B	A	D			S	P	A				H	I	P
I	T	E	M		C	H	O	R	E		P	A	R	E
N	O	N	E		R	A	N	T	S		A	L	I	T
	M	Y	S	T	E	R	Y		C	A	S	T	S	
		S	E	E	P		W	A	N	T				
	S	T	I	N	K		C	A	P	T	A	I	N
S	T	E	E	D		B	A	R	E	S		G	O	T
P	I	E	R		D	O	R	M	S		B	L	U	R
Y	E	T		T	E	X	A	S		P	E	O	N	Y
	S	H	E	R	B	E	T		S	O	L	O	S	
		N	E	A	R		C	O	O	L				
	S	W	E	E	T		B	U	R	R	I	T	O
S	E	A	M		E	L	A	T	E		E	A	S	T
E	N	V	Y		S	A	L	E	S		S	I	L	O
A	D	E			P	E	R				L	O	P	

CROSSWORD 8

	S	O	S		K	E	G			P	A	L
	T	A	X	I		I	R	A		W	I	D	E
	G	A	Y	E	R		M	E	R	R	I	E	S	T
S	O	L		N	E	R	O		Y	I	P		
I	N	K	S		N	I	N	A		P	E	E	R	S
P	E	S	T	S		D	O	G	S		D	R	O	P
		I	L	L		S	E	L	L		I	D	A	
W	A	R	R	I	O	R		S	O	O	N	E	S	T
A	B	E		T	I	E	S		B	O	A			
D	E	A	L		S	A	M	E		P	I	N	E	D
S	T	R	A	P		D	E	L	I		L	I	A	R
		P	A	W		A	I	D	A		C	R	Y	
T	O	G	E	T	H	E	R		A	N	G	E	L
O	R	A	L		O	N	E		H	E	I	R	
W	E	B		A	D	D		O	W	N			

CROSSWORD 9

```
B E A   S O W   A N D
L A Y S   O A R   C U R L
H A R E S   A T E   O N I O N
I N N   U M P   N O R   E V E
D E S T R O Y   A N D R E W
    H E M   L A S S O
A C H E D   D E S I   C U B A
C O O   S I N K S   S A N
T Y P E   W E D S   C L E A N
    B L I S S   A H A
B A R B E R   S L O G A N S
A X E   S L Y   T A P   R U E
G L A S S   A P E   P R I D E
  E C H O   W E E   E A S E
  H E N   N A P   D Y E
```

CROSSWORD 10

```
R E A P   B O U T   M A D
Y A L E   H O U S E   C O N E
E V E R   E N T E R   H O N E
  E X H A L E   D R A I N E D
    A S P     A I M
E L A P S E D   S C R E A M
P I G S   R I F L E   S P A R
I K E   V I E   R I O
C E N T   C A R E T   T I N A
  S T O N E S   P E D A L E D
    W I N     N A B
A C C E P T S   C A B L E S
R O A R   R O M A N   E X A M
E A R S   A D A P T   T I N E
A L L   L A T E   S T E W
```

CROSSWORD 11

```
B U N   F A R M   P U C K
A L T O   I D E A   A R R O W
G O A T   G A S P   S N A R E
O T H E R   M I L L S   M E L
  S U B   G E E   O P A L
E L F   T O W N   G A L
L A R K   B A S H   R E S T S
L I O N E S S   A L C O H O L
A R M O R   P A R E   S U R E
  B A H   V E E R   T E D
C A T S   I V E   S A W
A L E   S M A R T   W I N G S
L I N D A   P A I L   T I R E
M A S O N   O G L E   C L A W
  S E E K   R E E D   H E Y
```

CROSSWORD 12

```
A B L E   S O R T   E J E C T
L O A N   O H I O   M O V I E
P A N T   N O O N   B E E T S
S T A I R   T E A R   N E T
    C A R P   S L A B
C H E E T A H S   S C R A M S
O U R   S H O W S   E A S E L
I R A N   S T I L T   D I N E
L O S E S   O M A H A   D U E
S N E A K S   S P A R S E S T
    T A K E   S W A T
D A M   T I L L   B E G I N
U N I T E   B O D Y   E L S E
O T T E R   O B O E   R U L E
S I T E S   W E T S   S E E D
```

344

CROSSWORD 13

```
LANDS   BROW   SWAB
AWAIT   LIMA   COLE
TAMPA   AGED   OVEN
IRE  YAM  NEGLECT
NEST  REF  DAD
    IRISES  PETAL
DRAMAS  DUG  DONE
EAT GEM MOW   ITS
AVOW NOT  TABLES
REPEL PANTRY
   TIC  BEE  EACH
PHANTOM  ANY  WOE
RICE  BOAR  ABOVE
ODES  RAIL  RAKED
MESS  ANDY  DRESS
```

CROSSWORD 14

```
BIG    DID   SAD
ARE  NICE  OPEN
TON  AMEN  LEWIS
 NERVE   LID  NOS
 ROY  RAID  SEAT
GROW  HOSE  RISKY
YOU  PUSH  AIL
MESSAGE  DIPLOMA
 HUE  LODE   PAR
STOOL  MINE  PEEK
HOBO  CAPS  TAR
YEA  FOR  RADAR
 SMELL  LOOM  TOO
 AWED  OWLS   OLD
 EDS  TEL   RED
```

CROSSWORD 15

```
LASS   HATS   CHAT
OCEAN  ARIA  HERO
SHAME  LONG  RAMP
TEN WHOM   OILY
  LEI  ACIDS
 GRASPS  IDO   PIT
ALERT  ACTOR  HOE
WORD  SNAIL  HOWL
AVA  SPINE  CANAL
YEN  NUT  STEVEN
  MARYS  ADE
 GRIP   TUNA  BAD
REIN  STAG  RAISE
INTO  PULL  SATIN
BEER  ABLY   HEAT
```

CROSSWORD 16

```
 ILL  POE   CAB
 KNEE  RID  ANEW
SIDES  ELI  STRAW
ALI SAY TOT  EVA
PLACES  SALUTES
  UNITS  KEG
VERB  ARTS  SHAPE
IRA  NIECE   DAN
ARMED  MEAL  MOLD
 ORE  DROVE
MANNERS   POTATO
ABE  SEA  KEY  MAN
PEALS  VAN  ALONE
 TREE  EGO  GONG
 SOS  SET  EGG
```

CROSSWORD 17

```
S T A R S ■ O R A L ■ Z O N E
C A R O L ■ R O D E ■ E V I L
A L I B I ■ G U S T ■ R A C K
B E D ■ D R A G ■ F O L K S ■
■ ■ L I O N E S S E S ■ ■ ■
A S C E N T ■ M O E ■ B A A
S W U N G ■ G R A B ■ A R M S
H E R D ■ S O U L S ■ G A B S
E E L S ■ N O E L ■ T I T L E
S P Y ■ H I S ■ S U N S E T ■
■ ■ R E P E A T I N G ■ ■ ■
O C C U R ■ D A R N ■ R I M
A L A N ■ H A M S ■ E L U D E
R U S T ■ A L I T ■ L A D L E
S E E S ■ D A T E ■ S W E E T
```

CROSSWORD 18

```
H O P ■ ■ S H E ■ ■ M O B
A X E ■ T O U C H ■ A W E
Y E T ■ S O O T H E D ■ T N T
■ N E W T O N ■ O L I V E S ■
■ R O O T ■ ■ P E A S ■
■ O W E D ■ B E S S ■
T A P S ■ D I N E R ■ E A R S
W H O ■ ■ V A T ■ ■ T I E
O A T S ■ P A T T Y ■ M E O W
■ T E A S ■ Y A L E ■
■ F I R S ■ ■ C O M B ■
■ M E R I T S ■ T H R O A T
N O W ■ C O M P E T E ■ R O D
A P E ■ R U I N S ■ B O A
P E R ■ ■ G E T ■ ■ S L Y
```

CROSSWORD 19

```
L O A F ■ T W I N ■ ■ L A P
E L L A ■ B R A V O ■ B A L E
F E A R ■ A I R E D ■ O V E R
T O M ■ G N A T ■ B O A S T
■ S O C I A L ■ B I A S ■
■ A N N ■ S E N D ■ W E E
H A R P ■ A W N I N G ■ I D A
I V I E S ■ H O G ■ E A S E S
K I D ■ T R I B E S ■ R E N T
E V E ■ R U N S ■ C U E ■
■ B A B E ■ S E S A M E
A L L E Y ■ V I N E ■ I M P
L O I S ■ A G I L E ■ O N C E
D O N T ■ D U C K S ■ F E E T
A P T ■ D Y E S ■ ■ F R E E
```

CROSSWORD 20

```
G A L ■ ■ P A W ■ ■ B U T
U T A H ■ M O S E S ■ S U R E
N O T E ■ U P S E T ■ P O N D
■ M E D A L ■ D E C O Y S ■
■ G L E A M ■ P R O ■
D U E L ■ R I P ■ E L M S
B A N S ■ T E X A N S ■ A L P
A R C ■ B E N ■ R U T ■ G E E
G E L ■ R E A G A N ■ V I E W
D E S I ■ S O D ■ N E C K
■ A N D ■ D E M O N ■
■ L I N E R S ■ I R I S H
C A R D ■ I T E M S ■ C L I P
O K A Y ■ P O R E S ■ E A V E
P E N ■ ■ P A N ■ ■ B E G
```

CROSSWORD 21

```
GRIEF LADY  ACTS
LOCAL ERIE  NOAH
OPERA AIMS  NOPE
WED MOPS   JOKED
  BID ESSAY
MARINES CAW ALS
ALONG PARIS DOE
JOBS LACED POSE
OHO RENEW CURED
RAT INK SCORERS
  BLAST OUR
ANNIE ATOP REF
SEEN TAXI LEAVE
PROD AGED EAGER
SONS BODY STERN
```

CROSSWORD 22

```
SLAT ISLE COD
STAIR STAY LIAR
PANDA SOME ANNE
OLD PLUMP BIKED
TEST YEA TIM
  HUE CRIB PAD
SALEM THEN POLO
EXAMPLE EERIEST
ELSE EARL ALTOS
PET FARE EWE
  IRK LED SAWS
DANNY FALSE LIP
AVID CITE AWARE
BONE ALEC CORED
WAX REST HEMS
```

CROSSWORD 23

```
MOW ARK LID
AIDA DON ARAB
MINDS OWE GENES
ADE HIP WAG CAT
RESPECT REMEDY
ARE SLIDE
PAIRS FLEA WISH
ASK LOANS DUO
THEY AUTO STONE
AMPLE BEE
BLAMES LULLABY
AAH LEG AYE ROE
TREAT EBB CROWN
DAVE RYE TAMS
DAD MEL SPA
```

CROSSWORD 24

```
SPAT ACHE SOS
ELBOW WAIL MIST
TEETH ANTE OGLE
SAT IRIS MINNOW
KNIT CENT
TREND PONCHOS
WEEPY BOOTH BAD
EXIT BOWLS SALE
TAG PARES SIMON
SNEAKER SEDAN
AGES PANE
SOFTER LADS GAP
ABLE IVAN ERASE
MOON EONS DAVIS
SEW SWAY NEAT
```

CROSSWORD 25

```
C R U D E ■ S M O G ■ E D G E
R E R U N ■ I O W A ■ F R O G
A N G E R ■ L I L Y ■ F A N G
M O E ■ A D O S ■ L O B E S
■ ■ E G O ■ T A P E R ■ ■
S C R E E C H ■ T E E T E R S
C H I L D ■ A L T A R ■ L E E
O I L S ■ S N E A K ■ S A G A
O N E ■ M U S I C ■ P E T A L
T A D P O L E ■ K E R N E L S
■ ■ A N K L E ■ V E T ■ ■
S P A R K ■ R E A P ■ F L U
H A V E ■ A B E L ■ A D I O S
O P E N ■ R A C K ■ R I N S E
P A R T ■ M A T S ■ E N D E D
```

CROSSWORD 26

```
■ B E G A N ■ N U T ■ P O W
P A L A C E S ■ A N Y ■ I R A
A R A B I A N ■ T I P T O E D
I T S ■ D R A G ■ T E E N ■
N E T S ■ S K I E S ■ L E T S
T R I C K ■ E R R ■ S L E E P
■ S C O O P ■ L I S T ■ R A Y
■ ■ T R E K ■ C O A T ■ ■
W A S ■ E P I C ■ B R E E D ■
E X T R A ■ N A B ■ T A M E R
B E A U ■ S K I L L ■ M E M O
■ L I F T ■ N E E D ■ R O B
A V E N U E S ■ A G I T A T E
H A S ■ S E A ■ T A M A L E S
A N T ■ S L Y ■ L E N D S
```

CROSSWORD 27

```
S C A R S ■ T I C S ■ R I P E
A R G U E ■ E L L A ■ E D E N
L A R G E ■ A L A N ■ S L E D
A T E ■ S A P ■ P E S T E R S
D E E R ■ R O D ■ R I O ■
■ ■ U N I T E S ■ T R O T S
P I A N O S ■ L I E ■ E V I L
A N N ■ D E F I N E S ■ E L I
S T E M ■ N A G ■ R O A R E D
S O W E D ■ T H R I L L ■
■ ■ T I E ■ T O E ■ A S H E
G A T H E R S ■ D R Y ■ P I N
O H I O ■ R O M E ■ A P A R T
L O R D ■ O L E O ■ W I D E R
D Y E S ■ R O T S ■ N E E D Y
```

CROSSWORD 28

```
H A M ■ A D S ■ ■ C A M E R A
A L I ■ V I A ■ ■ O M E L E T
Y E L L I N G ■ S P I N A C H
■ D I V E ■ H O E D ■ T E E
I T E M ■ S T A N D ■ F I N N
N O S E S ■ R I G ■ S L O T S
N O T ■ P A I L ■ T H A N ■
■ ■ H A L O ■ B O O T ■ ■
■ H A R P ■ G A P E ■ S H E
S N O R E ■ R I B ■ S C O U R
T E N D ■ L I V E S ■ L A T E
A W E ■ V A N E ■ A J A R ■
R E S P O N D ■ P I A N I S T
E S T A T E ■ E L M ■ N U N
S T Y L E S ■ A S S ■ G E T
```

CROSSWORD 29

B	R	E	W			R	U	B			A	T	O	P
E	A	V	E		M	A	R	R	Y		L	A	V	A
A	G	E	D		A	N	N	I	E		A	M	E	N
	E	N	D	I	N	G		G	A	R	D	E	N	
		I	V	Y		S	H	R	E	D				
S	H	I	N	E		W	I	T		P	I	L	O	T
L	O	N	G		Y	A	P		V	E	N	I	C	E
A	N	D		K	E	Y		G	A	L		T	E	N
N	O	I	S	E	S		R	A	T		M	E	A	T
T	R	A	C	E		B	A	G		W	A	R	N	S
		O	P	R	A	H		G	I	N				
	C	L	O	S	E	R		A	U	G	U	S	T	
M	O	A	T		A	G	O	N	Y		A	L	I	T
O	N	C	E		L	E	A	D	S		L	I	M	A
B	E	E	R			S	K	Y		S	T	E	P	

CROSSWORD 30

K	I	T			H	O	G			L	O	S
I	R	O	N		O	D	E	S		A	U	N	T
D	A	R	E		N	O	E	L		S	T	A	R	S
	N	E	A	T	E	R		U	G	H		R	U	E
		R	O	Y		E	R	A		A	L	E	X
L	O	B	B	Y		L	A	S	S	E	S	
A	W	A	Y		N	O	R		P	A	P	E	R
P	E	R		P	A	W		B	E	T		D	U	G
	D	E	B	U	T		W	E	D		H	I	D	E
	U	N	I	T	E	D		H	O	T	E	L
F	A	C	T		V	I	E		G	E	M
I	D	A		B	E	N		B	E	R	E	T	S
B	A	N	J	O		E	A	R	N		R	O	A	M
M	O	A	N		S	C	A	T		S	O	F	A
	E	Y	E		E	D	S		T	E	D

CROSSWORD 31

W	O	R	E		T	I	E	R		D	R	U	M
B	A	R	O	N		A	C	R	E		E	A	S	E
A	N	G	E	L		V	E	I	N		F	R	E	E
Y	E	A		A	P	E		E	E	R	I	E	S	T
	S	N	O	R	E	R	S		W	I	N	
	A	G	E	N	T	S		M	E	O	W	S
B	A	R	R	E	L		R	O	W		D	R	O	P
A	R	E		D	E	C	I	D	E	D		A	V	A
T	I	E	D		D	A	D		T	E	L	L	E	R
S	A	F	E	R		B	E	E	T	L	E	
	F	A	D		S	L	E	I	G	H	S
S	H	A	R	P	E	N		A	R	C		O	H	O
T	A	C	O		S	O	F	T		A	R	R	O	W
A	R	T	S		K	N	E	E		T	A	S	T	E
B	E	S	T		S	E	E	D		E	W	E	S

CROSSWORD 32

S	C	A	B			C	H	I	N			H	E	Y
T	O	T	A	L		L	E	N	O		C	O	L	E
A	L	O	H	A		I	R	K	S		H	O	S	T
Y	A	M		D	O	M	E			S	I	T	E
		S	L	A	B		W	A	I	L	
	S	W	E	E	T		B	E	L	G	I	U	M
A	C	H	E	S		F	L	A	S	H		S	O	S
P	R	O	P		C	A	I	R	O		B	U	M	P
T	E	L		S	O	N	N	Y		D	R	A	M	A
	W	E	D	L	O	C	K		D	A	I	L	Y
	E	A	S	Y		F	O	R	M	
	C	A	M	P		S	I	G	N		D	A	N
H	O	B	O		L	I	A	R		E	R	A	S	E
O	M	E	N		A	C	N	E		D	A	V	I	S
W	E	T			B	Y	E	S		N	E	A	T

349

CROSSWORD 33

```
BAR    HIP      PAY
DAVID  ARAB  SAVE
ELOPE  NERO  TWIN
NEW  PEG  ERRAND
   FOG    RAG
  PHOTOS  MOMENT
PLEAS  THAWS  OIL
ROLL  VEILS  MORE
OWL  GEESE  BASED
 SOARED  SALTED
  MAR    DOT
 RABBIS  DON  BAA
SELL  NINA  DROLL
ANTE  GLOW  SEALS
MOO    OWN    FRY
```

CROSSWORD 34

```
 FED      TAB
 POLES   CHIRP
DARKENS LOUDEST
AGE  PONDERS  WAR
MESS  BOONE  RELY
 STOP  RED  GERM
 SOLVES  ANTS
  NEED  CHAR
 BEAT  GRATES
 BUST  POE  SACK
LIFT  ROADS  TANS
ELF  DIRTIER  TEA
ELEMENT TWEETED
 STANK  NAVEL
 SPY      PAR
```

CROSSWORD 35

```
ASK    SEE      BOA
DIET  ALONE  SOUR
ENVY  LANDS  PARK
SKILLETS  KNITS
 SNEERS  DIAL
  ROT  GAMBLERS
ABE   FIDO  EXIT
HERB  CORDS  DALE
EARL  HOLY   MEW
MUSICALS  GAB
 SUNS  CARESS
 OFTEN COMMENTS
ABLE  ELUDE  POOL
DEER  LOBES  SOLO
DYE    GAS    PEW
```

CROSSWORD 36

```
DEW    PAT      PAL
IVAN  RIO   SIRE
GIVES  ORE  SHEET
 LEAPED  SAHARA
 DRUG    LIPS
 EDGY   CAPE
REAR  SAGAS  SAND
OLD    ROB    LEI
DISC  IDOLS  CITE
 ANNS  ECHO
 ERIC    AIMS
TROPHY  ENTICE
HURLS  EVE  SCOTS
ONES   AIL   SUCH
PAD    HAS    THE
```

CROSSWORD 37

```
T U B       A S H
I R A       B E E
  C E N T S   L E A N S
I L L   S O L   E L M   W I T
T O U R   N A G S     M I K E
S T E A M   M O S S   A M E N
  S T I R   T E P E E S
      T I C   N O D
    B O T T O M   T E N D
W H O A   A L E S   N U R S E
H O O K     U T A H   T E A R
Y E S   T O M   S E T   A T E
    T W A I N   H I R E D
      A L L     R I B
      S L Y     S O B
```

CROSSWORD 38

```
O A T H S   S K I P   M E M O
G R O A N   L O D E   O V E N
L I N D A   I R A N   D E A L
E D S   R O M E     B E N N Y
        F L U   A C T O R
O M E L E T S   L I O N E S S
L I V E D   O D O R S   L I E
I D E A   A R I S E   W A R N
V A N   S C E N E   C I T E D
E S T A T E S   R E O P E N S
        D U S T S   A Y E
C O L O N   H E R O   W H O
A V E R   A V I V   T R I E D
G E N E   L I N E   E A S E D
E R A S   P E E R   S H E D S
```

CROSSWORD 39

```
M I S S     P A P A   S L U G
A T O P   S O R E R   L A N E
S C A R   U T T E R   E D I T
S H R I M P   S L O W E S T
    N A P S   S W A T
  A C T I O N S   S L I C E S
F I R   D R A P E   K N E L T
A D A M   T R E N D   G A V E
R E B E L   E A T E N   S I P
E S S A Y S   R E S I D E S
    T E A M   R I C E
  B O B S L E D   R E N T A L
L A V A   A R O S E   I O W A
O R A L   M I N U S   A N E W
W E L L   I T E M   L E S S
```

CROSSWORD 40

```
P E G     L A B     A V A
E X A M   G A S E S   L I E D
W I P E   R I P E N   A D E S
  T E L L E R   F O N D E R
    O A T     O I L
  B A D G E S   A P P E A R
T O N Y   L O B B Y   S N O B
I R K     R I O     G A Y
E E L S   A R G U E   M E R E
  D E P U T Y   T A P E R S
    A S H     S A T
  S T R E E T   C I N E M A
M A R E   N O B L E   R A I D
A V I D   S M E A R   S I D E
P E P     S E W     D A N
```

CROSSWORD 41

N	I	N	J	A	■	S	P	U	R	■	F	A	D	S
O	C	C	U	R	■	L	A	K	E	■	A	L	O	T
R	E	I	T	E	R	A	T	E	D	■	I	O	W	A
A	S	S	■	A	O	N	E	■	E	S	T	H	E	R
■	D	R	U	G	■	A	S	P	H	A	L	T		
A	L	L	O	U	T	■	B	I	A	S	■			
B	E	I	N	G	■	A	L	I	G	N	■	T	E	E
C	A	R	E	■	H	A	Y	D	N	■	D	R	A	W
S	P	A	■	P	U	R	E	E	■	R	E	E	S	E
■	D	E	M	O	■	M	E	E	K	E	R			
A	R	T	I	S	A	N	■	D	E	P	P	■		
N	E	U	R	O	N	■	L	I	A	R	■	A	L	A
G	E	N	E	■	I	D	E	N	T	I	F	I	E	S
E	V	E	S	■	T	I	N	A	■	S	I	N	A	I
L	E	S	T	■	Y	E	A	H	■	E	X	T	R	A

CROSSWORD 42

K	I	M	■	■	R	A	G
I	R	O	N	■	R	O	M	A
N	A	V	Y	■	E	S	P	Y
E	E	K	■	N	E	M	E	S	I	S	■	B	B	S
B	E	N	T	■	S	P	R	E	E	■	P	O	R	E
B	L	O	O	D	■	H	A	L	■	E	R	N	I	E
S	T	R	I	P	S	■	L	U	R	I	N	G
O	N	O	■	M	O	M
M	I	N	G	L	E	■	U	P	D	A	T	E
D	U	S	T	Y	■	J	A	R	■	E	R	E	C	T
O	S	L	O	■	H	E	R	B	S	■	Y	A	R	N
C	E	E	■	L	U	C	I	A	N	O	■	R	U	T
M	A	R	T	■	N	A	P	S
A	I	L	S	■	E	R	I	K
E	R	S	■	L	E	I

CROSSWORD 43

K	E	Y	■	E	S	S	A	Y	■	S	E	D	A	N
O	L	E	■	S	T	O	V	E	■	U	S	A	G	E
A	L	L	■	P	E	R	I	W	I	N	K	L	E	S
L	I	L	T	■	R	E	D	■	S	L	I	E	S	T
A	S	S	U	M	E	S	■	T	R	A	M	■		
■	■	B	O	O	■	D	I	A	M	O	N	D	S	
S	C	R	A	P	■	J	U	L	E	P	■	O	O	H
L	O	I	S	■	Q	U	E	L	L	■	S	O	S	A
O	A	T	■	S	U	I	T	S	■	L	I	N	E	D
P	L	A	S	T	I	C	S	■	S	O	X	■		
■	■	L	A	C	Y	■	S	E	T	T	L	E	D	
A	M	B	U	S	H	■	A	I	R	■	H	O	N	E
C	O	L	D	H	E	A	R	T	E	D	■	A	N	N
R	O	U	G	E	■	D	I	A	N	A	■	T	U	T
E	R	R	E	D	■	D	A	R	E	D	■	H	I	S

CROSSWORD 44

A	V	E	R	S	■	S	O	P	S	■	I	L	L	S
R	E	V	U	E	■	C	A	A	N	■	N	O	A	H
C	R	A	M	P	■	O	H	N	O	■	L	A	N	E
E	N	D	■	T	U	T	U	■	R	W	A	N	D	A
D	E	E	P	E	S	T	■	S	K	E	W	■		
■	■	U	T	E	■	B	E	E	R	■	A	B	S	
C	R	E	S	S	■	C	Y	C	L	E	■	H	U	E
L	A	D	S	■	N	E	W	T	S	■	C	E	L	T
O	V	A	■	T	U	N	A	S	■	B	O	M	B	S
G	E	M	■	A	R	T	Y	■	S	I	D	■		
■	■	O	R	T	S	■	W	A	G	E	R	E	D	
N	A	S	S	A	U	■	A	R	L	O	■	A	D	O
E	M	M	A	■	R	A	R	E	■	T	A	C	I	T
A	M	O	K	■	E	G	G	S	■	E	L	E	C	T
T	O	G	A	■	S	O	O	T	■	D	I	R	T	Y

CROSSWORD 45

W	I	D	T	H		P	O	P	E	S		B	R	A
A	D	I	E	U		A	L	O	N	E		R	I	B
R	E	A	L	M		P	I	N	S	T	R	I	P	E
P	A	L	E		W	A	V	Y		T	E	N	E	T
		P	H	A	S	E		R	E	I	G	N	S	
N	A	T	H	A	N			T	E	E	N			
A	F	O	O	T		H	E	R	A		C	A	D	S
G	R	I	N		R	E	M	A	P		A	G	U	E
S	O	L	E		E	A	S	Y		G	R	O	P	E
		C	H	E	R			D	A	N	G	E	R	
A	S	S	A	I	L		P	A	U	L	A			
S	T	A	L	K		D	A	S	H		T	H	A	W
S	I	L	L	I	N	E	S	S		T	I	A	R	A
E	L	L		N	O	L	T	E		S	O	L	A	R
S	L	Y		G	R	E	A	T		K	N	O	B	S

CROSSWORD 46

G	O	A	L	S		G	Y	R	O		I	C	E	D
U	P	S	E	T		L	U	A	U		D	A	T	A
L	A	T	T	E		E	M	E	R	G	E	N	C	Y
F	L	O		E	T	N	A			O	A	T	H	S
		S	P	U	N		O	V	A	L				
D	O	G	L	E	G		S	A	D	S	A	C	K	
E	R	R	O	R		F	A	C	T	S		R	A	N
B	L	O	W		A	V	A			M	E	R	E	
R	O	W		F	I	L	E	R		R	E	N	E	E
A	N	S	W	E	R	S		D	E	L	A	Y	S	
		A	L	E	E		Q	U	I	D				
A	T	A	L	L		B	U	D	S		K	I	D	
T	I	C	T	A	C	T	O	E		S	I	N	G	E
A	N	N	E		O	O	Z	E		U	N	I	O	N
D	Y	E	R		D	O	O	R		E	N	T	R	Y

CROSSWORD 47

B	A	R	D		S	E	L	M	A		C	H	U	G
A	L	O	E		T	R	E	A	T		E	A	R	L
L	U	M	P		A	R	E	N	T		L	I	N	E
I	M	P	O	S	T	O	R		A	V	E	R	S	E
		S	A	U	L		S	C	A	B				
C	L	A	I	M	S		P	A	K	I	S	T	A	N
R	E	N	T		K	A	R	E	N		O	N	E	
E	A	T	S		V	I	C	A	R		E	D	G	E
P	S	I		N	I	N	T	H		V	O	I	D	
E	T	C	H	I	N	G	S		C	H	A	S	E	S
		A	L	E	S		F	A	I	L				
N	U	T	M	E	G		M	U	R	M	U	R	E	D
O	R	A	L		A	B	O	D	E		A	I	R	Y
O	G	R	E		R	I	N	G	S		T	O	M	E
K	E	P	T		Y	O	K	E	S		E	T	A	S

CROSSWORD 48

S	A	L	S	A		S	H	A	V	E		E	L	F
O	C	E	A	N		C	A	B	I	N		L	E	I
C	H	O	W	D	E	R	H	E	A	D		L	A	S
K	E	N		P	E	A			I	R	I	S	H	
		B	R	E	W		D	Y	N	A	S	T	Y	
D	E	G	R	E	E		R	O	U	G	E			
A	D	L	I	B		W	H	I	M	S		L	A	B
S	N	U	G		V	I	O	L	A		F	A	R	E
H	A	M		G	I	D	D	Y		T	R	I	T	E
		P	A	S	T	E		K	E	E	N	E	R	
D	E	B	O	R	A	H		T	I	E	D			
A	V	O	I	D		C	A	W			H	I	S	
L	E	G		N	O	N	E	X	I	S	T	E	N	T
E	R	E		E	V	A	D	E		H	O	R	N	E
S	T	Y		R	A	G	E	D		Y	E	A	S	T

CROSSWORD 49

```
A L E C   Z E A L   A B B A
L I M O   E Y R E   F E E L S
I N E P T N E S S   T R A I T
K E N Y A   T O T S   T U B A
E N D   P I O N E E R   G I N
      Z E R O   R E E S E
T E R I   A T E   P A U S E D
A L I N E   H E W   R E T R O
T I N G L Y   K I M   D E N T
    T Y L E R   S A T E
P S I   A N O T H E R   B A A
L A N K   S N O B   E A R N S
U N T I E   A N O N Y M I T Y
S T I L L   L E N O   E D I E
  A N T S   D R E W   N E S T
```

CROSSWORD 50

```
E R R S   S T R A W   T I P
R O O T   A R O M A   O D E S
I M P E R S O N A L   L O L A
K E E N E S T   S K I L L E T
    O U I     S E R B
S R O   S E E D   D O O D A D
L A D I E S M A N   N O R S E
A N O N   T I M E R   T O O T
T O R C H   T E L E P H O N E
E N S U E D   S L U R   P E R
    B E E P     N U T
A L F A L F A   S I D E C A R
P O E T   O B L I T E R A T E
T O T O   G L A R E   S L O B
  P A R   S O W E D   E L M S
```

CROSSWORD 51

```
S K I S   S O F A   S M A S H
C A R T   P L O T   H E L L O
A R E A   I D E S   E L V E S
M A N I A C   S E L L   A W E
S T E N C I L   A I L S
      S H E A F   T A L E N T
S E W   E S S A Y   C A R O M
P R O P   T E X A N   V A N E
A L O H A   R E C A P   S O N
R E L I S H   S H R E W
      S O U L   T R A I N E E
A S H   C H A D   A S T E R S
S C I F I   M O S T   H E N S
K O R E A   B R I E   E D I E
S T E E L   S A S S   R Y E S
```

CROSSWORD 52

```
E L S A   S P A T E   G R A M
G U N S   O A S I S   R O B E
G L U T   B Y T E S   O M I T
S U B U R B   A D E Q U A T E
      T E E S     N U N
A T T E N D T O   C I D E R S
M A R L O   I N L E T   V E E
O B E Y   A N T I S   W A S P
N O S   V I T A L   R A D I I
G O S P E L   P A S A D E N A
    R A M   C A S E
I N S O L E N T   T H I R S T
S E E M   N O I S Y   N O A H
L I M O   T E N O R   T O G A
E L I S   S L E D S   O M E N
```

354

CROSSWORD 53

```
      P I E     R A P
      T O O L   O G L E
      P R U N E   T R Y S T
    H E I R   C L U E   S O P
H A R M   A T O N E   N O T
A R I   A C R I D   C H I L I
T E L E T H O N   D E U C E S
    L O O N   B O D E
A P O L L O   A L L E Y W A Y
F A T A L   G R E E D   H I E
T N T   B L I N D   W I M P
    T E N   L A D D   D O N S
      R A D A R   S M O K Y
      G A M E   I O U S
      B E D   N O G
```

CROSSWORD 54

```
              P O E
            P I K E R
          C H A R L I E
        D I A N A   G A L
        T O R S O   S H R E K
        T R U C E   O U T L I N E
A R U B A   D A I L Y   O A K
D U S T   P U T T Y   A C T I
S E T   C A C H E   T A K E N
R E W O R K S   S I R E N
    D E L E S   S C R O D
      B A N   S H E E N
        S T R A I N S
        S A I N T
          E D S
```

CROSSWORD 55

```
P U S S   S P R E E   A S P S
I S L E   P R I G S   S W A T
S E A R   R O B O T   S A T E
A R M A D A     H E I G H T
    P U N   P E E L S
B A D E G G   H E R I T A G E
A L I     N O R   Z E B R A
L O V E S   O B I   A D I O S
E N A C T   L I E     D O E
S E N O R I T A   M O D E M S
    N U D E S   A N Y
C O Y O T E     S E E S A W
O V U M   A N T E S   I N C H
D A L I   L E A V E   N O M E
A L E C   S E X E S   G W E N
```

CROSSWORD 56

```
A P E R   G A M M A   S T A N
D E M I   I V I E S   T A L E
D R A G   V E N T S   U S E S
S U N   T E R I   W A K E S
    C H R I S   D Y E R
O H I O A N   H E A R T E N
R E P L Y   T A B L E   G I G
S L A Y   A E R I E   L O C O
O P T   A V A S T   N A C H O
    S E L F I S H   C A R E E N
      E A V E   H A Y D N
E D G A R   F I R S   T R A
P O O R   S W I N G   E R I N
I V A N   L E T G O   R I C E
C E L T   Y E S E S   S C O W
```

CROSSWORD 57

I	C	E	S	■	R	A	P	I	D	■	C	H	A	T
N	I	C	E	■	O	B	E	S	E	■	O	U	C	H
D	A	R	T	■	D	E	C	A	L	■	O	G	R	E
Y	O	U	T	H	■	K	A	T	H	L	E	E	N	
■	■	L	I	R	A	■	C	A	A	N	■	■		
A	L	O	E	V	E	R	A	■	S	H	E	A	T	H
L	O	W	■	E	D	I	T	H	■	A	S	T	R	O
A	G	E	S	■	S	E	T	U	P	■	S	L	I	T
M	O	N	T	E	■	S	I	M	O	N	■	A	T	E
O	N	S	I	T	E	■	C	A	R	O	U	S	E	L
■	■	P	O	P	E	■	N	E	O	N	■	■		
L	O	V	E	N	O	T	E	■	K	E	E	L	S	
A	L	A	N	■	C	H	U	T	E	■	V	I	A	L
S	E	N	D	■	H	E	R	O	N	■	E	R	M	A
T	O	S	S	■	S	L	O	W	S	■	N	E	A	T

CROSSWORD 58

C	R	O	P	■	I	M	A	G	E	■	C	O	R	D
H	O	P	I	■	N	I	C	E	R	■	O	D	I	E
O	V	E	N	■	V	E	I	N	S	■	L	O	L	A
W	E	N	T	■	E	N	D	E	A	V	O	R	E	D
■	■	S	A	R	I	■	S	T	A	G	■	■		
A	C	E	■	U	G	L	Y	■	Z	I	N	N	I	A
S	O	S	■	B	L	E	A	K	■	N	E	E	D	S
O	R	A	L	■	E	A	R	N	S	■	S	W	A	Y
N	A	M	E	S	■	K	N	O	T	S	■	S	H	E
E	L	E	C	T	S	■	S	W	A	P	■	L	O	T
■	■	T	I	N	G	■	R	A	V	E	■	■		
N	A	T	U	R	A	L	I	S	T	■	I	T	C	H
A	J	A	R	■	F	I	N	A	L	■	S	T	A	Y
N	A	P	E	■	U	N	C	L	E	■	T	E	N	D
A	X	E	S	■	S	T	A	T	S	■	A	R	T	E

CROSSWORD 59

P	E	R	M	■	S	A	Y	■	S	L	A	V		
A	R	E	A	■	P	E	D	A	L	■	T	A	K	E
T	I	N	T	■	S	N	O	W	Y	■	E	M	I	T
S	E	E	T	O	I	T	■	N	E	A	T	E	N	S
■	■	H	I	S	■	T	E	S	T	S	■	■		
■	A	B	E	L	■	K	I	D	■	B	O	A	R	
C	R	E	W	■	D	I	E	■	H	A	N	G	A	R
A	I	R	■	T	U	T	■	B	U	Y	■	I	V	Y
P	A	R	I	S	H	■	L	E	G	■	G	L	E	E
■	S	A	R	A	■	F	I	N	■	T	E	E	N	
■	■	A	R	N	A	Z	■	P	E	N	■	■		
T	R	A	N	S	O	M	■	T	U	X	E	D	O	S
H	I	F	I	■	R	I	V	E	T	■	R	O	S	E
I	D	E	A	■	A	L	I	A	S	■	I	D	L	E
S	E	W	N	■	Y	A	M	■	C	O	O	P		

CROSSWORD 60

Y	E	T	I	■	E	S	S	A	Y	■	A	F	R	O
A	P	E	S	■	N	I	T	R	O	■	L	A	I	R
R	E	A	R	■	S	P	U	R	N	■	E	L	S	A
D	E	R	A	I	L	■	B	O	D	Y	■	L	E	N
■	■	E	T	A	■	W	E	E	D	I	N	G		
S	E	A	L	E	V	E	L	■	R	A	I	N		
O	D	D	■	M	E	T	E	S	■	H	E	L	L	O
D	I	V	E	■	S	N	A	P	S	■	T	O	A	D
S	T	I	L	L	■	A	S	I	A	N	■	V	I	E
■	S	K	I	S	■	E	N	L	I	V	E	N	S	
D	R	E	S	S	U	P	■	A	L	A	■	■		
R	I	M	■	A	R	L	O	■	R	E	L	I	E	S
A	G	E	D	■	F	U	N	G	I	■	I	O	W	A
M	O	N	A	■	E	M	C	E	E	■	S	T	E	W
A	R	T	Y	■	R	E	E	L	S	■	E	A	R	S

CROSSWORD 61

T	A	B		S	T	E	A	L		I	S	L	E	S
A	W	E		T	O	S	C	A		V	I	O	L	A
D	O	G		I	M	P	R	U	D	E	N	T	L	Y
A	L	I	E	N	S		O	R	E	S		T	I	N
		N	O	G		S	N	A	G		S	O	S	O
L	Y	N	N		T	H	Y		R	I	P			
O	U	I		A	H	E	M		A	R	O	M	A	S
A	M	N	E	S	I	A		E	D	I	T	I	O	N
D	A	G	G	E	R		A	R	E	S		G	N	U
		G	A	S		L	O	S		G	R	E	G	
P	A	S	S		T	A	T	S		B	O	A		
A	D	E		H	E	R	E		S	E	T	T	E	E
C	O	N	S	I	D	E	R	A	T	E		I	R	K
T	R	O	O	P		N	E	V	E	R		O	L	E
S	E	R	B	S		A	D	A	M	S		N	E	D

CROSSWORD 62

H	E	R	A		E	T	H	E	R		F	L	A	B
A	R	A	B		B	E	A	D	Y		R	E	N	O
L	I	P	S		B	A	R	G	E		I	N	T	O
O	C	T	O	P	I		D	E	B	O	N	A	I	R
			L	O	N	G		D	R	U	G			
L	A	S	V	E	G	A	S		E	R	E	C	T	S
O	C	T	E	T		P	U	M	A	S		H	I	T
A	T	A	D		T	E	P	I	D		S	A	N	E
N	U	T		D	O	S	E	S		C	O	N	G	A
S	P	E	W	E	D		R	E	R	O	U	T	E	D
			E	N	D	S		R	E	A	P			
B	O	B	D	Y	L	A	N		S	T	E	P	O	N
A	P	E	D		E	R	O	D	E		D	A	M	E
T	I	L	E		R	A	V	E	L		U	T	E	S
H	E	L	D		S	H	A	W	L		P	E	N	T

CROSSWORD 63

S	C	O	T		A	L	O	H	A		B	O	O	M
K	E	N	O		L	E	T	I	N		U	R	G	E
I	D	E	N	T	I	F	I	E	S		D	I	L	L
D	E	S		A	N	T	S		W	E	D	G	E	D
		T	H	E	Y		D	E	L	H	I			
C	U	R	I	O	S		G	A	R	L	A	N	D	S
A	S	I	D	E		W	A	N	E	S		A	A	H
R	A	C	E		R	O	U	N	D		O	T	T	O
E	G	O		N	E	R	D	Y		S	H	E	E	P
S	E	C	R	E	T	L	Y		A	T	O	D	D	S
		H	O	A	R	D		B	L	A	H			
F	E	E	B	L	E		S	E	E	K		S	A	D
A	C	T	I		A	P	P	A	R	E	N	T	L	Y
W	H	E	N		T	R	U	S	T		E	A	S	E
N	O	D	S		S	O	R	T	S		T	R	O	D

CROSSWORD 64

S	L	U	R		S	W	E	A	T		V	I	S	A
W	I	S	E		E	A	R	T	H		A	S	I	S
A	M	E	N		A	G	R	E	E		N	E	A	P
B	A	D	E	G	G		S	U	M		G	E	M	S
			G	O	O	D		P	E	R	U			
F	R	E	E	B	I	E	S		S	H	A	F	T	S
L	O	N		I	N	E	P	T		O	R	L	O	N
A	U	R	A		G	R	O	U	P		D	A	T	A
S	T	O	R	E		S	O	N	I	C		P	E	R
H	E	L	M	E	T		L	A	C	R	O	S	S	E
			S	L	A	B		S	C	A	N			
S	C	A	R		C	A	D		O	M	E	G	A	S
L	A	V	A		O	N	E	A	L		W	I	N	E
E	P	I	C		M	A	M	B	O		A	B	E	T
W	E	V	E		A	L	I	A	S		Y	E	W	S

CROSSWORD 65

```
M O S S   B R O W   M E O W S
A M O K   L E I A   A L P H A
S I S I   U R N S   S T E E P
S T A R T R E K   S C O N E S
    T A R A   K H A N
I D A   T E D   N O R   A D D
S I N B A D   R E T A I L E R
L A N A     S O W   O I L Y
A N I M A T E D   T O U S L E
M A E   S E A   D O N   T A R
    S C A M   O P U S
S H R I E K   G U M S H O E S
M O U R N   H O B O   O K R A
O W L E T   O R T S   R A I L
G L E N S   W E S T   T Y K E
```

CROSSWORD 66

```
S H O W   W H A T   M O B S
C O D A   R I C O   C O M E T
A N D Y   A N T I C I P A T E
R O N   F I G   L A G   R A P
E R U D I T E   N A T
    M Y T H   M I C R O B E S
V I B E S   L I R A   T E R I
A V E   S I M O N   F A T
S A R I   O V E N   N O O S E
E N S L A V E D   P O U R
    L E I   L U S T E R S
S P A   R E V   A T E   H U E
A R C H I T E C T S   P A I N
M A M I E   N A T O   I N N S
E Y E D   T M E N   E D G E
```

CROSSWORD 67

```
    W O O   A N D
    C I A O   R O O T
  M O N T H   C R E A K
  W E I G H   S A M   P E A
M I E N S   F I N S   I R A
A P T   D O L E   E A T E N
N E S S   I L K   O R P H A N
    A B E D   O R S O
A D A G E S   F I B   P R O F
M E L E E   P O L S   A R I
P A D   Z O O S   R E L A X
  F E Z   A I D   Y O U L L
  R A N I S   T E A R Y
    G E R E   E L M O
    W E D   E L S
```

CROSSWORD 68

```
S T O P   M A Y S   H O S T
I O W A   A L A I   E N T E R
P R E P   M A P S   L O O P Y
S O N A T A S   T E L   C E E
    Y E S   M E N   U K E S
T E X A N   B U R L A P
O A R S   B A N   I S S U E D
T R A   Y I D D I S H   S K I
O N Y X E S   A R T   S E E M
  I N T O N E   P A S S E
T H U S   R O E   M A C
E A R   P O D   P O T H O L E
S I G M A   L O I S   E D I T
S T E E R   E A T S   T I N A
  I D L E   S T A Y   S E E S
```

358

CROSSWORD 69

```
ZIP   ARF   MARS
ERIE  FLORA ALAN
NICK  REBEL TADA
 STENO SELF RIP
 ODES  SALAMI
SIR ETON HUG
POI  SNOB SODAS
UTAH TIE  GIVE
DALES OSLO SOL
 RUT YARD OWL
 REOPEN  DAUB
HAL SAYS EDGED
AGUE CLARA LYES
REDO HOTEL YEAH
EDEN  NED  DRY
```

CROSSWORD 70

```
AWL  ITEM ELLA
HOE  NORA MIAMI
SEX  LONG CEDARS
 ICE EPEES ZAP
ASCOT IVE MONA
BLOB THEE RUNIN
CAN DAIS SOS
SYSTEMS BEAKERS
 IFS GOAD LEO
ELECT DRAT SLIM
GUNK DUO  WHINE
ALI PIECE YEP
DUGOUT EMMA SUB
 SMART RIOT EMU
 AFRO STET SPY
```

CROSSWORD 71

```
 CBS      ORR
 SALAD   PLEAD
PARADES CREATED
RUSH BUSHY PAPA
ONE   RAE  TOM
 AAH CELEB CAT
 TENOR KAPUT
  FIR  SOP
 ATLAS ATTIC
 GUY LEASE DOC
HUT  ICY   MIA
ASHY KNEES OPTS
STOOLIE TINGLES
 ORGAN  DELES
 SIS    TEX
```

CROSSWORD 72

```
APED STAG  AWOL
PERU PORED URGE
PROGRAMMER DERN
LID EWES IRISES
ELEVENS AFOOT
 EDS RITA LED
TANGS IDENTITY
IDEA LONER ANNE
LAWSUITS SUGAR
EMS NOTE RUN
 RHINO PARTNER
CREATE HANG ORE
HOED SMATTERING
ISLE SUITE ASIA
SASS GRID  HEEL
```

CROSSWORD 73

```
F A S T ■ ■ S A N ■ E G G S
E L I S ■ A M B E R ■ C O L E
Y O D A ■ L E E C H ■ S T O W
■ T E R E S A ■ K O W T O W ■
■ ■ I V O R Y ■ S E A ■ ■ ■
D I A N E ■ S A P ■ E S S A Y
E R R A N D ■ Y E T ■ Y A L E
G I N ■ T A T ■ N I P ■ V I M
A S I F ■ Y U L ■ C A P O N E
S H E L F ■ B A G ■ S I R E N
■ ■ I O N ■ P E S T S ■ ■ ■
■ R E P E A T ■ T E E T E R ■
E A R P ■ M O U S E ■ O D O R
B I L E ■ E A T I N ■ L I M A
B L E D ■ ■ D E N ■ ■ S E A N
```

CROSSWORD 74

```
P E C S ■ E D D I E ■ T R O D
A C H E ■ L O Y A L ■ H O B O
S H E A ■ U N E N F O R C E D
T O R N A D O S ■ ■ T O K Y O
■ ■ ■ P O E T ■ J O H N ■ ■
D E F E N D ■ L A K E E R I E
I R E N E ■ R A D A R ■ U R N
C A A N ■ H O M E Y ■ G R A D
E S S ■ S A T E D ■ C R A T E
D E T E C T O R ■ J A I L E D
■ ■ V E E R ■ W E R E ■ ■ ■
O N I O N ■ A A R D V A R K
B A C K T R A C K S ■ I V A N
I S E E ■ A G R E E ■ N E R O
T A R S ■ T E E N Y ■ G R E W
```

CROSSWORD 75

```
B R A N ■ C A L F ■ C E L T
E I R E ■ E A S E L ■ A R I A
A S E A ■ P R O X Y ■ R A M P
M E A T L O A F ■ P A U S E S
■ ■ N E X T ■ J A B S ■ ■
H E R E S Y ■ C U P B O A R D
A M A S S ■ A L L E Y ■ B I O
D O N S ■ S T A I R ■ G A G S
O T T ■ P H O N E ■ B A T H E
N E S T L I N G ■ B E R E T S
■ ■ H O P E ■ G O A L ■ ■
E M B O D Y ■ F U R N A C E S
L O O M ■ A L L E N ■ N O A H
S O S A ■ R E U S E ■ D I V E
A R C S ■ D I E T ■ S L E D
```

CROSSWORD 76

```
■ M A P S ■ B A L M ■
■ G A S U P ■ A L I A S
■ C R I N G E ■ N I E C E S
P A I N E ■ W I D E N ■ S E T
L I N E R ■ T I N ■ T A P E
A N D ■ F A C T ■ J A M I E
N E S S ■ U G H ■ K O R E A N
■ E U R O ■ V E E P ■ ■
C R E A K S ■ D I N ■ S E M I
O H A R E ■ S E C T ■ R I D
D O T S ■ S U M ■ S M A L L
A D S ■ U N L I T ■ P E S K Y
E A G L E T ■ A G A T E S
T U N E R ■ U N D E R
M A R Y ■ S U E D
```

CROSSWORD 77

```
R A Z Z ▪ ▪ H E Y ▪ ▪ C R O W
A V O I D ▪ O V E N ▪ H O M E
M A R G E ▪ N I N E ▪ E D I T
S I R ▪ I D O L ▪ W R E S T S
▪ L O D G E R ▪ P S I S ▪ ▪
▪ ▪ E N S ▪ L U M B E R S ▪
C O L A S ▪ S I T E S ▪ A H A
A P E R ▪ D A M O N ▪ S P I N
R I G ▪ F E L O N ▪ W A S N T
▪ E S C A P E S ▪ V A L ▪ ▪
▪ ▪ E D A M ▪ B A T T E R ▪
G A R N E R ▪ C A N E ▪ L O G
E G O S ▪ T H A I ▪ R O U G E
T U T U ▪ S I L L ▪ Y O D E L
S E E S ▪ ▪ E L S ▪ ▪ H E R S
```

CROSSWORD 78

```
A C M E ▪ T W A S ▪ M A L E S
L O O P ▪ O H N O ▪ E D I T H
I D L E ▪ P O O R ▪ M I N C E
T E L E P H O N E B O O T H ▪
▪ ▪ ▪ S O A P ▪ E R S ▪ ▪ ▪
L O S ▪ S T I F F L Y ▪ D U H
A W A K E ▪ L I L ▪ B E T A
U N D E R S T A T E M E N T S
D U L Y ▪ A H S ▪ O N S E T
S P Y ▪ D I E H A R D ▪ E R E
▪ ▪ ▪ A I L ▪ T O E S ▪ ▪ ▪
▪ T R E A S U R E I S L A N D
T W I R L ▪ S E A L ▪ O L E O
R O S I E ▪ E L S E ▪ T E A L
A S K E D ▪ D Y E D ▪ S E L L
```

CROSSWORD 79

```
A L T O ▪ S H A M E ▪ P I S A
L I E U ▪ N Y L O N ▪ R O L L
O V E R C O M P E N S A T E D
H I T ▪ O W N S ▪ O T T A W A
A D H E R E S ▪ O B O E ▪ ▪
▪ ▪ P A D ▪ G A L O S H E S
S N A I L ▪ H O T E L ▪ U M A
T A L C ▪ P A T H S ▪ F L U S
E T A ▪ S O L O S ▪ T R A S H
P O S I T I O N ▪ M A O ▪ ▪
▪ ▪ T E N S ▪ F O R G E R Y
B A S S E T ▪ A U T O ▪ N E E
U L T E R I O R M O T I V E S
S O I L ▪ N I G E R ▪ R O V E
S E R F ▪ G L O S S ▪ E Y E S
```

CROSSWORD 80

```
S O D A S ▪ A S I A ▪ S C A N
A D U L T ▪ N O O N ▪ T A C O
V I L L A I N O U S ▪ A R T S
E E L ▪ S C O T ▪ W I L L I E
▪ ▪ W H E Y ▪ P E C K ▪ ▪
▪ S H O E S ▪ M A R K S O F F
S H O O S ▪ B O G E Y ▪ C A L
L O L L ▪ S A L A D ▪ O T T O
A V E ▪ L O R E N ▪ S L E E P
W E S T E R N S ▪ M E E T S
▪ ▪ O N E S ▪ R U E S ▪ ▪
R O D M A N ▪ B I L K ▪ A S P
E X E C ▪ E B U L L I E N C E
B E L A ▪ S O L E ▪ N A T A L
S N I T ▪ S O L D ▪ G R I M E
```

CROSSWORD 81

M	O	S	T		W	A	Y	S		P	A	S	T	A
A	S	T	O		A	L	A	I		U	L	C	E	R
A	L	A	N		R	E	N	D	I	T	I	O	N	S
M	O	T	I	F		K	N	O	T		R	O	O	
		C	O	L	L	E	E	N		T	E	R	N	
A	B	C		G	O	O	E	Y		O	R	B		
M	A	R		H	U	G	S		S	M	O	O	T	H
P	R	O	M	O	T	E		D	I	E	T	A	R	Y
S	K	I	E	R	S		C	U	R	L		R	I	P
	S	A	N		T	E	P	E	E		D	O	E	
V	A	S	T		P	A	R	E	N	T	S			
I	R	A		P	A	R	T		S	P	I	T	E	
C	O	N	T	E	N	T	I	O	N		O	D	E	S
A	S	T	E	R		A	F	R	O		R	E	A	P
R	E	S	E	T		R	Y	E	S		E	A	S	Y

CROSSWORD 82

B	R	A		A	S	H	E		W	I	L	E
C	A	A	N		D	A	I	S		A	G	E	D
D	U	C	H	Y		O	R	S	O		G	O	A	D
I	R	K		T	E	R	I		T	H	O	R	N	Y
D	E	S	P	I	S	E		L	E	O	N		
		U	M	P		M	E	R	E		Y	E	A
S	H	O	N	E		R	E	G	I	S		E	R	R
C	O	P	Y		R	E	L	I	C		B	A	I	T
A	B	E		W	Y	A	T	T		M	U	R	K	Y
R	O	N		H	E	M	S		S	O	L		
		B	O	B	S		G	A	R	B	A	G	E
D	O	G	E	A	R		E	L	M	O		T	A	G
A	W	L	S		E	M	M	A		C	R	A	I	G
N	E	A	T		A	I	M	S		C	O	L	T
E	N	D	S		D	A	Y	S		O	Y	L

CROSSWORD 83

L	A	C	E		A	C	R	E		D	I	M	S	
A	T	O	M		W	O	O	D		E	D	I	C	T
B	O	M	B	A	R	D	E	D		C	A	N	O	E
S	P	E	E	D	Y		I	L	K		E	R	A	
		A	R	E		I	S	E	E		T	R	E	K
P	A	L	S		T	S	K		D	A	N			
O	B	I		O	I	L	Y		I	T	A	L	Y	
R	E	V		U	S	E		D	A	D		M	O	O
E	L	E	C	T		L	U	R	E		B	A	G	
		U	S	A		I	N	K		T	I	N	A	
D	E	P	P		D	A	Z	E		F	I	G		
E	V	E		M	O	M		R	I	T	U	A	L	
M	E	T	O	O		U	N	D	E	R	L	I	N	E
O	N	T	A	P		S	O	O	N		E	T	N	A
	T	Y	K	E		E	D	G	E		D	Y	E	R

CROSSWORD 84

R	O	M	P		O	F	F	E	R		W	A	V	E
A	V	E	R		P	U	L	S	E		O	R	A	L
J	E	D	I		E	R	A	S	E		O	T	I	S
A	R	I	S	E	N		P	A	S	A	D	E	N	A
		O	M	A	H	A		Y	E	L	P			
M	A	C		S	O	U	L	S		M	I	L	L	S
O	R	R		T	U	N	E		A	S	L	E	E	P
V	E	I	L		S	T	A	N	D		E	A	V	E
E	N	T	I	R	E		R	E	D	S		D	E	N
S	A	Y	S	O		S	N	A	R	L		T	E	D
		T	A	R	T		P	E	A	C	H			
H	A	L	L	M	A	R	K		S	P	H	E	R	E
E	R	I	E		T	O	N	E	S		A	W	E	D
E	L	L	S		E	V	O	K	E		R	A	I	N
D	O	T	S		S	E	W	E	D		M	Y	N	A

362

CROSSWORD 85

A	C	H	E		L	I	B	E	L		A	H	E	M
S	L	A	V		A	D	O	B	E		B	O	R	E
T	A	R	A		C	O	W	B	O	Y	B	O	O	T
A	N	D		C	E	L	L			O	O	P	S	
		B	E	A	D			A	B	U	T			
A	M	O	N	G			A	V	E	R	T	E	D	
W	A	I	V	E	R		M	I	R	E		L	I	P
O	R	L	Y		O	L	I	V	E		L	A	V	A
L	I	E		C	U	E	S		T	R	I	B	A	L
	A	D	V	I	S	E	S			O	Z	O	N	E
		E	V	E	R			B	O	A	R			
	Z	I	T	I		S	P	O	T		A	D	S	
M	O	N	O	L	O	G	U	E	S		S	T	O	W
O	N	C	E		L	O	I	N	S		P	E	R	U
D	E	A	D		D	O	T	T	Y		A	D	A	M

CROSSWORD 86

V	A	L	V	E		J	E	A	N	S	
L	I	L	I	E	S		A	G	R	E	E	S
C	O	N	T	E	X	T		C	O	M	P	E	T	E
R	A	T	E	D		E	E	K		S	A	T	A	N
A	F	A	R		D	E	G	A	S		L	O	R	D
M	E	G		F	E	M	A	L	E	S		I	V	E
P	R	E	S	U	M	E	D		V	E	N	T	E	D
		U	S	E	D		L	E	N	O				
V	E	N	E	E	R		M	I	N	S	T	R	E	L
A	T	E		D	I	N	E	T	T	E		A	V	A
S	H	I	P		T	O	O	T	H		S	L	A	B
E	I	G	H	T		O	W	L		W	A	L	D	O
S	C	H	O	O	L	S		E	A	R	L	I	E	R
S	E	T	T	E	E		S	H	A	V	E	D	
D	O	S	E	S		T	A	P	E	D	

CROSSWORD 87

S	P	E	W		S	A	G	S		O	B	A	M	A
A	L	S	O		T	W	I	T		N	A	V	A	L
R	I	S	K		R	A	N	I		T	R	O	L	L
G	E	E		R	E	R	A	N		H	O	N	E	Y
E	S	S	A	Y	E	D		G	W	E	N			
		E	A	T		B	R	I	G		W	E	B	
A	C	O	R	N		S	O	A	P	O	P	E	R	A
H	O	P	I		K	A	N	Y	E		L	E	N	S
A	L	I	E	N	A	T	E	S		D	O	P	E	S
B	E	E		E	L	I	S		C	R	Y			
		P	I	E	R		S	L	A	S	H	E	D	
A	I	M	A	T		I	N	T	O	W		O	A	R
C	R	A	S	H		Z	O	O	S		A	U	R	A
N	O	R	S	E		E	D	I	E		I	S	N	T
E	N	T	E	R		S	E	C	T		L	E	S	S

CROSSWORD 88

			N	U	N				
	O	F	F		A	T	A	D	
	L	U	L	U		P	U	M	A	S
	W	I	R	E	S		P	R	E	P	A	Y
Y	O	N		A	S	H	E	N		P	L	E	A
A	R	G	O		P	A	D		M	E	A	T	Y
K	N	O	W	H	O	W		B	I	R	D	I	E
			L	I	T		T	A	N				
G	A	B	B	E	D		P	S	Y	C	H	I	C
A	P	A	R	T		I	O	U		E	U	R	O
P	E	S	O		D	O	W	N	S		M	A	Y
R	I	N	G	E	D		A	L	L	A	N	
S	C	I	F	I		M	O	A	N	
	O	V	E	N		I	T	S	
		E	R	E				

363

CROSSWORD 89

```
A D D S   B A S T E   V O T E
R O U T   U L N A S   A L E E
I N S E R T I O N S   N E A L
A S T R O   T O N   O D O R S
      E L F   P E G G Y
S C H O L A R   D A R K E S T
T A O S   B U M   T E E T E R
E R N   B R E A T H S   H I E
A L K A L I   O R E   P E N N
M Y S T I C S   A R M O R E D
      A S S E S   S I P
O P A L S   N O S   K O R A N
K E N O   P A U L R E V E R E
R A T S   A T S E A   E D I T
A L E S   R E A D Y   R O D S
```

CROSSWORD 90

```
S C A L E   O D E S   A S H E
H A D O N   P I T A   T H U G
A R I S E   I S O L A T I N G
M O E   R A N O N   M E E T S
S M U G G L E R   W A N D
      R Y E   G L E N D A L E
T O M E   X R A Y E D   W A X
O M E G A   A N N   A G A T E
F I N   D O Z I N G   L Y E S
U T A H J A Z Z   O V A
      G O U T   A N T I D O T E
A M E N S   S T O O L   L I D
M A R K T W A I N   L O D G E
O D I E   A L O E   A L I E N
S E E D   R E N T   S E E R S
```

CROSSWORD 91

```
R A B I D   S H U T   C O I L
A L O N E   T U T U   L A N E
S A L S A   A B E T   I S E E
H I T O R M I S S   S M I R K
      L A I D   R O A S T S
I N D E B T   B R O N X
D O E   B E I R U T   E C R U
L E A K Y   V I M   I S L E S
E L L A   K A N S A S   O N E
      T Y I N G   T R A D E R
S T A Y E D   B O A S
C O L D S   T R I M E S T E R
A N T I   F O U R   L E A V E
R E A D   O W E D   I N D I A
E R R S   E N D S   S T A L L
```

CROSSWORD 92

```
N A D E R   R E B A   A S E A
A L I V E   E R I C   T M A N
I D E A S   T I L T   L I S T
L A D L E   R E L O C A T E S
      U N D O   R A S H L Y
S O N A T A   T A S K
A B I T   M A R C   E A G L E
N O N E   P L U M E   N O O K
G E E S E   A N E W   N A P E
      D I S K   E M O T E S
D E F O G S   B R A Y
R E L A Y R A C E   N A S A L
I R I S   A L O T   I N A N E
P I N E   E V E S   A C I N G
S E T S   L A D Y   C E D E S
```

CROSSWORD 93

```
VIE . HUH . ROB .
. FIRE . USE . EWES
SOLAR . MAC . INGOT
ARE . IMP . KEN . ERA
MERGERS . . LITTER
. . ASS . LIENS .
WREST . ZINC . KNOT
AIM . MEANT . . AWE
GOUP . EARS . BAGEL
. . EARLS . TAM .
COURIC . . RESPITE
ART . DYE . AXE . SHY
PATTI . TAD . MELEE
. LEAN . ARI . EVEN
RUG . SKI . NAT .
```

CROSSWORD 94

```
ZERO . PEWS . . BELA
AXED . AXIOM . OPEN
ICED . CELLO . REND
REV . HIRE . NINETY
ELEGANT . DOLE .
. AGO . BECKONS .
PLUMS . WALLS . OUI
EIRE . ROSIE . COIF
PEN . TAMES . AUNTS
. USURPED . TUB .
. RUIN . DETESTS
LOBBED . RENO . MEL
ASIA . LLAMA . CIAO
PLAN . YUKON . ALMS
POSE . . GENT . MESH
```

CROSSWORD 95

```
BANG . SAMOA . AFEW
RICO . CRAWL . COLE
EDITORIALS . IRKS
DES . TEEM . ODDEST
. AHAS . CRESS .
. SALEM . GRAB . HEW
RADAR . FRONTPAGE
IRON . SLOWS . EDGE
FALSEHOOD . SCOOP
THE . DOOM . SPAWN
. SANER . LEON .
FACIAL . SEEK . OPT
EVER . APPARENTLY
TONE . CAUSE . ATOP
ANTS . ENDED . POPE
```

CROSSWORD 96

```
SAIL . IRATE . ITEM
NATO . NIVEN . CAPE
IRAN . SPANS . EXIT
POL . DUE . LYRICS
SNIVEL . CHAOS .
. CENT . LEVY . CAT
AMITY . CAMEO . OUR
BOZO . TIRED . CURE
ERE . SATIN . ARRAY
LES . CLEF . SLOT
. MOLDY . ETCHES
ALCOTT . PRO . ORT
SOLO . AGILE . TUNA
PLOD . LEDON . ASIF
SAYS . ELATE . BEEF
```

CROSSWORD 97

```
C E L E B ■ A D L I B ■ M A T
A R O M A ■ N I E C E ■ E G O
I L L U M I N A T E D ■ N E D
N E L L ■ O I L S ■ R H I N O
■ ■ A G U E ■ ■ P O I N T S
S T A T U S ■ A P L O M B ■
T O T E M ■ B L O O M ■ L I T
E G A D ■ K I T T Y ■ P A N E
P A L ■ K I T E S ■ M E C C A
■ L E N D E R ■ V O D K A S
S A C R E D ■ D E M I ■ ■
T B O N E ■ S O U R ■ C U B A
A H S ■ L O O N E Y T U N E S
L O T ■ E N A C T ■ I R I S H
E R S ■ D O P E S ■ P E T T Y
```

CROSSWORD 98

```
A N N A ■ M O L E ■ C O D A
L E E C H ■ A P E X ■ A B E D
P R A T E ■ Y U M A ■ R I L E
S O P ■ R I B S ■ M O U S E
■ ■ W A V E ■ P I G S ■
F U T I L E ■ S U N R O O F
O N E N D ■ T E P E E ■ M A R
A T A D ■ C O R P S ■ L I R A
L I L ■ T A N G Y ■ B O T C H
■ E S C A P E E ■ R E U S E S
■ ■ A R I D ■ W H A T ■
■ G R E A T ■ R I O T ■ P S I
E L I S ■ O L E S ■ I D O L S
B E T A ■ L E A P ■ T O K E N
B E A R ■ S I P S ■ N E W T
```

CROSSWORD 99

```
S O D A ■ M I M E D ■ K I D S
O D O R ■ A D O R E ■ E D I E
L I L T ■ L A B O R ■ A L E E
D E L I L A H ■ S E P T E T S
■ ■ F I D O ■ L E O ■ ■
G R A I N Y ■ F A I R N E S S
O U N C E ■ T R I C K ■ A L I
U R G E ■ S H A L T ■ S T A T
G A L ■ S C A N S ■ S T E V E
E L E C T R I C ■ S P I N E S
■ ■ R A E ■ M A U L ■ ■
B A L O N E Y ■ O W N E D U P
O L E O ■ N U T T Y ■ T Y K E
M O N K ■ E L I T E ■ T E E S
B E S S ■ D E C O R ■ O R S O
```

CROSSWORD 100

```
C A R S ■ I F F Y ■ L A S T S
A R E A ■ D A L I ■ U L T R A
M I S T L E T O E ■ M E R I T
P A T I O S ■ L A P ■ A T E
■ O R B ■ R O D S ■ A W E D
A C R E ■ L I D ■ H U B ■
C H I ■ J A N E T ■ S C A L D
H U N ■ E S S ■ I R E ■ R O E
E G G E D ■ E A G E R ■ G I N
■ V I A ■ V E X ■ N E S T
F L E E ■ P I E R ■ S O N ■
L A X ■ O T T ■ A O R T A S
A D I E U ■ C R O S S W I S E
S E L L S ■ H O L E ■ A N T E
K N E L T ■ Y O D A ■ Y E A R
```

CROSSWORD 101

W	A	K	E	N	■	S	H	R	E	D	■	A	F	T
I	M	A	G	E	■	L	A	U	R	A	■	P	E	R
S	O	N	G	W	R	I	T	E	R	S	■	P	A	Y
E	K	E	S	■	A	C	E	S	■	H	A	L	T	S
■	■	■	T	S	K	■	■	S	O	R	E	S	T	
B	U	R	L	A	P	■	B	L	U	F	F	S	■	
A	S	H	E	N	■	G	R	I	E	F	■	A	R	E
R	E	A	D	■	Y	E	A	S	T	■	D	U	E	L
E	S	P	■	M	A	R	I	A	■	R	A	C	E	S
■	S	O	A	K	E	D	■	P	A	M	E	L	A	
A	C	O	R	N	S	■	B	A	G	■				
M	O	D	E	M	■	S	P	U	R	■	O	R	A	L
P	O	I	■	A	T	T	E	N	T	I	V	E	L	Y
L	E	E	■	D	R	A	N	K	■	M	E	D	A	L
E	D	S	■	E	A	R	N	S	■	P	R	O	S	E

CROSSWORD 102

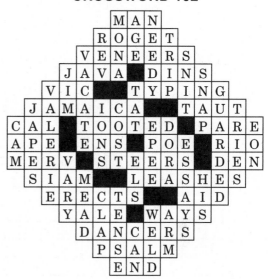

```
        M A N
      R O G E T
    V E N E E R S
  J A V A   D I N S
  V I C   T Y P I N G
  J A M A I C A   T A U T
C A L   T O O T E D   P A R E
A P E   E N S   P O E   R I O
M E R V   S T E E R S   D E N
  S I A M   L E A S H E S
    E R E C T S   A I D
      Y A L E   W A Y S
        D A N C E R S
          P S A L M
            E N D
```

CROSSWORD 103

C	R	A	F	T	■	O	S	L	O	■	L	A	V	A
R	A	T	I	O	■	U	T	A	H	■	A	W	E	S
E	P	O	X	Y	■	T	R	I	O	■	C	O	N	K
P	I	N	■	S	I	D	E	D	■	B	E	L	T	S
E	D	E	N	■	L	O	W	■	T	E	D	■		
■	■	E	L	K	■	E	K	E	D	■	N	A	B	
S	C	A	R	Y	■	E	D	N	A	■	D	I	N	O
N	A	I	V	E	T	E	■	O	R	I	E	N	T	S
A	N	N	E	■	S	L	A	W	■	L	E	A	S	H
G	E	T	■	V	A	S	T	■	E	L	M			
■	B	A	R	■	T	U	T	■	S	U	E	S		
M	E	R	Y	L	■	M	I	L	A	N	■	S	A	L
A	L	O	T	■	W	A	R	N	■	A	B	A	S	E
C	L	U	E	■	I	D	E	A	■	P	A	G	E	D
E	A	T	S	■	N	E	S	S	■	S	H	E	D	S

CROSSWORD 104

D	A	V	I	S	■	Y	O	U	R	■	E	V	I	L
E	V	I	C	T	■	U	N	T	O	■	N	A	S	A
P	E	S	K	Y	■	C	U	E	S	■	W	I	L	D
O	R	T	■	M	A	C	S	■	E	A	R	N	E	D
T	S	A	R	I	N	A	■	A	B	B	A	■		
■	■	Y	E	N	■	S	C	U	L	P	T	O	R	
G	O	B	A	D	■	D	O	U	S	E	■	E	V	A
A	V	O	N	■	F	I	L	T	H	■	B	R	A	Y
G	E	L	■	M	E	L	E	E	■	W	A	I	L	S
A	N	T	H	I	L	L	S	■	D	A	B	■		
■	A	M	O	S	■	M	O	S	A	I	C	S		
W	A	R	R	E	N	■	O	U	C	H	■	S	A	P
A	V	I	V	■	I	N	K	S	■	E	N	S	U	E
N	I	N	E	■	E	A	R	S	■	R	O	U	S	E
E	D	G	Y	■	S	T	A	Y	■	S	T	E	E	D

CROSSWORD 105

```
O U R           D E S
P R E P         T I M E
S P O N S O R   C H A S T E N
H A S   T O E N A I L   T W O
E L S E   L E E R S   N E E D
  M U T E   F A R   V E E R
  M E N U   T O T E M S
  R A M P   T U N E
  E N C A S E   B O S C
  M E A T   Y U L   M E O W
G I R L   S C R O D   S T E M
A R I   J E H O V A H   T A R
B E E L I N E   E N A M O R S
  S I L T       E R I N
  T E L         D A Y
```

CROSSWORD 106

```
Z E N           B O W
T O R C H       I O W A N
P E O N I E S   E V O L V E D
R A M   S L A N D E R   E W E
O M I T   D R U G S   B R E W
S N O B   O N E     B E E R
  G L E A N S   W I N D
  S A N G   T O R N
  S T U D   S A N D E D
M O O S   P H I   S T E P
D E F Y   I R O N S   T A R P
O A T   S C O O T E D   F E E
E L E C T E D   S A D D E S T
  S N E E R     M A I N S
  S E T         Y E S
```

CROSSWORD 107

```
Y A P S   C E D A R   K N E E
E R L E   A M U S E   N E A R
A L O E   R I O T S   A L S O
H O T S H O T   R I P P L E S
      A I M   C O N E S
S C O W L   B B S   S A M O A
T A D   O D O R   G O C A R T
A D D S   A G A I N   K I D S
T E E M E D   D A U B   Z E E
S T R A Y   S I N   O P E R A
    L E D T O   B O O
C H E L S E A   W I N E S A P
H A R E   B R E E D   T A L E
A L M S   R E E V E   I V A N
P E A T   A S K E D   C E N T
```

CROSSWORD 108

```
I N C A   A L O N E   S L I D
T E A L   S I T I N   Y O D A
E R I E   C O I L S   S O O T
M O N S O O N S   N E T T L E
        I T S   R A G E
F I N A L S   C E R A M I C S
E V E R Y   C U B E D   D U E
L I V E   L O P E D   T A T A
L E I   P E R I L   H O H U M
A S S E R T E D   C A N O P Y
    L E S S   C O N
A L L O Y S   T R U S T E E S
H O O P   L O R E N   E C R U
O G L E   I N E P T   S H A M
Y E A S   P O E T S   T O S S
```

CROSSWORD 109

```
D A L Y ■ A C R I D ■ S C A B
O P I E ■ R H O D A ■ T H O U
D E F T ■ C A T A M A R A N S
O D E ■ O A R S ■ ■ M O N E T
■ ■ J O I N T ■ S L A V ■ ■
E N A B L E ■ C A U S E W A Y
T A C O S ■ B A L L S ■ A L A
H I K E ■ R E P E L ■ S T I R
A V E ■ P A C E S ■ F I E N D
N E T W O R K S ■ P A D R E S
■ ■ H U E Y ■ C H I E F ■ ■
G R A I N ■ D O O R ■ A P T
R O U N D A B O U T ■ S L E W
E A R N ■ H A R P O ■ P L E A
G R A Y ■ S A K E S ■ A S P S
```

CROSSWORD 110

```
M O C H A ■ R O S A ■ H A L O
E T H E R ■ O N Y X ■ O M A R
S T O I C ■ L I M E ■ L I M A
H O P S ■ S L O B ■ M E D A L
■ ■ T I M ■ N O R A ■ ■ ■
E D A S N E R ■ L U S H E S T
R E D ■ N A Y S ■ T H I N L Y
A C E S ■ R E A C H ■ S N A P
S A L A M I ■ Y O L K ■ U K E
E L E G A N T ■ D E I T I E S
■ ■ A G U E ■ S T Y ■ ■ ■
G R O O M ■ R A G S ■ R I P S
L U L U ■ A N T E ■ G O O S E
I D E S ■ R E I N ■ A N T I C
B E S T ■ E R N E ■ Y E A S T
```

CROSSWORD 111

```
C H A D ■ L E O S ■ R O M A
R O T E ■ N O T C H ■ A H A B
A P O P ■ A G A T E ■ C O L E
G E M I N I ■ S E A R C H E D
■ ■ C U R L ■ T R I O ■ ■
G R O T T O E S ■ S N O O P
L I D S ■ B A T H ■ K N I S H
O L D ■ I D E A S ■ L A Y
W E L S H ■ S A T E ■ Y E L P
■ D Y L A N ■ M E L T O R M E
■ ■ E R I C ■ S L E D ■ ■
S C H E M E R S ■ E N E R G Y
A L O T ■ C U T E R ■ L O R E
W I S E ■ E D E N S ■ E D I T
S P E D ■ S E W S ■ D E M I
```

CROSSWORD 112

```
C H I P ■ G E E S E ■ T A D A
L O G O ■ A V A I L ■ E V I L
A M O S ■ M E T R O ■ R I L E
P E R T A I N S ■ N E E D L E
■ ■ P U N S ■ A G E S ■ ■
S T R O N G ■ S C A L A W A G
L E A N T ■ S L I T S ■ E L L
I N G E ■ R H O D E ■ D A L I
C D E ■ K E E P S ■ M O V E D
E S S E N C E S ■ R E D E Y E
■ ■ M E A N ■ N E R D ■ ■
S T R E W N ■ S O U V E N I R
P O O R ■ T E L L S ■ R A C E
A G O G ■ E L I T E ■ E T O N
R A T E ■ D I M E S ■ D O N E
```

CROSSWORD 113

S	T	U	B		R	A	N	I		A	T	B	A	Y
M	E	N	U		E	W	E	R		T	R	U	C	E
A	X	I	S		V	A	S	E		H	E	N	N	A
C	A	T		A	I	R	S		H	E	A	T	E	R
K	N	E	A	D	E	D		S	A	I	D			
			C	A	W		S	C	I	S	S	O	R	S
C	H	A	R	M		Q	U	A	R	T		O	U	I
Z	O	N	E		P	U	L	L	S		O	P	T	S
A	B	E		B	R	O	K	E		S	U	S	H	I
R	O	W	B	O	A	T	S		T	A	T			
			E	T	N	A		S	A	U	S	A	G	E
U	N	P	A	C	K		C	O	W	L		B	E	N
S	O	U	T	H		T	O	L	D		H	I	N	D
E	M	C	E	E		H	E	I	R		O	D	I	E
D	E	E	R	S		E	D	D	Y		W	E	E	D

CROSSWORD 114

S	H	A	P	E		F	A	R	E		A	S	O	F
C	U	B	A	N		A	W	O	L		D	O	L	E
A	L	E	R	T		M	A	Y	F	L	O	W	E	R
M	A	L	A	R	K	E	Y		O	R	S	O	N	
			L	A	I	D		C	O	I	N			
M	U	S	L	I	M		T	R	A	N	S	M	I	T
A	S	P	E	N		C	H	E	F	S		A	N	Y
P	H	I	L		S	H	O	E	S		W	R	A	P
L	E	N		S	O	U	N	D		M	A	I	N	E
E	R	E	C	T	I	N	G		P	U	R	E	E	D
			H	U	L	K		L	U	S	H			
A	L	L	A	N		R	A	T	I	O	N	E	D	
M	O	U	N	T	E	D	U	P		C	R	A	V	E
M	A	R	T		L	Y	L	E		A	S	N	E	R
O	N	E	S		K	E	E	L		L	E	A	R	N

CROSSWORD 115

E	M	A	I	L		C	I	T	E		U	M	P	S
D	E	B	R	A		R	O	I	L		N	O	A	H
N	A	B	O	B		A	W	E	D		L	A	V	A
A	L	A	N		U	S	A		O	P	I	N	E	D
			H	I	T	S		B	R	I	T			
U	N	S	A	F	E		F	R	A	T		P	R	O
R	O	A	N	S		H	E	A	D	Y		L	I	P
G	O	L	D		R	A	D	I	O		C	A	N	T
E	S	S		R	E	R	U	N		P	O	I	S	E
S	E	A		H	A	R	P		V	E	N	D	E	D
			N	O	S	Y		D	I	N	S			
E	L	P	A	S	O		T	R	A		U	S	E	R
R	A	I	N		N	A	S	A		A	M	I	G	O
O	P	E	N		E	D	A	M		B	E	R	G	S
S	P	R	Y		D	O	R	A		C	R	E	S	S

CROSSWORD 116

W	A	G	S		J	A	D	E	S		S	T	E	M
I	R	O	N		A	T	O	L	L		T	Y	K	E
L	E	N	O		C	A	G	E	Y		A	P	E	R
D	A	G	W	O	O	D		V	E	R	B	O	S	E
			J	A	B		P	E	R	I	L			
R	O	B	O	T		B	U	N		D	E	S	K	S
A	R	A	B		G	A	B		Y	E	S	M	A	N
I	L	L		J	A	Y		W	A	S		A	T	E
L	O	S	S	E	S		R	I	M		E	R	I	E
S	N	A	K	E		R	I	G		T	A	T	E	R
			I	R	K	E	D		F	O	R			
W	A	R	M	S	U	P		W	I	N	D	S	U	P
A	L	U	M		D	A	M	O	N		R	O	L	E
R	O	S	E		O	S	A	K	A		U	R	N	S
N	E	E	D		S	T	E	E	L		M	E	A	T

CROSSWORD 117

A	S	P	S		S	C	R	A	M		L	A	M	P
R	E	E	L		W	O	O	D	Y		O	P	A	L
T	E	R	I		A	V	A	S	T		V	E	T	O
S	M	U	G	G	L	E	R		H	E	E	D	E	D
		H	A	L	T		B	I	A	S				
G	R	O	T	T	O		S	U	C	C	E	E	D	S
R	E	B		E	W	I	N	G		H	A	B	I	T
A	C	E	D		S	T	I	L	T		T	O	R	O
S	U	S	A	N		E	P	E	E	S		N	E	W
P	R	E	M	I	U	M	S		S	A	T	Y	R	S
			A	N	N	S		S	T	I	R			
B	A	L	S	A	M		T	W	I	L	I	G	H	T
A	L	E	C		A	E	R	I	E		B	L	U	R
B	E	A	U		S	O	U	R	S		A	U	T	O
A	S	K	S		K	N	E	L	T		L	E	S	T

CROSSWORD 118

A	Y	E		A	B	O	V	E		Y	O	D	A
O	W	E	S		L	O	R	E	N		A	P	E	X
V	E	N	T	I	L	A	T	E	D		N	I	N	E
A	S	S	E	S	S		P	O	C	K	E	T	S
		L	E	E	K		R	O	E				
D	E	P	L	E	T	E	S		S	M	E	L	L	S
A	X	L	E		T	H	R	E	E		A	L	I
T	A	U		R	A	C	I	E	S	T		T	A	N
E	L	M		A	S	H	E	S		A	C	M	E
S	T	E	E	R	S		R	I	C	K	S	H	A	W
		L	E	I		N	E	A	P				
C	Y	B	O	R	G	S		A	N	E	M	I	C
L	O	O	P		N	A	N	O	S	E	C	O	N	D
O	G	R	E		E	L	A	T	E		T	O	T	S
T	I	E	D		D	E	B	T	S		S	R	O

CROSSWORD 119

O	R	A	L	S		W	H	E	W		S	A	N	G
M	O	V	I	E		E	U	R	O		I	R	A	N
I	D	O	L	S		A	F	R	O		E	M	M	A
T	E	N		S	E	R	F		A	S	S	E	T	
		A	I	R	Y		W	I	L	T				
	L	O	G	O	N		V	I	O	L	A	T	E	
L	I	K	E	N		D	A	N	N	Y		A	V	A
E	G	A	D		B	A	N	K	S		D	I	A	L
S	H	Y		B	A	R	N	S		F	E	N	D	S
	T	S	A	R	I	N	A		C	R	E	T	E	
		O	I	L	S		Q	U	A	D				
S	H	A	R	E		H	U	B	S		O	W	N	
W	A	I	T		C	I	A	O		I	D	A	H	O
A	L	D	A		A	C	T	I		E	E	R	I	E
P	E	A	S		N	E	S	T		R	E	S	T	S

CROSSWORD 120

T	O	G	A		C	A	T	C	H		G	L	E	N
A	H	A	S		O	M	A	H	A		L	I	M	O
L	I	L	T		Y	O	K	E	S		I	R	I	S
C	O	L	A	S		R	E	D		A	B	A	T	E
			M	E	A	N	D	E	R					
R	U	S	S	E	L	L		A	V	I	A	T	E	D
U	N	W	E	L	L		O	R	E		P	R	A	Y
S	T	I	N	T		E	D	S		D	R	I	V	E
T	I	P	S		B	U	D		L	O	I	T	E	R
S	L	E	E	P	E	R		W	I	T	L	E	S	S
			A	G	O	N	I	Z	E					
A	L	L	O	W		P	I	N		S	L	O	P	E
V	I	E	W		B	E	T	T	E		E	K	E	D
O	V	A	L		B	A	R	E	R		G	R	E	G
W	E	D	S		S	N	O	R	E		S	A	K	E

CROSSWORD 121

```
S O C K . R E V S . H E A T
E M E N D . A L O T . I D L Y
M E L E E . B E T A . D I L L
I N T E L L I G E N T . T O E
. . . T A D A . Z E P H Y R
B U R E A U . N E A R S . .
E T A S . D A T A . M Y R N A
S A R C A S M . R E S C U E S
S H E A R . P A P A . H I R E
. . P O S S E . G L E N D A
S C H E M E . R I L E . .
T E E . A R M O R E D C A R S
E L L A . V I S A . O R B I T
A L M S . E T O N . N O L T E
L O S S . D E L I . W E E P
```

CROSSWORD 122

```
N E T . . D E S . . P S I
M O L A R . Y E L P . S L I D
O O M P H . A R I A . H U L A
O N O . Y A R N . . P E S O
. . A M I D . F A R E .
R U L E R . W I D E N E D
S A L A D . W E N D Y . D U O
A N T I . L I E N S . E S P Y
N O R . S E E P S . C R E E L
N A S T I L Y . C H I L D
. L O A D . N O U N .
P L O P . P E N N . T H E
S L I P . P O U R . K N E E L
L E N S . A R G O . Y E A R S
Y A K . M R S . . E M S
```

CROSSWORD 123

```
M O E . M A S H . M E E T
O U T . E C H O . E A G E R
W R E N C H E S . D R O N E S
. R A C Y . P A I N . O N E
C O N G A . L I S A . B R E W
O B I S . M U C H . V A S E S
N O T . L O G E . B E T .
K E Y H O L E . C O N S U L T
. A N T . D O L T . N O W
S C O R E . R A P T . E T N A
L E F T . T O N Y . B E R G S
A L L . Z I N C . Z U L U
P L A C E D . E V A N S T O N
. S T A R E . R E N T . H U E
. E R O S . S E E S . S I D
```

CROSSWORD 124

```
S W I S H . N A P E . S E L L
T A L K Y . O W E N . I D E A
A D L I B . B A N D S T A N D
Y E S . R E L Y . N O M A D
. . D I K E . T H E N .
I N S I D E . F R E E . U M P
S A T E S . F R I A R . S E A
L I E D . F L O O R . L I D S
E V A . S L A T S . M Y N A S
T E D . H I G H . T A N G L E
. . H I T S . M I N X .
O S C A R . D U C K . P O L
S T O C K R O O M . I R E N E
L U R K . A L U M . N I E C E
O D E S . E D G Y . D O L E S
```

CROSSWORD 125

```
L O O K S ■ S P A T ■ O B I T
A G R E E ■ A O N E ■ C O D A
P L A N T A T I O N ■ C A L M
P E T ■ T R A ■ N A T U R E S
■ D E C L I N E ■ C A R D ■
■ ■ L E D ■ N E I L ■ G A P
C U P I D ■ S T A T E F A I R
A T O M ■ F O R T Y ■ A M M O
M E M B R A N E S ■ C R E S S
E S P ■ E L S E ■ D O C ■ ■
■ O T I S ■ S L I D E R S
S P U R N E D ■ A N D ■ E W E
W I S E ■ T R A N S L A T O R
I S L E ■ T I R E ■ E R R O L
M A Y S ■ O P T S ■ S C O N E
```

CROSSWORD 126

```
S C A M S ■ L A B O R ■ S R O
M A R I O ■ E X I L E ■ T A U
U N E X P L A I N E D ■ I T S
R A N ■ E R S ■ ■ F A C E T
F L A T T E N ■ F L O C K ■
■ ■ E E K ■ F L I R T I N G
A N N E X ■ T R E N D ■ E A R
M A A M ■ A R O S E ■ A S I A
E S S ■ B R U S H ■ A P T L Y
N A T T I E S T ■ A B E ■ ■
■ I O T A S ■ M I S D E E D
K A N Y E ■ T A D ■ A D O
A L E ■ O B L I T E R A T E D
L A S ■ F R A M E ■ O W I N G
E N S ■ F A X E S ■ T E N S E
```

CROSSWORD 127

```
    S P A       H A M
    S T A B     O W E S
  S H O V E L   S P E A K S
A W A R E ■ E A T ■ S L A T E
D A R E ■ S A L E S ■ S T A R
O N E ■ S T R E E T S ■ E Y E
    D E M O N   P A W N S
    W A R       T I E
    D E L I S   P I N T S
Z O E ■ L E A K I N G ■ C A B
A D A M ■ S T I N G ■ L A C E
P O L E S ■ A D E ■ C A R E D
    R E T U R N   S T O N E S
    R A R E       O R E S
    L E D         Y E S
```

CROSSWORD 128

```
B L U R ■ B L A D E ■ T U B A
R I S E ■ A I R E D ■ O P E N
A S E A ■ S T I N G ■ T O N Y
T A R P ■ T E D ■ E V E N T ■
■ ■ P E E R ■ S W A M ■ ■
■ A V E R S ■ T H I S ■ S H Y
S H E A R ■ C H O S E ■ P E A
L E E R ■ A L I C E ■ S E A N
O A R ■ S N A C K ■ S P A R K
E D S ■ P I N K ■ L E A R N
■ ■ H A M S ■ L A W N ■ ■
C H I N A ■ H O G ■ G R O W
S O A R ■ T E A S E ■ L O V E
P L I E ■ E A T E R ■ E V E N
Y A R D ■ D R E S S ■ D E N T
```

CROSSWORD 129

```
C O K E   O R A L   W H A M
A H O Y   R O D E   H I R E
L I N E S   R O L E M O D E L
L O A F E R   M I R E   E A T
    U T A H   B E R M
P R E L U D E S   D I E S E L
A H A   P A R T S   T E P E E
C O S T   R O O T S   T A R N
K N E E S   N O R T H   R I D
S E L L E R   P E R I G E E S
    L I E S   W I L L
S P A   N A P S   P L A T E N
H O U S E C O A T   S C O R E
A L T O   T U N A   I R I S
M O O D   S T E P   S E N T
```

CROSSWORD 130

```
B A S S   U R N S   T H E M
E X I T   A F O O T   R O V E
A L T O   R O U T E   A P E S
R E S O R T   T E R R I E R S
    G A I T   S E A L
O F F E N S E S   O P E R A
P A L S   T E N T   T R U M P
A C E   S T O O P   R U E
L E E R S   H O U R   M A S T
  S T E P S   P R O F I L E S
    L I E N   S C A N
C A L E N D A R   E N I G M A
A R E A   A V O W S   V I E W
P I N S   N A P E S   A B L E
E A S E   S L E D   N E T S
```

CROSSWORD 131

```
W A L L S   S H A M   D E E P
E L I O T   T I R E   I D L E
L O D G E   E L M S   V E S T
L E S   E A R L   S H I N E S
    S P I N   L A U D
S T R O L L   S U G G E S T S
C R I M E   C A R E S   C O O
R A V E   C A F E S   H E A R
A C E   H O L E S   D E N S E
P E R F O R M S   G R E E T S
    R U N S   F E E D
A S P I R E   P O T S   R O W
P A L E   R O A R   S T O V E
O M E N   E D I T   E A S E S
D E A D   D E N Y   S P E N T
```

CROSSWORD 132

```
S W A T   C A B L E   P E R U
W A S H   A G A I N   A M O S
E S T E   R I L E D   S I T E
E T E   B O L L   E A S T E R
P E R C A L E   M A M E
    A L E   B E V E R A G E
S T A L K   S O L O N   G O D
T O L L   T E N O R   H E R E
O R E   S E V E N   L O D E N
W R E S T L E D   K O S
    P I E R   A R R E S T S
R E T O R T   A L O E   M A T
A M O K   H E R O N   V A S E
T I N E   O V I N E   A S T A
E R I N   N A D E R   T H E M
```

CROSSWORD 133

H	A	R	T		M	U	T	E	D		A	S	P	S
O	P	U	S		I	N	A	N	E		B	L	O	W
M	E	S	A		N	I	G	E	R		B	A	L	I
E	X	T	R	A	C	T	S			D	E	P	O	T
		G	E	E		B	U	O	Y					
S	T	E	W	E	D		C	A	R	E	S	S	E	D
L	U	R	I	D		S	H	I	N	S		A	X	E
A	L	I	T		S	E	A	L	S		G	L	I	B
I	L	E		S	T	I	R	S		V	I	O	L	A
N	E	S	C	I	E	N	T		B	A	N	N	E	R
		H	A	M	E		A	L	I					
S	C	R	A	M		C	R	I	N	K	L	E	D	
T	O	E	S		S	T	A	I	N		H	O	S	E
A	D	I	T		A	I	R	E	D		A	N	T	E
B	A	N	E		C	L	A	S	S		N	E	A	R

CROSSWORD 134

S	C	O	W		U	R	A	L	S		T	W	O	S
H	O	N	E		P	I	L	O	T		O	H	I	O
O	R	E	S		E	N	O	L	A		W	I	L	L
W	R	I	T	I	N	G	T	A	B	L	E	T	S	
M	A	L		O	D	O				T	R	E	K	S
E	L	L	E	N			S	P	A	S		L	I	T
		D	I	G	I	T	A	L		A	I	N	U	
	S	P	A	C	E	C	A	P	S	U	L	E	S	
S	E	A	M		N	O	T	S	O	L	D			
O	A	K		L	A	N	E		N	A	S	A	L	
S	W	I	P	E			A	S	A		T	I	A	
	A	S	H	O	T	I	N	T	H	E	D	A	R	K
O	T	T	O		A	D	E	L	E		E	L	I	E
D	E	A	N		N	O	M	A	D		L	E	E	R
E	R	N	E		G	L	O	S	S		E	R	R	S

CROSSWORD 135

T	R	A	P	D	O	O	R		S	H	A	V	E	N
A	I	R	R	I	F	L	E		C	A	P	O	N	E
S	P	R	I	N	T	E	D		A	T	T	I	R	E
S	P	I	C	E		A	W	A	R	E		C	O	D
E	L	V	E	S		N	I	L	E		B	E	L	L
L	E	E	S		E	D	N	A		S	A	B	L	E
		C	R	E	E		H	O	B	O	E	S		
C	A	M	P	H	O	R		R	E	L	A	X	E	S
O	P	E	R	A	S		G	E	N	E				
M	I	S	E	R		I	R	I	S		V	I	E	S
R	A	S	P		S	C	A	N		M	A	N	N	A
A	R	M		F	I	E	N	D		O	U	S	T	S
D	I	A	L	E	D		D	E	F	I	L	E	R	S
E	S	T	A	T	E		P	E	A	R	T	R	E	E
S	T	E	W	E	D		A	R	R	E	S	T	E	D

CROSSWORD 136

A	C	C	O	L	A	D	E	S		A	W	A	R	D
C	O	R	R	U	G	A	T	E		D	O	G	I	E
C	L	E	A	R	E	Y	E	D		D	E	I	C	E
E	L	A	T	E		R	A	P		S	T	E	P	
N	A	M	E		C	O	N	N	E	D		A	C	E
T	R	Y		C	A	N	A	S	T	A		T	A	N
		K	A	B	U	L		S	T	R	O	K	E	
C	A	M	E	R	A	S		S	T	E	E	R	E	D
O	N	A	G	E	R		C	H	O	R	D			
A	N	N		T	E	T	H	E	R	S		M	U	M
R	O	E		S	T	R	I	D	E		M	A	N	E
S	T	U	D		S	A	M			T	E	R	R	A
E	A	V	E	S		D	E	N	S	I	T	I	E	S
S	T	E	E	L		E	R	I	E	C	A	N	A	L
T	E	R	R	Y		S	A	L	E	S	L	A	D	Y

CROSSWORD 137

```
M A S S I V E ■ S P H E R E S
I M P E R I L ■ E L E G A N T
S N A C K E D ■ T O R O N T O
C E N T S ■ O U T D O ■ R E O
A S K S ■ E R N E S ■ T I N G
L I E ■ B L A D E ■ W R O T E
L A D ■ L A D E ■ S A U T E S
■ ■ M O T O R C A D E ■ ■
S P R I T E ■ T A X I ■ R A P
T R A M S ■ B O R E S ■ E L I
R I T E ■ T I N E S ■ L U L L
A C T ■ R E P E L ■ T A N G S
U K R A I N E ■ E R O S I O N
S L A P P E D ■ S O M E O N E
S E P T E T S ■ S T E R N E R
```

CROSSWORD 138

```
F U S S P O T S ■ A F L A M E
O N T A R G E T ■ C L O V E R
A L A C A R T E ■ T A P I R S
M A T ■ M E R E ■ U N P A C K
I T E M ■ S A L S A ■ E T U I
E C L A T ■ S E C T ■ D E R N
R H Y M E S ■ D A I S ■ D Y E
■ A S H Y ■ T O T S ■
R A M ■ T A O S ■ N E C T A R
A R A B ■ R Y A N ■ W O R S E
F R E E ■ P O L E D ■ W I S P
F A S T E N ■ A G O G ■ B U R
L I T T L E ■ M A N I C U R E
E G R E S S ■ I T E R A T E S
S N O R E S ■ S E E D B E D S
```

CROSSWORD 139

```
A S H C A N S ■ N I A G A R A
S C U L P I N ■ E N G A G E S
T H R E E L I T T L E P I G S
R E L A X ■ F A M E D ■ T I E
A M E N ■ D F L A T ■ D A M S
L E D ■ C O L O N ■ R A T E S
■ R A V E N ■ S E R E N E
A C C U S E D ■ D E T E S T S
P H A S E S ■ Y E A R S ■
P E S T S ■ H O T L Y ■ C U R
E A S Y ■ T O G A S ■ J U N E
A P E ■ I O N I C ■ V E R D I
S E T S O N E S H E A R T O N
E S T A T E S ■ E R S K I N E
S T E W A R T ■ D R E S S E D
```

CROSSWORD 140

```
C L A S S R O O M S ■ G E T S
L A S T H U R R A H ■ A V O W
A N T O I N E T T E ■ P O L E
S C I O N ■ R I D ■ C E E
H E R D ■ S T R O K E ■ A R T
■ S P A I N ■ S A T A N
S N A P P I N G ■ F I N I T E
P O T I O N S ■ D E R I V E S
E N T E R S ■ T O N E L E S S
E V E R T ■ C O L D S ■
D I N ■ E M O T E S ■ R O A N
B A D ■ D I M ■ N U R S E
O B E Y ■ D E C E L E R A T E
A L E E ■ S T A L E M A T E D
T E S T ■ T O M F O O L E R Y
```

CROSSWORD 141

```
S L O B ■ K E B O B ■ P H E W
P I P E ■ A L I V E ■ H A S H
A R E A ■ P A G A N ■ A N T I
S A N C T U M ■ ■ J U N K E T
■ ■ O R T ■ S H I R T ■ ■
P A N N E ■ O H O ■ N O H O W
A V A ■ A L L E G E ■ M Y T H
M E T ■ D A D ■ N E E ■ E T E
P R A M ■ S H O U L D ■ N E T
A T L A S ■ A R T ■ G N A R S
■ ■ G E S T E ■ T E E ■ ■
D E M E A N ■ ■ P E R C H E D
E L A N ■ A G A I N ■ T I R E
F I S T ■ F U R L S ■ A K I N
T A T A ■ U N C L E ■ R E N T
```

CROSSWORD 142

```
A L M S ■ S T E A M ■ B E A N
T O O T ■ T H I N E ■ L A N E
O D O R ■ E R R E D ■ A C T S
P I N E T R E E ■ D A S H E S
■ ■ N O N E ■ S L I T ■ ■
B A R G E S ■ S T E M ■ S H Y
O M I T S ■ C H A R S ■ C O E
O U C H ■ R O A R S ■ N O V A
T S K ■ C O U R T ■ F I N E R
H E Y ■ H A N K ■ R A C E R S
■ ■ M I S T ■ L A C K ■ ■
C L I E N T ■ L A V E N D E R
H I R E ■ I R A T E ■ A R L O
E M I T ■ N A V E L ■ M A S S
F E S S ■ G E A R S ■ E W E S
```

CROSSWORD 143

```
A C E S ■ F L I R T ■ L E T O
C O T E ■ R A C E R ■ O D O R
R A N G ■ O M E G A ■ R I F E
E X A M I N E ■ I M P E T U S
■ ■ E N D ■ I M P E L ■ ■
F R A N K ■ O N E ■ D E A L T
L E N T ■ M U D ■ S A I L O R
E G G ■ N A T U R A L ■ A G O
C A L L O W ■ L I D ■ E M I T
K N E E S ■ E G O ■ B L O C H
■ ■ G E E S E ■ B A Y ■ ■
A D J U S T S ■ B A N S H E E
L O A M ■ H E A R D ■ I O W A
T O N E ■ A N G E L ■ A W E S
A R E S ■ N E E D Y ■ N E S T
```

CROSSWORD 144

```
S A G E ■ B R O A D ■ A P S E
A L A S ■ E A G L E ■ B E A N
L I P S ■ H I L L S ■ A R L O
A C E ■ C A S E ■ I S S U E S
D E S E R V E ■ A G E E ■ ■
■ ■ T O E ■ S E N T D O W N
A L L O W ■ H E R E S ■ H I E
L O A N ■ D A V I D ■ S I N S
P O T ■ M E L E E ■ S H O E S
S K E L E T O N ■ M A O ■ ■
■ ■ E W E S ■ D I M P L E S
E G R E S S ■ D O L E ■ E R A
B O A R ■ T E A S E ■ O V A L
B A K E ■ E S T E R ■ R E S T
S L E D ■ D E E D S ■ T E E S
```

CROSSWORD 145

```
G A P   O A F S   S H A V E D
A T E   D U E T   M O R E N O
G A R B A N Z O   A S P E C T
A D V E R T   R A R E   R O T
    A V E   H I N T   M E R E
J O D Y   C O E D   J A D E D
A D E   W A N D   F U R
M E S S A G E   C O N T R O L
    A G E   D A R K   E V A
P A C K S   F I N E   F L A X
A S H E   J I V E   S E E
U S A   H E R E   S P A N K S
S I S T E R   R E P A R T E E
E S T H E R   G O U T   E R A
S T E E L Y   E N D S   D I M
```

CROSSWORD 146

```
S A W S   C A R I B   S P A R
O P A L   A G I L E   L O C O
L A D Y   R A I S A   O L E O
O R E   H E R S   R E P A S T
S T R A I T S   P A L E R
      I T S   B A R K   B E T
L A P S E   B R I M   F E A R
O R A L   B E A N S   R A T E
T I N E   E A S T   H O R S E
S A D   D A D S   S I N
    A P E R S   R E N T E R S
A M B U S H   S A L T   R A W
L I E N   U N T I L   R A N I
S C A T   G E E S E   A S K S
O A R S   S E W E R   M E S S
```

CROSSWORD 147

```
R O S S   S P A T S   V E D A
A L I T   P I V O T   E V E R
P E A R   A L O N E   R E A M
T O M O R R O W   V A I N L Y
      D I R T   S E R F
T O L E D O   F A N C I E S T
A R E   S W E L L   H E L L O
C A V E   S L E E P   S L A W
I T E M S   Y E M E N   E V E
T E L E C A S T   D O N N E D
    R A G E   F I R E
D E B A T E   S E G M E N T S
O R A L   N E W E R   D I A L
M I N D   T R A D E   E L L A
E N D S   S E N S E   D E E P
```

CROSSWORD 148

```
N I T E   J A M B   S E R G E
O D I N   A L O E   E P E E S
L A M B   C O A T   G I V E S
A H I L L O F B E A N S
N O D O U B T   R O O T U P
    C D S   A U K   D A R E
A A H   W E I S S   S I N G S
D R O P I N T H E B U C K E T
D E F O G   L E D A T   S S S
I N F O   E L S   S U P
S T A L E R   A E R O S O L
    R U N O F T H E M I L L
V I S O R   H A H A   M E S A
A C H O O   I V O R   E V E N
T E E M S   O A S T   L E N O
```

CROSSWORD 149

```
T R A D E █ S W A M █ S A R I
R A C E R █ C O N E █ A G E D
E T H E R █ R O T S █ V E A L
K E E P A T A D I S T A N C E
█ E N E M Y █ M O N T H S █ █
B L O N D E S █ D A R N █ █ █
O A K █ █ █ P I T T A N C E
S C R A T C H O N E S H E A D
S E A T R O U T █ █ █ A N N
█ H A R E █ S A G E T E A
A B B E Y S █ A L L A N █ █
L O U I S A M A Y A L C O T T
A X I S █ G O R E █ L A N A I
M E L T █ E R O S █ U S U R P
O D D S █ S E N T █ P E S T S
```

CROSSWORD 150

```
S E A P L A N E █ R O S T E R
C A R O U S E L █ A W H I L E
A S T E R I S K █ G L A N D S
R E D M E A T █ D E E P S E T
A D E █ N E M O █ T E T R A
B U C K S █ D A N E █ S A L T
S P O I L S █ N E A L █ R Y E
█ █ P I T C H E S I N █ █
R A G █ T A R O █ T R I A D S
E E L S █ G E L S █ E X C E L
T R U T H █ P E E R █ E L I
R A T R A C E █ R E F U T E D
A T T I L A █ G E N E R A T E
C O O P E R █ A N T E A T E R
E R N E S T █ R E S T L E S S
```

CROSSWORD 151

```
S H E A R E D █ S C H O L A R
C A N N I E R █ E R U D I T E
R I G I D L Y █ R E L E N T S
E R O S E █ R E E L █ K I T
A C R E █ W R E N S █ M A M A
M U G █ B R A V E █ C A G E R
S T E E R A G E █ D I V E S T
█ █ W A T E R G A T E █ █
T H R E S H █ S U R E N E S S
R O A R S █ S A L E S █ P A T
O T I S █ N U L L S █ P I T A
O L D █ H O E S █ V I T A L
P I E B A L D █ A B A L O N E
E N R O U T E █ S A L A M I S
R E S O L E S █ P R E F E C T
```

CROSSWORD 152

```
S T A L E M A T E S █ L A D S
C H L O R O F O R M █ A L I T
O R A N G E T R E E █ P A G E
L E T G O █ C A T █ B E E
D E E S █ C A S T R O █ A S P
█ █ M O I L S █ T A S T E
F I S C A L L Y █ M A R T I N
I M P A L A S █ R E L I E V E
S M A R T S █ C O L L A R E D
H O R D E █ B O O T Y █ █
E V E █ S P O O K S █ C H A T
R A T █ E R R █ B L A R E
I B I S █ I N F A T U A T E S
E L M O █ S E A S E R P E N T
S E E D █ M O T H E R S D A Y
```

379

CROSSWORD 153

```
S U C H ■ S I G H T S ■ O H M
A B L E ■ C A N A R Y ■ P E A
G O O F F O N A T A N G E N T
E A S T E R ■ R E C O U R S E
S T E E L E D ■ S E N S E ■
■ ■ D O P E S ■ S Y S T E M
A C E ■ N A T A L ■ M E T R O
W O M B ■ D E G A S ■ T A I L
L O B E S ■ R A Z O R ■ S E T
S L A L O M ■ S E R I F ■
■ T I N E S ■ D E T R A C T
A N T E N N A S ■ N E E D L E
F A L S E I M P R E S S I O N
A P E ■ T A B O O S ■ C E D E
R E D ■ S L A T E S ■ O U S T
```

CROSSWORD 154

```
G R A P H I T E ■ F E A S T S
R E T A I L E R ■ U R G E O N
A N T I L L E S ■ S I E R R A
S T U N T S ■ K N E E D E E P
P A N E S ■ D I E D ■ N A P
S L E D ■ M A N E ■ G L I D E
■ ■ R I T E ■ S U I T O R
A S A R U L E ■ M A R T Y R S
P E C A N S ■ P E R U ■
P A C T S ■ M A G I ■ B A S S
E M U ■ C A S A ■ T A C I T
A I R D R O P S ■ L A T T E R
S E A E A R ■ E R U P T I V E
E S C A R P ■ R E L I E V E S
S T Y L E S ■ S O U R N E S S
```

CROSSWORD 155

```
■ P R O ■ ■ ■ B E T ■
■ B O A R D ■ P A G E S ■
B A R G A I N ■ T A R G E T S
A R T ■ L E A D E R S ■ N A P
T E A M ■ S T A L K ■ G A L A
S L O W ■ I L L ■ C A G E
S T R I V E ■ P O L E
H I D E ■ P A I L
L E T S ■ C A L L O N
F I R E ■ B U S ■ S N O W
L E S S ■ P U R S E ■ S T O P
O A T ■ P O S T E R S ■ H U E
S T E P O U T ■ S A I L I N G
S N E E R ■ S P E N D
S A T ■ ■ S A G
```

CROSSWORD 156

```
L E F T ■ D E G A S ■ P E O N
A L O E ■ E R U P T ■ U R G E
C L U E ■ A G R E E ■ L A R A
Y A R N ■ F O U R P O S T E R
■ ■ I S L E ■ S I V A ■
C A N ■ E N D S ■ N E T T E D
E T H ■ D E A N S ■ N E W E R
C O A L ■ D R O O D ■ S O R E
I N N E S ■ T R A I L ■ B I G
L E D G E S ■ E R S E ■ Y E S
■ I C E D ■ S E R F ■
F O U R S Q U A R E ■ I O W A
A L T O ■ U N I O N ■ D U O S
L I E N ■ E C L A T ■ G R O H
L O S S ■ L E E R S ■ E S S E
```

CROSSWORD 157

```
C A S H   T A L E S   A R I D
A L T O   O L I V E   L O D E
K E E N   S T E E R   A B E L
E X P E N S E S   V A S S A L
      S E E R   S A C K
S L A T E S   S A N T A A N A
W O U L D   C A N T S   B I N
E D G Y   R O V E S   P O E T
A G E   S E V E R   T R U C E
R E R O U T E D   G R A T E S
      P E R T   B A I T
C H E E S E   D E V O T I O N
R O A N   A D A G E   L O V E
E L S E   T O T A L   E W E S
W E E D   S C A N S   D A R T
```

CROSSWORD 158

```
I N C H   H A T E   R O O T
C O L A   S O D A S   E N V Y
Y E A R   I R O N S   S L A P
  S W E A R S     S T Y L E
      L E E S   C U E
C A R B O N   A B A N D O N S
O C E A N   E X I T   P E P
B R A G G E D   D E C L A R E
R E D   D E E S   H A L V E
A S S U M I N G   M I S S E D
      M A T   O P E N
S L O P E   L O A D E D
T A X I   S T R A W   A R E A
E V E R   L E A N S   M I L L
P A N E   Y A N K   P E E L
```

CROSSWORD 159

```
S C A T   R A P I D   R A C E
C O L A   A L O N E   E T O N
A L A N   W I N K S   S O L D
M O M   H E A D   E R U P T S
P R O C E S S   P R O M
    H A T   T A T T E R E D
R A D A R   P I N E S   A D O
E X I T   C U R E D   S I G N
A L E   C A R E S   B A L E S
R E T U R N E D   R A N
    N O T E   F I N D E R S
R E C I P E   T A N K   L A P
E D I T   R E E L S   L O V E
B I T E   E R A S E   O P E N
S E E D   D A R E D   B E N D
```

CROSSWORD 160

```
  S P A R   T R I M   S T E P
S P A C E   R I C E   T I L L
T I N E S   A D E S   A L S O
A T E   P O D S   S A L T E D
R E S T O R E   M A L E
    O N E   R E G A R D E D
B L A N D   B I T E S   A V E
R O S Y   P O S E S   T R E E
A R K   T O N E R   F I E N D
D E S C E N D S   Y A M
    E N D S   D E T E S T S
P A R A D E   S A S H   T O E
U S E S   R A P T   O R A T E
N I N E   E R I E   M U T E D
T A T S   D E N S   S E E S
```

CROSSWORD 161

S	L	E	D		L	I	K	E	S		S	A	G	S
P	A	R	E		A	M	O	R	E		A	R	E	A
A	R	I	A		T	A	K	E	S		T	I	N	S
S	A	N	D	I	E	G	O		S	H	A	D	E	S
		L	O	S	E		L	I	O	N				
S	P	R	I	N	T		B	O	O	S		S	E	C
L	I	E	N	S		B	E	A	N	S		P	A	R
A	L	E	E		R	E	A	D	S		F	A	T	E
T	E	D		T	E	A	R	S		M	A	R	E	S
E	S	S		O	A	T	S		D	E	S	E	R	T
		L	E	S	S		H	I	N	T				
E	L	P	A	S	O		W	O	N	D	E	R	E	D
L	O	I	N		N	O	I	S	E		N	E	R	O
L	O	N	E		E	L	D	E	R		E	D	I	T
A	M	E	S		D	E	E	D	S		D	O	C	S

CROSSWORD 162

W	A	S	H		A	H	E	A	D		S	H	O	P
A	R	E	A		M	E	R	C	I		L	U	R	E
S	L	A	T		B	R	I	T	S		A	L	A	N
	O	R	C	H	I	D	C	A	P	I	T	A	L	
		H	A	T	S		O	D	E					
R	A	B	B	I	S		M	I	S	S		A	R	N
E	C	L	A	T		D	O	N	A		C	L	E	O
T	H	E	C	I	T	Y	O	F	L	I	L	I	E	S
R	E	E	K		R	E	D	O		R	O	S	S	I
O	D	D		P	A	S	S		J	E	S	T	E	R
		L	A	D		S	O	N	E					
	B	R	I	D	E	O	F	T	H	E	S	E	A	
I	R	O	N		O	N	I	O	N		O	L	G	A
C	A	V	E		F	E	L	O	N		U	S	E	D
E	Y	E	S		F	I	L	L	Y		T	E	S	S

CROSSWORD 163

S	E	C	R	E	T		L	I	T	E	R	A	T	E
A	S	H	O	R	E		A	T	O	M	I	Z	E	R
I	C	E	B	O	X		T	E	R	I	G	A	R	R
L	A	M		S	A	L	E	M		T	U	L	S	A
B	L	I	P		S	E	R	I	F		P	E	E	N
O	A	S	I	S		D	O	Z	E	S		A	R	T
A	T	T	E	N	D		N	E	W	T	S			
T	E	S	T	O	U	T		S	E	R	A	P	E	S
		Y	O	K	E	S		R	E	P	E	N	T	
O	F	T		T	E	N	O	N		W	I	N	C	E
B	L	A	B		S	T	R	O	P		D	A	L	E
J	A	M	E	S		A	R	G	O	N		L	A	P
E	V	A	N	E	S	C	E		R	E	V	I	V	E
C	O	L	D	C	A	L	L		C	R	A	Z	E	S
T	R	E	S	T	L	E	S		H	O	N	E	S	T

CROSSWORD 164

S	P	A	T	U	L	A	S		B	A	D	O	F	F
I	R	R	I	G	A	T	E		E	L	I	X	I	R
Z	O	O	P	H	Y	T	E		D	E	N	I	R	O
E	M	U	S		A	D	M	I	X		D	E	W	
S	I	S		S	K	I	B	U	M		L	I	M	A
U	S	E		P	A	N	E	D		D	O	Z	E	R
P	E	S	T	E	R	E	D		D	E	P	E	N	D
		H	E	A	D		L	I	F	E				
O	B	J	E	C	T		D	E	N	I	Z	E	N	S
B	R	A	S	H		B	E	T	E	L		M	A	P
L	O	V	E		F	A	C	A	D	E		P	R	O
I	C	E		P	E	R	I	L		N	E	R	O	
G	A	L	O	O	T		M	O	N	A	U	R	A	L
E	D	I	B	L	E		A	N	E	C	D	O	T	E
D	E	N	I	E	S		L	E	T	T	E	R	E	D

CROSSWORD 165

P	A	S	S	A	G	E	■	A	B	A	S	H	E	S
A	N	T	H	I	L	L	■	S	I	X	P	A	C	K
C	A	R	A	M	E	L	■	C	L	E	A	R	L	Y
E	L	A	P	S	E	■	S	O	B	S	■	D	O	C
C	O	N	E	■	O	T	T	O	■	M	E	G	A	
A	G	G	R	I	E	V	E	S	■	P	I	N	U	P
R	Y	E	■	R	E	A	P	■	M	O	S	S	E	S
■	P	I	L	L	A	G	E	R	S	■				
A	S	S	E	S	S	■	S	A	T	E	■	W	E	D
S	H	U	S	H	■	M	I	L	E	S	T	O	N	E
S	O	R	T	■	C	E	D	E	■	I	O	T	A	
I	O	N	■	H	A	R	E	■	R	O	L	L	E	R
S	T	A	T	U	T	E	■	M	A	R	L	E	N	E
T	A	M	A	L	E	S	■	A	C	C	E	N	T	S
S	T	E	W	A	R	T	■	D	E	A	D	S	E	T

CROSSWORD 166

C	R	O	S	S	B	A	R	■	E	S	C	A	R	P
A	I	R	P	L	A	N	E	■	B	U	R	N	E	R
R	A	D	I	A	T	E	S	■	B	E	E	T	L	E
E	L	E	C	T	■	M	I	L	■	T	W	E	E	T
S	T	A	Y	■	R	O	S	I	N	■	S	A	V	E
S	O	L	■	G	E	N	T	E	E	L	■	T	A	X
■	D	O	P	E	S	■	M	O	M	E	N	T		
R	E	S	E	A	L	S	■	D	E	P	A	R	T	S
I	M	P	E	D	E	■	R	E	S	E	T	■		
N	I	L	■	S	T	E	E	L	E	D	■	P	O	T
G	N	U	S	■	E	L	V	E	S	■	S	A	R	I
T	E	R	N	S	■	L	O	T	■	S	C	R	A	G
A	N	G	O	L	A	■	L	I	B	E	R	A	T	E
I	C	E	B	O	X	■	T	O	R	E	A	D	O	R
L	E	S	S	E	E	■	S	N	A	P	P	E	R	S

CROSSWORD 167

M	I	S	S	■	C	O	L	A	■	B	L	O	C	K
E	D	I	T	O	R	I	A	L	■	R	E	V	U	E
G	E	N	E	R	A	L	D	E	L	I	V	E	R	Y
A	S	S	E	N	T	E	D	■	E	M	E	N	D	S
■	P	E	E	R	■	D	A	M	E	■				
S	A	B	E	R	S	■	L	O	N	E	S	O	M	E
P	E	O	N	Y	■	R	I	L	E	D	■	P	I	N
E	R	O	S	■	D	I	N	E	D	■	H	A	N	D
L	I	T	■	D	I	C	E	S	■	D	O	L	C	E
L	E	S	S	E	N	E	D	■	R	O	U	S	E	D
■	I	C	E	D	■	S	A	G	S	■				
S	C	A	L	A	R	■	A	I	S	L	E	W	A	Y
C	O	M	E	D	O	W	N	T	H	E	P	I	K	E
A	T	O	N	E	■	A	N	A	L	G	E	S	I	A
R	E	S	T	S	■	G	A	R	Y	■	T	E	N	S

CROSSWORD 168

T	E	E	S	O	F	F	■	S	C	O	O	P	E	D
O	N	S	H	O	R	E	■	H	O	U	D	I	N	I
A	C	C	E	D	E	D	■	R	E	T	E	L	L	S
M	O	R	A	L	E	■	B	E	D	S	■	L	I	T
A	D	O	R	E	■	W	O	W	S	■	J	A	V	A
N	E	W	S	S	T	A	N	D	■	C	A	G	E	S
■	O	R	E	■	R	O	D	E	N	T				
T	R	E	B	L	E	D	■	F	I	N	E	S	S	E
R	E	P	A	I	D	■	B	U	N	■				
A	F	I	R	E	■	C	O	L	D	S	N	A	P	S
V	E	S	T	■	M	U	L	L	■	T	E	T	R	A
O	R	O	■	H	E	R	O	■	C	O	T	T	O	N
L	E	D	G	E	R	S	■	C	A	P	T	I	V	E
T	E	E	N	A	G	E	■	O	R	I	O	L	E	S
A	S	S	U	R	E	S	■	P	E	N	N	A	N	T